Language and Literacy in Social Context

This Reader is part of an Open University Course (E825) forming one module in the MA in Education Programme. The selection is related to other material available to students. Opinions expressed in individual articles are not necessarily those of the course team or of the University.

Other volumes published as part of this course by Multilingual Matters Ltd in association with The Open University:

Language and Literacy in Social Practice
    JANET MAYBIN (ed.)
Language, Literacy and Learning in Educational Practice
    BARRY STIERER and JANET MAYBIN (eds)
Researching Language and Literacy in Social Context
    DAVID GRADDOL, JANET MAYBIN and BARRY STIERER (eds)

Other books of related interest, published by Multilingual Matters Ltd:

Critical Theory and Classroom Talk
    ROBERT YOUNG
Language Policy Across the Curriculum
    DAVID CORSON
Language, Minority Education and Gender
    DAVID CORSON
School to Work Transition in Japan
    KAORI OKANO
Reading Acquisition Processes
    G. B. THOMPSON, W. E. TUNMER and T. NICHOLSON (eds)
Worlds of Literacy
    D. BARTON, M. HAMILTON and R. IVANIC (eds)

Please contact us for the latest book information:
Multilingual Matters Ltd,
Frankfurt Lodge, Clevedon Hall, Victoria Road,
Clevedon, Avon BS21 7SJ, England.

Language and Literacy in Social Context

Media Texts: Authors and Readers

A Reader edited by

David Graddol and Oliver Boyd-Barrett

at the Open University

MULTILINGUAL MATTERS LTD
Clevedon • Philadelphia • Adelaide
in association with
THE OPEN UNIVERSITY

Library of Congress Cataloging in Publication Data

Media Texts, Authors and Readers: A Reader/Edited by David Graddol and
Oliver Boyd-Barrett
p. cm.
'Language and Literacy in Social Context'.
Includes bibliographical references and index.
1. Mass media and language. 2. Discourse analysis. 3. Mass media–Authorship.
4. Mass media–Audiences. I. Graddol, David. II. Boyd-Barrett, Oliver.
P96.L34M38   1993   93-23199
302.2–dc20   CIP

British Library Cataloguing in Publication Data

A CIP catalogue record for this book is available from the British Library.

ISBN 1-85359-220-X (hbk)
ISBN 1-85359-219-6 (pbk)

Multilingual Matters Ltd

UK: Frankfurt Lodge, Clevedon Hall, Victoria Road, Clevedon, Avon BS21 7SJ.
USA: 1900 Frost Road, Suite 101, Bristol, PA 19007, USA.
Australia: P.O. Box 6025, 83 Gilles Street, Adelaide, SA 5000, Australia.

Selection, editorial material and commissioned chapters
copyright © 1994 The Open University.

Cover design by Bob Jones Associates.
Index compiled by Meg Davies (Society of Indexers).
Printed and bound in Great Britain by Short Run Press Ltd, Exeter.

Contents

Preface

This is one of four volumes of readings compiled as a part of an Open University MA course called *Language and Literacy in Social Context* (E825). The course draws on a variety of work in sociolinguistics, grammar, semiotics, media studies, anthropology, psychology and education and the interdisciplinary nature of the course is reflected in the articles collected together in this series. Each volume contains a mix of classic and newly published material which will be of interest to a wide audience.

Anyone who studies these papers will inevitably be drawn in to some of the most exciting intellectual debates of the closing years of the 20th century. The authors deal with many of the 'big issues' relating to life in the postmodern world — identity, social relations, social control, ideology, freedom, democracy, power, aesthetics, pleasure — but always with a concern for the way these very abstract notions manifest themselves in individual lives.

I would like to take the opportunity of thanking all those who, in various ways, supported, encouraged (and sometimes cautioned), the course team during the production process. In particular, I should mention Myra Barrs, Rebecca Bunting, Jane Cooper, Norman Fairclough, Gordon Gibson, Gunther Kress, Gemma Moss, Brian Street, Terry Threadgold, Gill Watson, many students and tutors of a predecessor course on language and literacy (E815), and colleagues in the School of Education at The Open University.

David Graddol
Course Chair

Sources

We would like to thank the authors and publishers concerned for kindly granting permission to reproduce copyright material in this reader. Every effort has been made to trace the correct copyright owners, both authors and publishers, as listed in the Contents and by chapter below.

1. Commissioned article.
2. Commissioned article.
3. Commissioned article.
4. From *Comprehending Oral and Written Language* by R. Horowitz and S. J. Samuels (eds). Orlando, FL: © Academic Press, 1987.
5. Extracts from Chapter 5 of *Language, Context and Text: Aspects of Language in a Social-semiotic Perspective* by M. A. K. Halliday and R. Hasan. Oxford: Oxford University Press, 1989.
6. Extracts from Chapter 9 of *Language in the News: Discourse and Ideology in the Press* by R. Fowler. London: Routledge, 1991.
7. From Chapter 8 of *The Language of News Media* by Allan Bell. Oxford: Blackwell Education, 1991.
8. From Chapter 3 of *Film as Social Practice* by Graeme Turner. London: Routledge, 1988.
9. First published this volume, © Author.
10. From *The Medieval Theory of Authorship* by A. J. Minnis. London: Scolar Press, 1984.
11. From *Image, Music, Text* by Roland Barthes. London: Fontana (An Imprint of HarperCollins), 1977.
12. From *Reading Saussure* by Roy Harris. London: Duckworth. (Reprinted by permission of Duckworth & Co. Ltd, London and Open Court Publishing Company, La Salle, Illinois.)
13. Edited version of Chapter 4 of *Un/popular Fictions* by Gemma Moss. London: Virago, 1989.
14. From *Culture, Media, Language* by Stuart Hall, Dorothy Hobson, Andrew Lowe and Paul Willis (eds). London: Hutchinson, 1980. © Authors.
15. Revised version of paper in *Language and Power* by Romy Clark, Norman Fairclough, Roz Ivanic, Nicki McLeod, Jenny Thomas and Paul Meara (eds). London: CILT/BAAL, © Author.
16. From Chapter 8 of *The Lively Audience* by P. Palmer. London: Allen & Unwin (Routledge), 1986.
17. From *Television Culture* by J. Fiske. London: Routledge, 1987.
18. From *Media, Culture and Society*. 12, 9-29. London: Sage, 1990.

Introduction

The collection of papers in this volume is the outcome of a collaboration between two editors: the first a linguist and the second a researcher in media studies. The papers reflect the growing convergence of the two disciplines in their treatment of the text. Analyses of film and television have for some time drawn on linguistic theory — particularly the structuralist model of language provided by Saussure. More recently linguists have themselves turned their attention to the kinds of text which pervade everyday life, and that has at last generated more principled accounts of the interaction between words and image, and more generally of the interplay and tension between verbal and nonverbal modes of meaning.

This anthology is thus concerned with the complex ways in which texts communicate; at how the verbal and visual element of texts can be theorised within a linguistic framework; and at postmodern approaches which strive to 'decenter' the text itself and explore the historical and social contexts of their production and consumption. The collection should be of wide interest to students and researchers in linguistics, media studies, and communication. Five of the papers are published here for the first time.

Section 1: Texts and Linguistic Theory

David Graddol

In *Three Models of Language Description* David Graddol outlines the history of structuralist approaches to language and describes the roots of sociolinguistic and postmodern theories. The article not only provides an overview of ideas about language and how communication works, but also sets out the wider intellectual context for the papers included in this volume.

Oliver Boyd-Barrett

One of the most notable features of media and literary studies in the late 20th Century has been what is sometimes called the 'linguistic turn'. Not only have researchers and theorists looked to linguistics for inspiration but, more recently, linguists themselves have turned their attention to the analysis of media texts. This article, written by a researcher and author in media studies, examines the contribution of three linguists — Allan Bell,

Roger Fowler, and Teun van Dijk — to the analysis of media texts. The work of the first two linguists is represented elsewhere in this volume.

David Graddol

In *What is a Text?* David Graddol discusses the ways in which definitions of the text have broadened in recent years — so that it is now possible to talk of a 'media text' and analyse it in ways broadly similar to a verbal text. The article will be useful to anyone coming to the area for the first time and is puzzled about the nature of the text in semiotic theory.

Section 2: The Structure of Texts

Michael Halliday

Michael Halliday's approach to grammatical description has been extremely influential in language education and text analysis. Indeed, several of the other authors in this volume (for example, Ulrike Meinhof) explicitly draw on his approach in their analyses of media texts. Many theorists have argued that texts encode not only ideas but also social identities, social relations, and wider ideologies. Halliday shows how this occurs within grammar. In this article he discusses some important differences in the rhetorical structure of oral and written language and concludes that they represent different ways of construing the world.

Ruqaia Hasan

Ruqaia Hasan has collaborated with Halliday in the study of *cohesion* in texts. That is, the pattern of words which provide interrelations between sentences and clauses and which distinguish a text from a list of sentences. In this article she describes a range of such devices which give a text 'texture'. Although her analysis relates only to verbal patterns in texts, many of the broader ideas about texture can be usefully applied more widely in the analysis of media texts.

Roger Fowler

Roger Fowler provides a linguistic analysis of newspaper journalism in his book *Language in the News*. In this extract he focuses on one particular event which he calls the 'Salmonella in eggs' scare. Fowler is concerned to describe the linguistic characteristics of a 'hysterical style in the press'. He takes account of lexical choice, grammatical processes such as nominalisation and passivization, and draws on theories of intertextuality to explain why accounts of salmonella were so terrifying for some readers.

Allan Bell

Allan Bell is unusual in being both an 'insider' — a practising journalist — and a respected linguist, known best perhaps for his work in sociolinguistics and his theory of 'audience design'. In his book *The Language of News Media*, from which this article is extracted, he gives a full account of the production and analysis of news from a linguist's point of view. In this article he analyses the story structure in press reports and concludes that it belongs to a long tradition of storytelling in the West. One major difference between oral narratives and news reports, however, is that the latter are not structured chronologically. Instead, the order in which the story is told reflects news values.

Graeme Turner

Graeme Turner explains how 'film languages' work. In doing so, he provides a straightforward account of the semiotics of the cinema, taking the reader through basic camera techniques, and discussing the role of editing, lighting, and sound in the construction of film.

David Graddol

This paper examines the visual and nonverbal construction of news reports, and builds on the preceding three papers. The persuasiveness of TV news as a factual account of events is commonly assumed to derive from the transparency with which images communicate. In this paper, David Graddol argues that the apparent transparency of images in TV news reflects the extent to which realist cinematic techniques have become naturalized in visual narrative, and that there exists a constant tension in TV news between the verbal and visual narrative and between objective and subjective modes of representation.

Section 3: The Problem of Authorship

A. J. Minnis

The extract from Minnis provides an intriguing insight into medieval notions of the author. In particular, we are reminded of the close connection between the words 'author' and 'authority'. In those days the best authors were dead ones. Texts contained within them authoritative wisdom, but they required a skilled interpreter to perceive it. In this way, the institutional authority of the Church, and of the educational establishment, was also maintained.

Roland Barthes

In this classic text, Roland Barthes plays with a theme which was later to become something of a preoccupation of poststructural theory. Can texts be said to have an identifiable author when they are necessarily heteroglossic? When the reader is required to do so much of the work in providing meaning? Have texts actually changed their character in response to literary criticism and as a reflection of the postmodern world ('the text is henceforth made and read in such a way that at all its levels the author is absent')?

Roy Harris

The inclusion of an extract from Roy Harris's book *Reading Saussure* is, it has to be admitted, partly a piece of mischief making. Has the author of structuralism, the theorist who made possible the analysis of culture as myth, thereby permitted himself to be theorised as myth? 'At the very worst, the Saussure of the *Cours* is a literary — and literal — fabrication of his editors', claims Harris. More seriously, the paper provides a relevant account of how the authorship of a particular work — of extraordinary influence on 20th Century thought — has been constructed and interpreted. Harris also addresses the question of when, and how, Saussure became 'the founding father of linguistics' by charting the pattern of influence which Saussure's work has had on linguists in the 20th Century.

Gemma Moss

Gemma Moss is concerned, like a number of researchers, with the effects of popular fiction genres on young people. For many, popular fiction provides a model for their own writing. The paper published here (extracted from Moss's book *Un/Popular Fictions*) provides a detailed examination of the writing of a black girl called Angelique. Moss shows how Angelique is able to modify and adapt the formulas of popular fiction, and use them to raise her own questions and to express her own purposes, about her identity and social relations with boys. Moss argues 'Angelique's writing cannot be understood in terms of passive consumers hopelessly trapped and subdued by an all-powerful popular fiction, relentlessly undermining their perception of the real world'. Instead, the detailed examination of a piece of writing, combined with interviews with the writer, argues for a 'far more complex interaction between the writer and the text than the customary arguments about popular culture and popular fiction allow for'.

Section 4: The Role of the Reader

Stuart Hall

This article by Stuart Hall is a classic one in the literature on texts and ideology. It argues that the ideological effects of TV texts cannot be explained as a straightforward result of encoding. Rather, viewers will react to a text according to the beliefs and ideological commitments that they already hold. Hall describes three positions which a viewer can take in relation to a text. They may be compliant, and accept the ideological position offered them by the text; they may be oppositional and resist the position offered; or they may enter a negotiated position, in which they are prepared to modify some of their pre-existing beliefs as a result of engaging with the text.

Ulrike Meinhof

This article begins with a review of some recent ideas about TV texts and how they are interpreted by viewers. Ulrike Meinhof is a linguist and takes a broadly Hallidayan view of the way texts encode social relations, but she argues that understanding how viewers interpret images on TV requires an understanding of the extent to which texts are heteroglossic: they can give different messages through the verbal and visual channels and the effect they have on a particular viewer can never be wholly predicted.

John Fiske

John Fiske examines the pleasures which TV texts give their consumers and describes a number of theoretical approaches. Pleasure is the location for many theoretical debates: is pleasure an ideological effect, a means of recruiting willing subjects to dubious views of the world? Or is pleasure a site of resistance, a space where individual subjects can experience a sense of control over their own lives?

Shaun Moores

In this last reading, Shaun Moores provides a useful overview of different theories of the relationship between texts, readers, and contexts. It describes the emergence of various schools of thought, and places recent ethnographic studies of media audiences into a wider perspective.

1 Three Models of Language Description

DAVID GRADDOL

Introduction

It has always been something of an embarrassment to language scholars that the definition of their object of study is itself a major part of intellectual dispute. That thing which we know as 'language' is a complex, multifaceted phenomenon which seems constantly to evade satisfactory description and explanation. Language is an important part of our individual identity and private experience, yet it also seems to exist 'out there' as a public entity. Individually we have limited control over its structure and workings. The complex manner of its existence means that we need to call on many forms of enquiry to picture language in the round: physiological, psychological, sociological, anthropological, mathematical, semiotic, geographical, historical, political.

In this paper I identify and sketch out three contrasting ways in which scholars have attempted to discipline the messy business which we call language, and provide some kind of coherent explanation of how it works. These three approaches are to be found in a variety of disciplines besides linguistics, such as literary theory, media and cultural studies, and anthropology. Wherever researchers have tried to describe and analyse human communicative behaviour broadly similar arguments have arisen. I refer to each approach as a *model of language*.

The first approach is one which focuses on the material substance of language. Verbal language is conceived as being some kind of autonomous mechanism, of which the cogs and pulleys consist of entities called 'phonemes', 'morphemes', 'clauses', 'sentences' and so on. By establishing a concern for material form, the flux of human experience that we call 'communication' can be made more manageable and concrete, and above all, made amenable to some kind of methodical analysis. I have called this structuralist approach *Model 1*. It has undoubtedly been the dominant model of language description in Western thought for many centuries.

The second approach I describe is one which arose in the middle of the 20th Century, partly as a reaction to the 'pure' linguistic approach. *Model 2* approaches do not abandon a broadly structuralist model of language, but they put forward the argument that linguistic structure alone cannot determine meaning: an account of social context — a social theory — is also required. The social theories which they draw on are broadly compatible with their linguistic theory: positivist and structural. In Model 2 I locate the tradition which has become known as *sociolinguistics* and some kinds of *ethnography*.

The third model, *Model 3*, I have loosely called *postmodern*. It represents an attempt to understand the fragmentary flux of language not by idealising simple underlying mechanisms but by attempting to tease apart and understand the nature of the fragmentation. It differs from Model 2 both in the way it conceptualises language and also in the ways in which it conceives of society and individual identity. Language, for example, is always diverse and unstable in structure, it is not clear where the boundaries of language and other forms of human communication lie. (Is the visual symbolism of films a form of language? Is architecture a language?) Human identity in postmodern theory is also seen as diverse, inconsistent, and unstable. The fragmentary nature of linguistic experience both reflects and is the cause of this fractured personal identity.

What follows is not to be taken as a comprehensive history of language study. Although I try to capture something of the historical development of ideas, I have focused particularly on those which relate to the nature of language, how meaning is conveyed by utterances and texts, and the role played by the individual language user. The main purpose of the paper is to place the models of the text which are described elsewhere in this volume within a wider historical context. One shortcoming of such a crude attempt at classification is that individual authors and researchers can rarely be easily categorised. The models I describe should be regarded as 'discourses' about language and texts which are drawn upon, often implicitly, by authors.

Model 1: Structuralism

In the 20th Century, two scholars have been of pre-eminent importance in developing modern linguistic theory. The first is the Swiss linguist Ferdinand de Saussure, whose *Course in General Linguistics* was published in 1916. The second is the American linguist Noam Chomsky, whose seminal work *Syntactic Structures* was published in 1957. Both have contributed to the structuralist enterprise: that is, the attempt to describe, analyse, and explain the complex *form* of language in ways which theorise it as an autonomous mechanism. In this part of the paper, I will try to set their respective approaches to language study briefly in intellectual context.

Pre-Saussurean structuralism

Many of the debates about the nature of language and how it conveys meaning which characterise present day linguistic theory are longstanding ones and can be seen already in the 17th Century where I will (somewhat arbitrarily) begin this account. The English philosopher, John Locke, for example, was interested in how language allowed people to understand and convey knowledge. In his famous *Essay Concerning Human Understanding* (1690) he sets out what would now be called a *semiotic* theory. That is, he conceives of communication in terms of 'signs': words are the signs of ideas, and ideas are the signs of things. The relation of the word to the idea is, for Locke, an arbitrary one — language is purely a semiotic device and its signs do not in any way try to mimic nature:

> Thus we may conceive how *Words*, which were by Nature so well adapted to that purpose, come to be made use of by Men, as *the Signs of* their *Ideas*; not by any natural connexion, that there is between particular articulate Sounds and certain *Ideas*, for then there would be but one language amongst all Men; but a voluntary Imposition, whereby such a Word is made arbitrarily the Mark of such an *Idea*. The use then of Words, is to be sensible Marks of *Ideas*; and the *Ideas* they stand for, are their proper and immediate signification. (Locke, in Crowley, 1991: 16)

The primary function of language is communication: language is 'the great conduit, whereby men convey their discoveries, reasonings, and knowledge, from one to another'.

Many of the post-renaissance scholars who published grammatical treatises in Britain were also scientists engaged in the huge project of ordering natural phenomena and rendering nature amenable to rational analysis. For example, John Wallis — a geometrician and also architect of the ingenious roof of the Sheldonian Theatre in Oxford — published his *Grammatica Linguae Anglicanae* in 1653; Joseph Priestley — the chemist credited with the discovery of Oxygen — published *The Rudiments of English Grammar* in 1761. This close link between the investigation of language and more general scientific enquiry explains why intellectual fashions in linguistic theory frequently mirror changing ideas about what constitutes science and scientific method. During the 18th Century language succumbed to the same mathematical enterprise which tamed the chaos of nature. Grammars and dictionaries which helped 'ascertain' and standardise the English language appeared at this time. Samuel Johnson wrote in his *Plan of a Dictionary*:

Thus, my Lord, will our language be laid down, distinct in its minutest subdivisions, and resolved into its elemental principles. And who upon this survey can forbear to wish, that these fundamental atoms of our speech might obtain the firmness and immutability of the primogenial and constituent particles of matter, that they might retain their substance while they alter their appearance, and be varied and compounded, yet not destroyed. (Johnson, 1747: 18)

Here language is clearly seen, metaphorically, as chemistry and approachable by similar analytical techniques. Texts and utterances are the compounds and substances in daily use, but they are constructed from chemical elements whose characteristics and patterns of combination can be described and explained by a general chemical theory.

In the 19th Century, language ceased to be regarded as a mathematical or logical device and became a living organism. Franz Bopp in 1827, one the major comparative linguists of the time, suggested that:

languages must be regarded as organic bodies formed in accordance with definite laws; bearing within themselves an internal principle of life, they develop and they gradually die out . . . (1827: 1)

Just as living organisms were of many species, so different kinds of language could be found in different parts of the world. During the late 18th and 19th Century many of these languages were discovered to be closely related. So was born the 'genetic' theory of language classification, which portrayed the languages of the world as belonging to different 'language families'. The genealogy of each language could be shown by means of the 'family tree'.

It seems likely that Charles Darwin was influenced by linguistic theory when he published *On the Origin of Species*. Certainly later discourses about the evolution of species and discourses about language became closely entwined. Linguists even began to talk about 'the struggle for survival' amongst languages in competition.

By this time language study was an historical enterprise rather than a comparative one, but one which examined only the inner, material substance of the language. Languages were theorised as evolving and changing over time according to definite laws, which admitted of no exception. By the end of the 19th Century, the metaphor of a language as a natural organism was a dying one. Partly, this stemmed from a growing appreciation that the mechanism of language change lay with speakers, rather than internal structural motives, but it has as much to do with the changing nature of science and increasing emphasis on technological progress. At some time in the industrial age, language seems to have become a mechanical device.

Language was now an intricate machine: made up of myriad component parts, each with their own special attributes and peculiarities, which together formed a complex interlocking mechanism. This model of language was supported by the growing study of dialects of Romance and Germanic languages. Study was focused on fairly isolated speech communities, and within those communities women and children were avoided in favour of male, often elderly, informants. Such techniques not only fitted the Romantic spirit of the times — the quest for pure language varieties from the mouths of rustic peasants — they also helped maintain the illusion that languages could be modelled as coherent structures.

Saussure's contribution to structuralism

This, briefly, was the intellectual legacy inherited by Saussure when he began working out his general linguistic theory at the very end of the 19th Century. Some of the story of how his ideas became published is described by Roy Harris (this volume). All his own analytical work was in the realm of historical linguistics, but in his general theory he sharply distinguishes between the historical (or *diachronic*) approach to language study, and the study of a language at a particular point in time (the *synchronic* approach). If one wants to understand how language 'works' then the latter is the only legitimate approach: speakers do not carry about with them a knowledge of the history of their language. This requires great intellectual labour to discover. It cannot form part of the 'knowledge of language' which individual speakers possess.

Saussure regards language as being a *system* of elements which conveys meaning through two basic mechanisms. First, a meaning is arbitrarily assigned to an element (let us think of these elements for the moment as 'words') through social convention. There exists a 'social contract' between speakers within a particular speech community which specifies these meanings. Second, the meaning of elements is modified to an important degree by their *opposition* with other elements in the system. If some elements in the system are withdrawn, or new elements are inserted, then the meaning of the original items must, according to Saussure's theory, change.

A simple example will illustrate the Saussurean notion of opposition. Titles for women in English used to include a simple distinction between *Mrs* and *Miss*. If a woman were not Mrs, then she had to be Miss. The introduction of the term *Ms*, however, has led to a perceptible shift in the meaning of Mrs and Miss in Britain and United States. Now, adopting Mrs or Miss as one's title can be interpreted as deliberately avoiding the designation Ms. The value of the original address terms has necessarily changed because of the availability of a third element.

The conventions, or rules, of language form a 'social contract' between speakers. Saussure called these conventions *langue*. The actual speech which forms the transactions between individuals on a specific occasion, he called *parole*. Saussure used the analogy of chess: whereas *langue* was equivalent to the rules of chess, *parole* was like a particular game. Thus an important theoretical distinction between language and text was born.

Post Saussurean structuralism

The empirical rigour of 19th Century European linguistics was taken to America by Leonard Bloomfield who, after being trained in Germany, returned to the United States to take up the study of American Indian languages. Like so many before him, Bloomfield was keen to establish linguistics as a *science*. In the 1920s and 1930s the dominant model in the human sciences was that of *behaviourism*: the doctrine that only observable human behaviour could be used as data when constructing theory. In linguistics, such an approach stressed the need for rigorous methodology in data collection, and the building of extensive 'corpora' of utterances collected in field trips to communities where exotic languages were spoken. Analysts necessarily then worked with a finite 'language' which was alienated from the social contexts in which utterances had been collected. This abstraction of text from context was not seen as being a weakness; it reflected behaviourism's lack of interest in meaning. Meaning was something suspiciously mentalistic and inaccessible to observation. For Bloomfield, meaning was essentially 'referential':

> The statement of meaning is therefore the weak point in language study, and will remain so until human knowledge advances very far beyond its present state. (Bloomfield, 1935: 140)

What he had in mind was the idea that, in order to understand the meaning of an utterance, one had to investigate scientifically the properties of the objects being referred to.

It was to this narrow conception of structuralism without meaning that Noam Chomsky reacted so violently. He argued that going to the field to collect a corpus of utterances was a fatally flawed enterprise. It would result in a very limited range of structures which the investigator happened to record during brief fieldwork. Furthermore the data would be polluted by numerous errors, hesitancies, fragmentary utterances and so on which did not reflect the real grammar of the language but rather the incidental effects of the non-linguistic real world such as lapses of memory, interruptions, and slips of the tongue. For Chomsky, the 'language' which was the object of study was not empirically directly accessible, since it consisted of every possible sentence which a speaker competent in the language could possibly ever utter. Chomsky urged the use of intuition and introspection to make judgements about grammaticality. He distinguished between *competence* (the underlying knowledge of grammar which every speaker possesses) and *performance* (the inconsistent use that speakers make of this knowledge in the real world). This distinction in many ways mirrors the one made by Saussure between *langue* and *parole*, but it more clearly identified the former as the proper object of study.

Chomsky's work marked a major departure for linguistic theory in the United States in many respects apart from methodology: it shifted the emphasis to syntax (sentence structure) from morphology (word structure); it sought universals of language structure rather than detailing the qualities of individual languages; it represented (self-consciously) a return to the mathematical models of the post-renaissance period.

The language machine which emerged from this intellectual revolution, was a computational one. The new technical terms and insights which Noam Chomsky introduced to grammarians were largely derived from computer studies. Sentences, or parts of sentences became 'strings' which underwent 'transformations' as various pre-specified processes and manipulations were applied to them. The grammar was seen as like a computer program, requiring an 'input' which after various kinds of computational processing, gave rise to 'output'. A grammar became the set of processes, or algorithms which could be applied to input.

Chomsky's denunciation of what he called 'structuralism' was so vigorous, and the alternative model of language which he provided so influential and intellectually imperious that it took critics a little while to summon up the courage (or perhaps find publishers with the courage) to point out that the Chomskyan paradigm looked like structuralism with a new flavour. It is true that Chomsky's grammar is not structuralist in the Saussurean sense, in which language is seen as a system of elements in certain structural relations. Language, rather, is seen by Chomsky as a system of rules or principles which guide the construction of sentences. But in hindsight, the Transformational-Generative Grammar (TGG) which Chomsky invented at the end of the 1950s can be seen as belonging to the same enterprise as the earlier 19th Century approaches to language structure. The theory may indeed be greatly more sophisticated, but the basic frame of reference has not shifted. Language is still an autonomous mechanism whose structure can be described and analysed independently of the social contexts of its use.

It has to be admitted that there was a certain convenience in the new orthodoxy to scholars who were no longer expected to endure the rigours of field trips. And it is perhaps ironical that the computer, which through metaphor enabled the rise of the abstract grammatical enterprise of TGG, has more recently acquired the sheer power to overcome some of the limitations of empirical corpus based linguistics which Chomsky rightly identified.

The new corpora of English usage being collected in computer databases for commercial and academic exploitation are vast, some approaching 100 million words. An early limitation of such computerised texts was their exclusion of spoken materials. That is also now being overcome with the generation of spoken language corpora. The *Longman corpus*, for example, commissioned a market research organisation to equip a cross section of the British population with portable cassette recorders, with which they were to record their own speech and conversational encounters continuously through a whole day. These tapes were submitted anonymously to the project for transcription and added to the database.

Dictionary making has been revolutionised by this new empiricism and several publishers have been engaged in a race to build a more complete and larger corpus than their rivals. More interesting, perhaps, is that some of the sentence structures found in real texts are not easily analysable by the grammatical models built using introspective data. In relation to spoken language in particular, it seems that linguists are often wrong in their intuitions of what can and can't be said. Not all the unexpected complexities found in speech can be put down to 'errors' and 'slips of the tongue'.

Structuralism in literary theory, cultural studies, anthropology

The movement which became known as 'structuralism' in literary theory and cultural studies in the late 1960s owes very little, if anything, to Chomsky and TGG. Rather, its intellectual roots lie in Saussure's 'general theory' formulated at the beginning of the century. Saussure, in one of the most quoted sections of his book, located language as just one among many kinds of sign system. In verbal language the signs were — more or less — words. But other kinds of sign system could be envisaged:

> A science that studies the life of signs within society is conceivable; . . .
> I shall call it semiology (from the Greek *semeion* 'sign'). Semiology
> would show what constitutes signs, what laws govern them. Since the
> science does not yet exist, no one can say what it would be; but it has
> a right to existence, a place staked out in advance. (Saussure, 1966: 16)

This broader semiotic perspective was imported to Britain in the 1960s from continental Europe where Saussure had always been more widely read and was taken up with some vigour in literary theory, media studies, and cultural analysis. For example, Graeme Turner (this volume) introduces an approach to film theory which builds on the basic Saussurean structural model.

Semiotics would still have emerged had there been no Saussure. In his writing, Saussure makes no mention of a long tradition in a semiotic approach to communication which flourished particularly in Britain in the Middle

Ages. Roger Bacon, for example, is credited with providing an analysis of shop window displays in his 13th Century *Ars signis*. At almost the same time as Saussure was formulating his semiotic theory, C. S. Peirce in the United States independently produced a much fuller semiotic treatise — one which in many ways focused more usefully on the nature of interpretation rather than the structure of languages or texts.

Model 1 as an ideology of language

Models of language are not just built to explain empirical data. Language is so intimately connected with social life and human behaviour that any model of language tends to embody assumptions and value judgements which cannot be challenged by empirical data because they already circumscribe what kind of data is regarded as relevant to the theory. In this respect, a model of language can also be said to represent an *ideology* of language. In this section I will explore some of the wider ideological implications of structuralism in relation to communication (how it imagines texts work), and the identity of individual speakers.

Model 1 as a theory of communication

In Saussure's *Course* there is a simple model of the communication process:

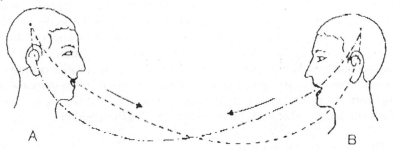

Figure 1

Essentially, the model embodies what Roy Harris describes as the 'telementation fallacy': the idea that human communication works by transferring ideas from the mind of a speaker into the mind of a listener. This idea has a very long history, and the metaphors used to describe the process have tended to reflect technologies of the times. John Locke used a plumbing metaphor in describing language as a 'great conduit'. We know that Saussure's model comes from the post electric age because he describes it as a speech *circuit*.

This model of communication became fully formalised by mathematicians and engineers working in the 1940s. Most famous and influential, perhaps, is the 'information processing' model proposed by Shannon and Weaver:

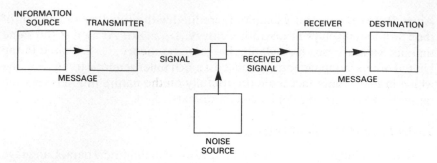

Figure 2 Schematic diagram of a general communication system

This is a very mechanical view of communication: messages are encoded by a speaker–writer–producer, transmitted through the ether and then decoded by a listener–reader–viewer. Miscommunication takes place principally for one of two reasons: there may be noise in the system which causes a breakup of the signal; the receiver may use an algorithm (system of rules) for decoding the message which differs from that used by the transmitter.

The transmission model of meaning is closely allied to structuralism in that both assume that meanings are encoded in texts and are readily recoverable by any reader who possesses the appropriate 'decoding skills' that literacy provides. In media studies, it corresponds to what has been called the 'hypodermic' or 'bullet' model of communication: the idea that TV programmes carry certain messages and that these messages will be understood in predictable ways and give rise to predictable reactions in the viewer. In traditional literary criticism it corresponds to the idea that texts contain definite meanings which can be recovered by a skilled reader or critic.

Model 1 concepts of the language user

Within such a model, the integrity and standardization of the symbolic stuff of language is essential for the continuation of communication, and hence culture and society. Structuralists approach this problem in a variety of ways. Many theorists disguise the problem by regarding it as marginal to the enterprise of understanding how language works. For them, the speaker–listener is an idealised communicative apparatus.

The speaker whose competence Chomsky attempted to describe was explicitly an idealised one:

> Linguistic theory is concerned with an ideal speaker–listener, in a completely homogeneous speech-community, who knows its language perfectly. (1965: 4)

Neither in Saussure's notion of social collectivity, nor in Chomsky's 'homogeneous speech-community' is there any notion of conflict or diversity, nor any sophisticated discussion of how the consensus about linguistic conventions is maintained. In the real world, where the transmission view of language seems to be a 'common sense' one, such issues are more central to people's interest in language.

John Locke, for example, conceived the language user as an individual who acts voluntarily in acts of utterance: the relation between sign and idea is chosen by the individual, usually in a way which conforms to the practice of others. This introduces a weakness in human communication and Locke was concerned with the dangers and imperfections of language as a transmission device:

> And every man has so inviolable a liberty, to make words stand for what ideas he pleases, that no one hath the power to make others have the same ideas in their minds, that he has, when they use the same words, that he does. (Essay Book III, Ch. 2, Section 8)

Because communication depends on everyone agreeing to use words to mean the same things, there is a moral responsibility placed on all language users to conform to agreed social practice. Those who attempt to meddle with the standard language, or pollute it, are guilty of acts of sabotage, if not treason (it is the Queen's English, after all). Washington Moon put this view forward forcibly in the 19th Century in his criticism of the English used by some contemporary grammarians. Quoting from an unknown, but 'educated American' writer he suggested:

> The corrupter of a language stabs straight at the heart of his country. He commits a crime against every individual of the nation, for he throws a poison into a stream from which all must drink. (Moon, 1892: ix)

More recent commentators seem to take a similar view. For example, Prince Charles, in his 'Cranmer' speech on the state of English, in which he laments a 'calamitous decline in literacy and the quality of English' suggests:

> The world of work demands high standards of accuracy in communication skills to deploy and transmit facts, to process information, to persuade people, to sell goods. Many of you are familiar with computers and know that if you give these machines inaccurate instructions, your wishes will not be obeyed. So it is with people. If we do not communicate effectively with one another then we create confusion and lose our way. (Prince Charles, 1989 as in text published in *Daily Telegraph*)

The transmission model of language which structuralism implies is thus close to the 'common sense' view of how language works. It can legitimate a social authoritarianism which insists on the *moral* correctness of strict adherence to a standard language.

Model 2: The Social Model

In an attempt to discover a language which is analysable and codifiable, structuralists have imagined that under the messiness of real life experience lies an ideal form. Such idealisations rest on the assumption that context and social processes are of marginal interest: they get in the way, in the course of real use of language, so that the data is impure and rough-edged. Such models do not necessarily suggest that social aspects of language are unimportant, but rather that they are unimportant for the purposes of linguistic analysis. Other disciplines can study social processes, if they wish, and find them of interest: mainstream linguistics has other concerns and interests. Hence, by rendering aspects of social context invisible, linguists make the task of analysing linguistic structure possible. Apparent messiness and loose ends in the data can be put down to incidental factors in the social environment, like noise on a telephone line.

Throughout the 20th Century, at least, there have existed alternative traditions of language study which reject this idea of an autonomous language mechanism.

Early anthropological linguistics

One such tradition began in the United States at the end of the 19th Century, when anthropological linguists like Franz Boas set out to describe the native languages of North America. This ambitious project required the training of numerous fieldworkers, who each investigated the language of a particular community. Very little, if anything, was known in advance about these languages except that they were very different from any European language. There was no recorded history (at least accessible to the fieldworkers), and little preconception about the structure and nature of the languages which were found. From this enterprise arose an important principle of relativism: that languages were diverse, that none was structurally more primitive than another, that each had to be approached on its own ground.

This concern for language and culture was almost extinguished by the behaviourist and positivist approach promoted by Bloomfield, but one of Boas' students — Edward Sapir — continued the tradition.

> Language does not exist apart from culture, that is, from the socially inherited assemblage of practices and beliefs that determines the texture of our lives. (1921: 207)

Britain's emerging tradition of language study also had anthropological roots. One of the major figures was Malinowski, who studied the culture of Trobriand Islanders in the Pacific. He developed a close interest in the role of language in their work and social practices. Malinowski appreciated that the Saussurean tradition of language, particularly in its 'philological' version, was of little help to his enterprise. He criticized two aspects of this tradition: first that it viewed language as primarily a vehicle for 'information communication'; second, that language study is essentially about the study of linguistic form.

> The false conception of language as a means of transfusing ideas from the head of the speaker to that of the listener has, in my opinion, largely vitiated the philological approach to language. The view here set forth [in *The Language of Magic and Gardening*] is not merely academic: it compels us, as we shall see, to correlate the study of language with that of other activities, to interpret the meaning of each utterance within its actual context. (Malinowski, 1935: 9)

Malinowski argued that to speak, particularly in a primitive culture is not to tell, but to do.

> In its primitive uses, language functions as a link in concerted human activity . . . It is a mode of action and not an instrument of reflection. (Malinowski, 1923: 312 — supplement to *Meaning of Meaning*)

Malinowski thus became interested in the functions that language was used for in particular social contexts. He identified three main functions to describe the language of the 'savages':

(a) Realizes action

(b) Expresses social and emotive functions (e.g. 'narratives express togetherness of society')

(c) Phatic communion — Malinowski invented this term in to show that even Trobriand islanders' idle gossip had a function in creating and maintaining 'bonds of sentiment'.

To Malinowski we owe the concept of 'context of situation' (Malinowski, 1923). Utterances become comprehensible only in the context of the whole way of life of which they form part. The focus of analysis is not a sentence but a 'speech event in a context of situation'.

The early anthropologists described a complex relationship between language, culture, and society, and their work has been drawn on by a number of more recent theorists. Here I will describe one direction which the study of language in social context took in the USA and the UK and which gave rise to what is now known as *sociolinguistics*.

Sociolinguistics in the USA

Although the rise of Chomskyan linguistics posed something of a threat to empirical studies of language in the USA, a number of scholars fought back. The ethnographer Dell Hymes complained that the kind of division which Chomsky made between competence and performance left out of account the kinds of cultural knowledge needed by speakers to talk in socially appropriate ways. This knowledge he termed *communicative competence*. The links between the 'ethnography of speaking' and earlier anthropological interests were evident:

> The ethnography of speaking is concerned with the situations and uses, the patterns and functions, of speaking as an activity in its own right. (Hymes, 1962).

But it was William Labov who provided the quantitative methodology which became dominant in sociolinguistic studies throughout the 1960s and 1970s. Labov examined the relationship between language and social context by correlating details of pronunciation with speaker identity and formality of situation. He was able to show that what had appeared as inconsistent patterns of behaviour appeared more orderly and predictable when aspects of speaker identity and social context were taken into account.

Sociolinguistics in the UK

In the United Kingdom sociolinguistics took a rather different direction, and one which has had considerable implications for the analysis of texts. As in the USA, the earlier anthropological tradition provided a starting point. Malinowski became Professor of linguistics at the School of African and Oriental Studies (SOAS) in 1927 and his interest in meaning and functionalism was taken up by J. R. Firth who also taught at SOAS and whose work influenced generations of linguistics scholars in this country. Firth was mainly concerned with studies of phonology, but he also wrote on subjects which would now be described as 'sociolinguistic'.

> Logicians are apt to think of words and propositions as having 'meaning' somehow in themselves, apart from participants in context of situation. Speakers and listeners do not seem to be necessary. (Firth, 1951)

Michael Halliday was a student of Firth's and he recognises the importance of both Firth and Malinowski in his own writing. Halliday, however, went further than either of them in attempting to build a formal model that showed how language and context were interlinked in the production of meaning. He claimed:

> After a period of intensive study of language as an idealized philosophical construct, linguists have come round to taking account

of the fact that people talk to each other. In order to solve purely internal problems of its own history and structure, language has had to be taken out of its glass case, dusted, and put back in a living environment — into a 'context of situation', in Malinowski's term. (Halliday, 1978: 192)

The context of situation, for Halliday, can be described in terms of three parameters:

Field: The ongoing activity and particular purpose language is serving within that activity.

Tenor: Describes the role and status relationships between participants. Tenor also includes other aspects of interpersonal relation, such as the social function of an utterance: is a speaker trying to persuade or warn someone, for example.

Mode: Includes the channel, such as speech or writing, telephone or face to face, but also the rhetorical mode conventionally associated with particular channels. Hence 'writing' and 'speech' routinely use different kinds of grammatical structure, and different ways of organising information and so on.

Another important feature of the Hallidayan model of language is the notion of the linguistic repertoire:

The social functions of language clearly determine the pattern of language varieties, in the sense of what have been called 'diatypic' varieties, or 'registers'; the register range, or linguistic repertoire, of a community or of an individual is derived from the range of uses that language is put to in that particular culture or sub-culture.

Halliday's ideas became extremely influential in educational circles in the UK and, later, in Australia. Halliday was the Director of the *Nuffield Programme in Linguistics and English Teaching* (1964–1970) whose work was developed by the Schools Council and disseminated widely through publications and in Teacher Training Colleges. The output from this programme was specifically directed at teachers, and the materials that were developed for language awareness work by secondary pupils (for example, *Language in Use*), probably provided the main vehicle for informing the educational profession about developments in linguistics during the 1960s and early 1970s.

Model 2 as an ideology of language

Model 2, like Model 1, embodies a number of ideas about language, society, and individual identity which are rarely subject to explicit explanation. Sociolinguistics starts from the premise that all language varieties merit study; that a standard language is one among many dialects; that the prime distinction between varieties has to do with the social and political contexts in which they are used, rather than some notion of intrinsic linguistic merit. Sociolinguistics therefore celebrates diversity and has an ideological commitment to pluralism.

In this respect sociolinguistics has proved to be a radical discipline. By making the study of nonstandard languages — dialects, black English, popular language forms, and so on — a respectable scholarly activity, such varieties become, to some extent, legitimated. Sociolinguistics fits well with progressive educational ideas, and conflicts with authoritarian and prescriptive views of 'correctness' in language use.

Model 2 as a theory of communication

Model 2 approaches to communication see meaning as arising from an interaction between language and social context. In other words, the same linguistic structure used in different social contexts of use, will carry different meanings.

Where structuralist linguistics marginalised the importance of the text, Halliday's model locates it as the central object of study. The grammatical and rhetorical form that a text takes reflects the three aspects of social context which he identified. Texts in this way encode not just ideas but also the social context and social relations between participants.

An important part of communication within sociolinguistic theory is the appropriate choice by a speaker of a particular language variety. These language varieties are assumed, in most cases, to be well defined 'codes'. In multilingual contexts, for example, they will be what are more traditionally regarded as 'languages'. Although pluralist, sociolinguistics does not seriously challenge the idea that language varieties can be identified as structural entities. It retains many of the traditional structuralist linguistic concerns.

Model 2 concepts of the language user

The model of society which sociolinguists appealed to was a structural one popular at that time within American sociology. Society was seen as containing well defined social groups ordered along lines of ethnicity, social class, sex and, to a lesser extent, chronological age. An individual's social identity was defined in terms of their membership of such groups.

Sociolinguistics thus appeals to a structuralist model of society and adds it to structural descriptions of language varieties. Its conception of speakers is not a radical one either. The speaker–listener is a humanist, rational being who displays communicative competence; who negotiates a social world and is responsible for personal actions. In this way, sociolinguistics is ideologically liberal. Speakers are, in principle, free to express their identity by choosing one language variety rather than another. The liberal-humanist ideal was perhaps most explicitly expressed by the British sociolinguist Robert Le Page:

> The individual creates his system of verbal behaviour so as to resemble those common to the groups or groups with which he wishes from time to time to be identified. (Le Page, 1968)

Model 3: The Postmodern Model

What I call the postmodern model of language has much in common with what is also sometimes called poststructuralism. I use the term postmodern, because such theory is not so much *post*-structuralist as simply embodying more recent conceptions of structure and world order. Postmodern approaches to language reflect wider trends in our understanding of the universe and the natural and social world. Just as Darwinian theory changed popular understandings of the world and the place of humans within it, so the Newtonian fixities were undermined by Einstein. The Cosmos has become infinitely large and incapable of human cognition; it has become a different place depending on the position adopted by the observer.

Popular models and representations of the Cosmos as a hierarchical, ordered universe, gave way to ideas of endless labyrinths and multi-dimensional structures. Novels acquired multiple endings. Diagrams in the form of branching trees had been used both by the early comparativists to represent language relationships, and by generative grammarians to represent phrase structure in sentences. The figures illustrating linguistic articles have since become more complex labyrinths; semantic networks in which paths cross and rejoin, in which an infinite number of different routes can be taken and experienced. Hence, postmodern approaches do not necessarily deny the existence of structure: they just conceive of it in ways which are more in keeping with new understandings of science and the universe.

Many of the articles in this volume illustrate the rise of the postmodern model. An attempt to describe a unified theory would be futile. It is easier to sketch out some recurrent theoretical preoccupations.

Postmodern theories tend to take a broader semiotic view of what language consists of. The concern with 'signs' rather than words, suggests that music, pictures, clothing, cuisine, even consumer durables, can be seen to belong to 'signifying practices' that is, processes of human communication which are language-like. Hence in postmodern theories, the boundary between language and non language is blurred.

Postmodern theories are concerned pre-eminently with texts, with how texts are produced, and with how texts are used and situated within other cultural practices. But the texts they are concerned with reflect postmodern conceptions of language and society. Texts are not internally homogeneous entities, but entities which draw on many sources, and which contain inconsistencies of structure and meaning. They are comprised (see article 3 in this volume) of more than one semiotic system interwoven (for example, a newspaper uses words, typographical conventions, conventions of page layout, photographs and so on).

Texts are historicised within Model 3. That is, they are produced by processes in which relations of power and social role apply, and in which a division of labour occurs. Bell (1991) describes the many people who take part in the production of a press report. Such multiple authorship is very common. Yet there is a social reluctance to admit this. There exists a romantic attachment to the idea of named authors. Within postmodern theory, it is impossible for a single text to speak with one voice: apart from the many people who have been involved in its production, such a text relies on a reader's experience of other texts and cannot be interpreted in isolation.

The postmodern model of language suggests that even acts of cognition — traditionally regarded as the most private and individual kind of behaviour — is socially and jointly constructed. For example, Coates (1994) describes how individual turns in a conversation may be constructed by more than one participant, so that it becomes difficult to allocate responsibility for a sentence structure or idea.

Model 3 as an ideology of language

Many of the reassuring ideas and assumptions which underlie Western liberal humanist thought are rejected by postmodern theory: ideas about the nature of individual autonomy and agency; ideas about the stable structure of the social world; ideas about the reliability of human communication.

Model 3 as a theory of communication

In postmodern theory communication is a great deal more precarious than in either of the previous models. In Model 1, communication is a transparent activity, provided both speaker and listener share the same code. In Model 2, the texts which form the messages exchanged between communicating parties encode social relations and identities as well as ideas. In Model 3 meaning arises ephemerally and precariously from an intimate interaction with context and the social activities of participants. Indeed, utterances and texts have no single unproblematical meaning: instead, different hearer/readers will respond to the materiality of a text in different ways, according to their ideological states and previous world experiences. Furthermore, meaning for each participant is not fixed but provisional and subject to further social negotiation, and such negotiation takes place in relations of power. For example, one person may say something and wait to see how others take it up. The original speaker may then agree when a particular interpretation is given to their words by a more powerful interlocutor but disagree when it is offered by a less powerful one. Meaning is thus, like texts themselves, jointly produced and negotiated.

Texts, within the postmodern model, are not simply read and understood, but consumed, used, exploited, provide a site of struggle. A text will take on a different life, new functions and new meanings, according to the social activities in which it is embedded. Scholars can never discover *what* texts mean, they can only build theories of *how* texts mean. In order to discover the latter, the analyst needs to make an ethnographic study of the social practices around texts, whether these be bed-time stories in families of different social classes; the variety of things people do whilst watching television; or the different social functions and social relations negotiated by greetings cards.

Model 3 conceptions of the language user

The postmodern model of the language user is far from the meaning machine of Model 1 and (to a lesser extent) Model 2. The postmodern language user cannot be said to have particular ideas, intentions and meanings which then become encoded in language since language users are not the authors of their own meanings: they use the words of others, their utterances and texts are populated with other voices, and they cannot guarantee how their texts will be received and interpreted.

The postmodern language user is often described as a 'speaking subject' and personal identity as their 'subjectivity'. Subjectivity is not given by their membership of well defined social groups but is constructed through discourse — the everyday experience of language interaction. But because texts are themselves so diverse and internally inconsistent, the subjectivities which they construct are similarly incoherent. The 'self' which, in Model 1 theories is idealised and homogeneous, and in Model 2 theories unified, rational, and in control of its own identity becomes in postmodern theory an internally contradictory, seemingly irrational, and discursively constructed subject. Some postmodern theories are explicitly anti-humanist. Others are reluctant to jettison the comforting beliefs of humanism, and just take a more complex view of the nature of identity and the limited powers of individual agency against the constructive potential of language.

The history of linguistic ideas

The problem with any attempt to provide a brief account of the 'broad sweep of history' is, as one historian wryly observed that 'history does not sweep'. A highly schematic overview of approaches to language study, such as offered here, cannot be read as a simple historical progression.

Ideas often run throughout history in tension and opposition to each other — though from time to time one seems to surface as the dominant one. In this way they help define each other. The three models described above are not therefore strictly a historical development, showing a steadily widening perspective on language and an increasing sophistication in linguistic analysis. Rather than being regarded as stages in history, the models are best thought of as 'discourses' about language: different ways of talking and thinking about language and how it works. In this way Model 2 can be seen to be something of a compromise, between structuralism and postmodernism. It is an uneasy compromise, which takes issue with the idea that language exists as an autonomous object, divorced from contexts of use. Yet sociolinguistics fails to challenge some of the ideological beliefs which support the structuralist enterprise: it maintains traditional western, liberal values of the self.

In notionally beginning this article in the 17th Century I have, of course, begun the story in *medias res*: the 17th Century was not in any sense the beginning of scholarly dispute about the nature of language. Nevertheless, the selected span of centuries enables us to see how some ideas recycle, and are given new significance as they become opposed to different antecedent ideas.

One of the first papers published by Noam Chomsky, was an article called 'Three models for the description of language'. In it he described in turn three mathematical approaches to sentence structure. The first two, he argued, were inadequate. The last — which formed the basis of his own later theoretical development overcame the manifest weaknesses of the first two. It may appear to some readers that I have attempted to accomplish the same rhetorical trick here, in positioning the postmodern model as the most powerful and most satisfactory approach to language study. Many scholars would be happy to concur with that sentiment, particularly in relation to the study of texts. However, postmodern theory is a fragmentary one which does not quite add up to a coherent whole. There are internal contradictions and points of theoretical inexplicitness and difficulty. It is too soon to say whether this arises from its essential nature or whether it marks the early stages of the development of a more coherent theoretical model.

References

Bell, A. (1991) *The Language of News Media*. Oxford: Blackwell.
Chomsky, N. (1965) *Aspects of the Theory of Syntax*. Cambridge, MA: MIT Press.

Coates, J. (1994) Lots of gap, no overlap. In D. Graddol, J. Maybin and B. Stierer (eds) *Researching Language and Literacy in Social Context.* Clevedon: Multilingual Matters.

Crowley, A. (ed.) (1991) *Proper English: Readings in Language, History and Cultural Identity.* London: Routledge.

Halliday, M. A. K. (1978) *Language as Social Semiotic.* London: Edward Arnold.

Johnson, S. (1747) (Facsimile) *The Plan of a Dictionary.* Menston: Scholar Press.

LePage, R. (1968) Problems of description in multilingual communities. *Transactions of the Philogical Society* 189–212.

Malinowski, B. (1935) *The Language and Magic of Gardening.* London: George Allen & Unwin.

Moon, G. W. (1892) (1st publ. 1867, 12th edn) *Learned Men's English: The Grammarians.* London: George Routledge & Sons.

Saussure, F. de (1966) (Edited by Charles Bally and Albert Sechehaye) *Course in General Linguistics.* New York: McGraw-Hill.

2 Language and Media: A Question of Convergence

OLIVER BOYD-BARRETT

Introduction

My concern is the relationship between language study and media study. There is plenty written about language in the media if the term 'language' is used to refer, principally, to features of discourse, narrative and genre, or to the 'languages of communication', meaning the cluster of different sign systems, verbal and non-verbal, encountered in the media. Corner (1986) for example, has looked at the discourse of television documentary; Turner (1988) and Scannell & Cardiff (1991) have contributed to our understanding of non-verbal languages of communication in broadcasting; Meinhof, in this volume, looks at how the interaction of text and visual communication contributes to the opening up of texts to different readings.

The contribution to media study of the study of language in its more restricted, linguistic, sense — as referring to phonetic, graphemic, lexical, syntactic and semantic features of words, sentences, and short passages of text, and studies of regular variations in such features, is much less common. In what follows I want to explore some contributions of linguistic analysis to media study looking first at work within media and cultural studies and then at recent work that has originated more directly from the field of linguistics proper.

Traditions of Media Study

Alvarado & Boyd-Barrett (1992) describe three major intellectual sources for the analysis of media in media education: the interpretive, social science and creative traditions. The creative tradition focuses primarily on media practice as vocational preparation, and is not relevant for this discussion. The interpretive tradition concentrates primarily on media *texts*; while the social science tradition is mostly concerned with *contexts*.

The interpretive tradition traces a line back to Leavis (see Leavis & Thompson, 1948) and the notion of textual discrimination, through the aesthetic analysis of early film studies, to a variety of neo-Marxist, structuralist, psychoanalytical, feminist and post-structuralist approaches to the reading of texts. In this tradition there may or may not be an attempt to relate the meaning of a text to features of the world beyond that text, but where it occurs it is in the text itself that evidence is sought.

The social science tradition is primarily concerned with the contexts of media production and the uses to which media texts are put. It ranges from macrosocial analysis of the various ways in which media interrelate with other social institutions, through the analysis of media as economic enterprises and as sites of professional practice, to sociological investigation of media consumers and the ethnography of media use. Despite the common premise that the media operate ideologically, the analysis of actual media texts in this tradition has often been unsophisticated. There is now growing evidence of work which productively fuses the best of both traditions.

Linguistics in the Interpretive and Social Science Traditions of Media Study

I have spoken primarily of different traditions within media studies. One is text focused, the other is context focused. Literary theory is very influential in the interpretive tradition, but linguistics far less so. The Birmingham Centre for Cultural Studies, whose work might largely be ascribed to the interpretive tradition, was established within the English Department of the University of Birmingham. An early summary of the Centre's work (bearing the word 'Language' in its title — Hall, Hobson, Lowe & Willis, 1980) uses the term 'language' as synonymous almost with 'representation' or even 'ideology'. Much of the volume wrestles with the uses and limitations of semiology. One contribution (Weedon, Tolsen & Mort, 1981) on theories of language and subjectivity analyzes Saussure and Derrida's critique of Saussure, and moves on to consider language in psychoanalytic theory and in the work of Foucault. There is no evidence of interest in analysis of particular linguistic variables or of language variation, whether internal to texts or in relation to social contexts. The theoretical debates represented in the volume do not encourage such attention, for they question whether semantic significance can ever be 'fixed', still less accessed by anything less than comprehensive analysis of a holistic discourse.

These debates accentuate doubt in the social science tradition that the 'meaning(s)' of texts can be satisfactorily accessed without investigating actual 'readers'. In a broad ranging survey of media analysis, McQuail (1983) has only a brief discussion relevant to language, this on news form, the determinants of primacy of news items, and strategies used to qualify a news text as 'objective'. A decade further on, McQuail (1992) still has relatively little to say about language analysis. There is reference to textual factors that aid recall and to methods of content analysis. There are references to the work of the Glasgow Media Group, and to that of van Dijk, of which more later, as well as to the work of Osgood (1957) and Val Cuilenburg (1986) on 'direct evaluation analysis'. This involves defining units of analysis (nuclear sentences) and within these identifying 'attitude objects' (persons or things which are the object of an evaluation), words of evaluation (adjectival or adverbial, having a 'common meaning' in the speech community) and connectors (language parts which supply the linkages between attitude objects and words of evaluation).

Social scientists generally have been reluctant to engage with texts using such methodological tools because they recognize the limitations of dependence upon specific textual samples for accessing the meaning of texts as a whole or, given the currently prevailing view that meanings are not fixed within texts but are the product of the interrelationship between texts and their different readers (Morley, 1980), for accessing the interpretation of texts by readers.

The work of the Glasgow Media Group (e.g. 1977), whose early work was primarily in the interpretive tradition, has often engaged with specific features of media language. Analysis of television coverage in three countries of the assassination by the Red Brigades of Italian premier, Aldo Moro, examined how the activities of the Red Brigades were linguistically 'excluded' in television bulletins from any concept of normal, everyday life (Davies & Walton, 1983) through such devices as linguistic markers or qualifiers: e.g. reference to 'self-styled' Red Brigades; heavily value-laden labels and stereotypes: e.g. 'criminal', 'killers', 'gunmen', 'murderer'; and use of words assuming the psychopathological nature of Red Brigades activity: e.g. 'fanatics', 'crazies', 'willing sadists', etc. These are valuable and legitimate insights, but suggest that a particular hypothesis (that of 'linguistic exclusion') has been formed and then applied to the evidence, rather than that a range of linguistic methodologies has been systematically applied.

The same might also be said of language analysis in work from the Leicester Centre for Mass Communications Research. Hansen & Murdock (1985) looked at how newspaper language supports the organizing oppositions of populist discourse in press coverage of urban riots. Their tools include: counts of the most frequently mentioned actors; counts of which actors' definitions of the situation are used in headlines; the presence or absence of 'distancing' quotation marks in quoting definitions of the situation; use of interrogative or imperative forms; use of photographs to provide information that is only inferred in the text; use of a proportionately greater variety of (negative) terms for the rioters; use of terms derived from particular paradigms such as that of warfare and insurgency; use of photos taken from behind police lines. The authors conclude that 'we have tried to show how the insights of linguists, structuralists and semioticians can be combined with the more established techniques of content analysis to produce a more detailed and sensitive account of the way that discourses are transformed and worked on as they pass through the news making process' (Hansen & Murdock, 1985: 255).

Three Approaches to the Language of News Media

Moving away from the interpretive and social science traditions of media study to explore contributions to the study of media language that have come more directly from linguistics proper, I will look at three relatively recent volumes which have all addressed the language of news media. As one of the three volumes relates closely to two others by the same author, I shall, in reality, be referring to five volumes altogether. These are not necessarily linguistic contributions; at least, not all of the time; but they are the contributions of scholars who have been trained in linguistics, and whose training, I believe, is very evident in ways in which they have defined problems. But the volumes are also significant in that they pose quite original questions, for linguistics as for media studies.

The volumes in which I am interested are Teun van Dijk (1988a, but also 1988b and 1991), Roger Fowler (1991) and Allan Bell (1991). I have chosen these because they are all approaches to the study of news; they concentrate on either print or radio but not television media; they are all works by authors with an academic background that includes linguistics; they are all recent. The work of van Dijk has a very ambitious theoretical objective, while Bell, significantly, leaves much of his theoretical 'preamble' to an end chapter; Fowler's theoretical interest is in the application of 'critical linguistics'. The works do not draw heavily on macro-theories from outside linguistics, such as those of the Birmingham Centre or of the Glasgow Media Group. Significantly, semiotics is almost without trace. While the relevance of semiotics has been threatened by post-structuralist critique, it might nonetheless have figured more prominently here had any of these works looked in detail at television news imagery or news photos. For development in this direction, one needs to turn to the work of Meinhof (a linguist), in this volume, whose genre is television news and who looks at how the degree of overlap between text and visual representation can influence the openness of texts for different readings, although Meinhof here is less concerned with specific, localized features of linguistic structure that are the main concern in this chapter.

On a different genre, the analysis by Guy Cook (1992) of still and television advertising provides highly specific integration of both verbal and
non-verbal modes of communication.

Teun van Dijk

Van Dijk's contribution to the study of news language is developed
through a number of publications. In his 1988 work, *News as Discourse*, he
attempts to integrate his general theory of discourse to the discourse of
news; application of this theory to concrete cases is provided by *News
Analysis* (1988) and *Racism and the Press* (1991). Van Dijk's range goes
beyond that of many discourse theorists in that he is concerned to integrate
within the concept of discourse the dimensions of production, content and
comprehension. His is an approach which respects the diachronic dynamism
of the communication process, that is, text as something which has a history
before it is realized as text and after it has been realized and commodified.
It is also a cybernetic history in that the production is informed by anticipation of its future. He recognizes, therefore, not only that utterances have a
context, which is the larger text of which they are a part, but that text itself
has a context.

Van Dijk's originality, however, rests in part in the fact that he does not
move to the macro-social level to establish this context, but pays close attention to more immediate features and processes of text production and reception. His intention, he says, is 'a new interdisciplinary theory of news in the
press'. He argues that mass communication research has paid only marginal
attention to its central object of research — the media messages themselves.
He calls for a detailed account of both textual structures and cognitive
processing, without which, he claims, we are unable to explain how news is
actually made. His approach 'is intended to bridge the gap between the
microlevels and macrolevels of news analysis and between media texts and
contexts' (p. 181).

Three levels of textual structure are identified. The first and most traditionally linguistic is the grammatic, referring to phonological or graphema-
tic, morphological, syntactic, semantic and lexical features of text. Here we
can examine how syntactic structures express underlying ideological positions, for instance through the use of passive constructions and deletion of
agents from typical subject positions in order to dissimulate the negative
actions of elite or powerful groups. Lexical choice is also significant here. A
second level, which need not detain us just now is that of speech acts. The
third level is that of macrostructures: topics or themes which are expressed
indirectly by larger stretches of talk or text. They have a hierarchical organization, defined by macrorules which represent what we understand intuitively by summarizing. In other words, they define the gist, upshot or most

important information of the news report. Three major macrorules that reduce information of a text to its topics are the processes of deletion, generalization and construction. But macrorules are subjective; their meanings are assigned by readers, and they call upon readers' world knowledge.

In news, macrostructures are revealed in headlines and lead paragraphs. The key concepts in news analysis are *topics*, which are structured according to *news schemata* and linked together by criteria of *relevance*, and given affective force by *rhetoric*. News schemata are based on a particular narrative structure made up of summary (headline and lead), main events, backgrounds (context and history), consequences (evaluation and prediction) and comment. Only some elements of this narrative are obligatory (summary and main events). Topics are linked according to principles of relevance: the most relevant information comes first. At the micro level, topics are made up of propositions which are of various complexity, usually come in sequences, and must display local coherence, matching the topic. But local coherence may be subjective: i.e. coherence is assigned by readers rather than directly stated in the text. It is in the gaps to which readers may assign their own coherence that texts may work ideologically.

News then, displays a top-down, schema-driven and relevance dependent realization of information that is not necessarily chronological or cause–effect in order. News rhetoric has to do with features that help to make stories more noticeable, hence more memorable and effective. News rhetoric includes issues of lexical choice; it is bound up with factuality — emphasizing the factual nature of events, building a strong relational structure for facts, providing information that also has attitudinal and emotional dimensions.

Van Dijk possibly makes too much of headlines and paragraphs, for there are exceptions to this traditional pattern, influenced by other forms of narrative, including documentary and drama. Any such variation in language merits investigation, and perhaps begs the question: what do we choose to mean by 'news'? It is also difficult to reconcile the view that macrostructures are represented in news headlines and lead paragraphs with the view that macrorules which generate macrostructures are subjective.

The identification of 'news schemata' as a non-chronological form of narrative should offer fertile opportunities for investigation of the conditions that govern use of the full schemata, or of variations from it. One case study in *News Analysis* shows how the omission or understatement of the context component radically affected the meaning of a given news story in mainstream Dutch media, on a highly sensitive news topic. Otherwise the concept of news schemata is not much exploited: a chapter on news schemata in 'Racism and the Press' quickly moves from news stories as such to the very different schematic categories of news editorials. However, it is significant that van Dijk can demonstrate the presence of identical news schemata in the media of several different countries.

The notion of local coherence, and the ways in which readers may be drawn in to the manufacture of news texts by supplying from their own world knowledge the linkages between different propositions and topics is also under-exploited in van Dijk's application of his theory to practice. It is an extremely important issue for it suggests that through devices of local coherence news texts are freer to work ideologically while adhering to the practices required to sustain claims to objectivity.

The role of rhetoric is strongly associated by van Dijk with strategies of 'factuality'. This should not obscure the limits of these strategies — the professional norm that news assertions should always be sourced is frequently breached or fudged (e.g. references to 'diplomatic sources') in ways which deliberately mask the weaknesses of working practices (e.g. where 'diplomatic sources' refers to the intelligence services of one particular embassy, and whose information 'disclosures' have highly specific objectives).

The role assigned to grammatic features is relatively modest, although this area often yields the richest data. Carefully sampled populations of news headlines of stories about ethnic affairs, for example, in *Racism in the Press*, yield evidence of the following statistical regularities in ethnic reporting: majority actors figure more prominently than minority; minority actors are mostly associated with negative predicates; majority actors are more often associated with neutral and positive predicates; minorities more often get first position in headlines as agents of negative actions. These are significant data.

Survey data is backed up by 'qualitative' data (where there is a risk that highlighting the 'interesting' examples, over-states their incidence and prominence). This reveals many examples of nominalizations (and other strategies that conceal responsible agency), ideological lexicalizations, and bias in the identification of colour, such that the colour of actors is mentioned when they are responsible for negative actions but not when they are responsible for neutral or positive actions. Van Dijk's linguistic background is clearly evident in later chapters where he examines the role of semantic features such as presuppositions, and features of rhetoric and style.

Interest in the compilation of information from diverse sources in news production prompts him to explore features such as the use of quotations and sources. Quantified analysis shows that minorities appear as speakers only in a fifth of all items in which they appear as actors (in ethnic affairs reporting), whereas majority group actors are shown in speaking roles in more than half of all items. The finding is more pronounced in some topics than others. Ethnic minority groups are not only quoted much less often than whites, but also on less important topics, even when one might expect minority actors to be the experts on these topics, such as prejudice, racism and ethnic social affairs. This form of analysis suggests to me that there is still a lot of life in more traditional forms of content analysis, even though the omission of more semiotically-charged investigation is regrettable.

In themselves both these quantitative and qualitative analyses can be criticized for their implicit assumption that text structure is related to how texts are read. This is indeed a matter for entirely separate investigation that may require observation and questioning of readers — the 'hypodermic needle' model of media effects has long been discarded in media study. While the notion of 'preferred reading' (Hall, 1982) refers to the ways in which texts are structured to predispose readers to interpret them in particular ways, such privileged 'preferred readings' do not determine the meanings that readers construct in interaction with texts. But if for lack of time or resource we have to disregard how readers actually interpret texts, there still remains more than an academic interest in establishing the range of texts that main-stream media provide: the spread of opportunities of exposure to different kinds of text.

Van Dijk attempts to integrate analysis of text with processes both of pro-duction and reading. Structures of news text derive from the structure of news sources and of the cognitive processing of journalists. Processing typi-cally involves: *selection* (according to criteria such as credibility, authority, availability); *reproduction*; *summarization*; *local transformation* (involving such things as deletion or addition); *stylistic and rhetorical* alterations. These processes are infused amongst other things by 'news values', and here van Dijk draws on the classic studies of news value by Galtung & Ruge (1965) (e.g. novelty, recency, presupposition, consonance, relevance, deviance and negativity, proximity). Some of this exploration derives from social psychology and its contribution to studies of media effect: e.g. perceived authority as supporting the credibility of information sources. Van Dijk's particular contribution is to the neglected area of what we might call the con-crete practices of journalistic writing, and their relationship, in turn, to such things as the concept of news story, the range and transformation of news sources (which generally take the form of other, existing, texts), news values, and anticipated readings. I am less convinced, however, that van Dijk has been able to apply his framework to processes of production with the same effect as he has to text. It does not address and therefore cannot answer the critiques of political-economy approaches to media production which would emphasize the ways in which media production reflect the interests of powerful social groups.

I am tempted to the same conclusion with respect to news comprehen-sion. The major processes of comprehension are identified as having to do with perception and attention, reading, understanding, mental representation. The process of reading involves decoding of surface structure, syntactic analysis, and semantic interpretation. It is related to the macrostructures of context and of news schemata. Readers bring to texts certain 'situation models' composed essentially of their mental representations of the macrostructures of broad news issues (e.g. the crisis in Northern Ireland, or in Bosnia) that readers have distilled from repeated exposure to long-running news stories over time. In the process of representation, situation models are updated, sometimes with the use of 'scripts' — e.g. a 'political assassination' script is the distillation of the key events typically involved in a political assassination. A new event may quickly be distilled in the form of a 'script' to update a 'situation model'.

Van Dijk reviews and adds to empirical evidence suggesting a correspondence between text structures and cognitive structures. Macrostructures, for example, are generally recalled best, and after the elapse of some time they are the only things which readers can retrieve. In many ways, what people remember best is precisely the things which were most 'newsworthy' in the first place (and which in the course of news production, journalists selected in anticipation of what would have most 'effect'). Readers tend to recall what they already know. News values such as negativity, surprise, and meaningfulness predict better recall. First items are best recalled. What is signalled to be the most important in news discourse, the information in headlines and lead paragraphs, tends to be the best recalled both in immediate and delayed recall. Either it is the structure of news presentation which causes these features of mental processing and recall, or there is a shared value system which explains both.

This view of comprehension, much influenced by psychological models, tends to focus on regularities observable in the behaviours of individuals, and in that sense it is very different from sociological models of textual reading which tend to focus on the influence of group membership (social class, gender, ethnic group, etc) on how texts are perceived and retained, on the social anthropology of how texts are used and what kind of status and purposes the activity of reading enjoys within particular cultures; van Dijk's concept, finally, does not incorporate reading as an interactive and creative process (see Meinhof in this volume) one which also occurs over time, often involving talk about texts with other people.

Roger Fowler

Fowler describes himself as a 'critical' linguist. His own language is at times clearly political. For example, in his introduction to *Language in the News* he makes the following statement: 'The government (during the 1980s) systematically depleted the resources and protections available for those in need.' This may be a defensible thesis, but the rhetoric is tendentious. Should this diminish one's confidence in an analysis of how language works? Does an author's political self-disclosure serve as a kind of caveat to the reader; could it be a sign of confidence that the logic and methodology are sufficiently beyond challenge that introductory political sentiments pose no difficulty for the main work? This may be less likely if the choice of the object of study is itself manifestly political (i.e. relates to government policies), and where one might predict that a person of political leanings X or Y will draw conclusions X + 1 or Y + 1.

Fowler adopts a case-study approach, which is informed by a section on analytical tools. While his description of the tools is a very useful guide for other media researchers, his application does not seem to require consistently rigorous sampling or survey techniques, or consistently rigorous identification of which media, and which sections of those media, are being drawn upon to support particular conclusions. There is also a tendency towards the classic fallacy of attributing particular 'readings' to readers, or media 'effects', solely on the basis of textual analysis. None the less there is much of value in this volume.

Fowler is interested in the use of conversational discourse to bridge the gap between what he calls the 'bureaucratic' and the 'personal' in news media. This is a form of inter-textuality, the use of *oral modes* in print to create the illusion of informality, familiarity, friendliness. Its underlying function is to neutralize the terms in which reality is represented. Conversation implies a commonly held view of the world, a shared subjective reality that is taken for granted and does not have to be proved. I agree that this may be the intent of oral mode, although I do not think we can ever assume it has this effect. The heterogeneous inter-textuality of particular texts is certainly a significant feature: modes (print, speech), registers (e.g. Scientific English) and dialects are all *in* texts, texts are not just one or other of these things. More precisely, they are *perceived* in texts, and perceptions are filtered by *schemas* which are developed through habitual use and experience, and which are activated by *cues*. The illusion of orality is cued by devices such as slang words, certain syntactic constructions and fragmented layout.

Textual mode is also a feature in Fowler's case study of news coverage of hospital admissions. He examines a newspaper which adopts a patient's perspective in its criticism of hospital admissions policy, but does so using a style of language which conveys the very same attitude towards patients as the hospital authorities which are being criticized. Relevant features of style included mechanisms of impersonality (e.g. assertion clauses, and obligation clauses), nominal expressions (e.g. 'cases', 'wait', 'matter' and 'list') which have negative connotations, uses of the pronoun 'it', constant use of plurals. By contrast, the politicians, administrators and medical staff are presented as people of high prestige, complete with their formal titles (an important individuating feature), and the predicates associated with them are much more active.

Fowler's principal case-study is of 1989 coverage of the salmonella-in-eggs affair which precipitated the resignation of a junior health minister. Fowler sets himself to describe the discourse; to answer the question 'what does the discourse really represent?', and to explore how the answer might be found.

A process of 'press hysteria', he argues, established a 'food poisoning' paradigm. This was achieved by means of (a) a vocabulary of 'hazard' and 'risk', (b) scare tactics that drew on the notion of rapid and large-scale growth of the problem ('astronomical increase'), (c) intimations of conspiracy (e.g. secret dealings between government departments and industry, (d) blame for the individual, in particular the housewife, (e) didactic instruction of the individual in dealing with the 'crisis', (f) globalization (e.g. linking up with the notion of ecological disaster).

To say that the affair is addressed 'hysterically' is justified by a high level of intensity, an 'excess of negative feeling'; discourse is permeated by terms denoting emotive reaction, always negative, clustering around the concepts of fear and confusion, e.g. 'scare', 'confusion', 'anxiety'. Another vocabulary set stresses 'danger', 'risk', 'hazard', and words which connote deliberateness or malevolence such as 'threat' or 'menace'. A multiplicity of technical and medical terms are used which many people find unfamiliar or disturbing (although I am unconvinced by this, as such a register could function to reassure where it connotes expertise and authority). There is also a rhetoric of animation: listeria bacteria are 'germs' or 'bugs' or 'killer bugs' (horror-film intertextuality); accompanied with linguistic transitivity, bugs deliberately do things to people. There is, finally, use of warlike metaphor: 'battlefield', 'minefield', 'uncontrolled'. The germs are portrayed as attacking the most vulnerable members of society, especially the housewife, in the kitchen, thus drawing upon stereotypes of femininity: e.g. women are supposed to be afraid of 'creepy-crawlies'; there are connotations of sexual assault (e.g. penetrate, invade). Finally, to all of this is added a rhetoric of quantification: very large numbers, generally rounded silently and upwards. These numbers are very *active*: they increase, rise, grow, spend, mount, expand, jump, multiply; there is astronomical increase, rampant size, exponential leap. The numbers appear to refer to lots of different things and to everything that is quantifiable.

Having described the discourse, Fowler then asks, what is the salmonella-in-eggs affair *really* about? He collected 560 noun phrases designating the subject: e.g. 'scare over infected eggs', or 'the poisoning of our world'. From these he noted the prevalence of a tendency to transfer the subject from a specific source of contamination to a more abstract and subjective state: e.g. the salmonella *outbreak*, and the *risk* of listeria. Similar abstract subjects include: crisis, danger, alarm, affair, scandal, incident, risks, increase, threat. Most common 'modifiers' were: poisoning, infection, contamination, pollution, health, safety, hygiene.

Such 'formula patterning' helps to give coherence to the text and to generate new instances of 'it' (the 'crisis' or whatever), so it is generative and has a levelling or equating effect, causing different matters to be perceived as instances of the same thing.

What then is the 'real' subject? It is a 'problem' that is an epidemic, something harmful, causing negative subjective reactions (confusion, uncertainty, loss of confidence), speech acts (allegation, warning, urging), and political events (scandal, muddle, fiasco).

So far, so good. But the abstract subject titles which Fowler identifies also apply to a broad range of press coverage: has he simply identified a common vocabulary which newspapers find useful in selling newspapers? The analysis does not discriminate very clearly between different media. Furthermore, there is an assumption that the language actually works in the way that Fowler believes is intended. But he is not actually content to leave his search for the 'real subject' at the analysis of headlines. He argues, instead, that it is about the ethic of personal responsibility and that it is related to a complex and ramified domestic stereotype of women, but this case seems to rest upon a more limited, less well specified sampling of press content.

The salmonella crisis is seen to culminate with a recognition of personal responsibility for diet, exercise, and health. This, rather than culpability of the industry, is the 'real' story. Readers are given instruction in culinary and dietary habits. The assumed addressee is a woman, because the instruction centres on issues to do with shopping and cooking, and who is also presumed to be extremely ignorant. She is implicated as a source of the problem because of her assumed dependence on convenience foods, a dependence which arises because she goes out to work. There is a link here with personal hygiene, which fits into a pattern of making women feel guilty about the possibilities of being unclean.

All this makes for a good hypothesis. If true, it should be dynamite. But by this stage of the analysis we have lost touch with systematic quantitative analysis, and with issues of representativeness (e.g. which methods of analysis expose which media as defining the situation in this way, how frequently, on which pages, in what manner?). Nor is there much sensitivity to actual or likely readings. The methodology for getting at 'what is it really about?' turns out to be less rigorous than appeared at the beginning, and has less to do with linguistic method. Is it reasonable to assume that there is one 'real' meaning rather than several meanings, some converging, others in competition?

Allan Bell

Bell is an unusual combination of linguist and journalist. In *The Language of News Media* he draws on his experience of working for a specialist news agency. He is often inspired by van Dijk, but extends beyond van Dijk. His thinking has a grass-roots feel to it, reflected in a less abstract, technical style. He is excellent on the integration of issues of text structure, production and audience. His conception of audience is less rooted in theories of cognitive processing, and does not have much to say about reading, but it does focus productively and imaginatively on media perceptions of audiences and how these perceptions influence media language. Characteristically, he looks not so much at abstract phenomena such as 'cognitive processing' but rather investigates physically observable phenomena of misreporting, mis-editing and misunderstanding of news texts.

Like van Dijk, Bell has three major themes: production, the texts themselves, and the audience, but he approaches them in a different order: news production, then audiences, then the texts themselves. Unlike van Dijk, he tackles both press and broadcast media.

Production

Bell stresses the multi-authored character of media texts. Text production brings together several different roles, of which the most important are: 'principals' (spokespersons, sources), authors, editors and animators (e.g. newsreaders). Through meticulous unpacking of the complexity of news processes, Bell provides a rich vein for the mining of ideas for future research.

News texts are texts which typically embed several different kinds of existing news talk within a single story. Bell classifies what these different sources are. Documents are especially important. Journalists prefer written sources which 'are already prefabricated in an appropriate news style', in particular agency copy, press releases, previous stories about the same topic lifted from press archives.

A key issue is how journalists use and interact with the various inputs that are available to them: this involves processes of selection or rejection, reproduction of source material, summarization in early parts of a story of information that is to be provided in greater detail later, generalization and particularization, re-styling and translation.

Editing primarily involves deletions (and, no less important, the repair of consequent ungrammatical constructions), lexical substitutions and syntactic editing rules. The latter are: applications, reversals or alternatives. Applications include: reduction of relative clauses; deletion of agents from passives; prepositional phrases proposed and reduced. Reversals occur where coordinated sentences are split and returned to separate sentences; previous attempts at summarization and synthesis are undone. Alternatives include selections of alternative output as where one verb tense replaces another; alternative determiners, coordinators or complementizers are chosen.

What functions are served by such processes? Why do journalists (or rather, sub-editors) edit? Editing serves to: cut news stories to the space available; maximize news value: e.g. to make a lead 'harder' and more striking; improve the credentials of a source; sharpen the writing; heighten audience appeal; standardize language in line with prevailing rules of syntax, lexicon, spelling, pronunciation; observe general guidelines for writing news; conform to 'house style'.

Audience

Bell recognizes that communication between producers and audiences is disjointed, dependent upon various forms of largely indirect feed-back, on the communicators' own limited images of the audience, and on routine professional practices and stereotyping.

There are multiple audience roles. A speaker on televison may be speaking to someone in the studio who is known, whose presence is clearly legitimate or appropriate (ratified), and who is addressed. This latter person is an *addressee*. But there may also be known and ratified members of the audience, perhaps in the studio, who are not addressed specifically. They are *auditors*. Then there are members of the audience who are known, but neither ratified nor addressed. They are *over-hearers*. These might include members of an audience to which a programme is targeted. Then again, there are audience members who are not known, not ratified and not addressed: these might include viewers in other countries.

Just as news sources are embedded in news texts so are audiences. That is to say, audiences for previous versions or sources of a news text remain in some senses embedded *in* the news text, as for example in the sense that a person to whom a letter is sent becomes embedded in the text of a news item that makes that letter public for whatever reason.

Communicators themselves have audience roles: as technicians, editors, animators, and authors (i.e. audiences for their own productions).

News programmes are designed to take account of audiences in various ways. Bell applies the well known sociolinguistic concepts of accommodation and divergence. An example of accommodation is the phenomenon of 'determiner deletion' in headlines. In the British press, the 'quality' news-papers typically exhibit relatively low rates of determiner deletion, while the tabloids exhibit high rates. Diachronic study shows how determiner deletion was a journalistic convention borrowed from the 'new journalism' style of the nineteenth century American popular press, and borrowed principally by the more radical English popular newspapers who were serving a much broader social class than the more established 'qualities'. Over time, the rate of determiner deletion has increased across all newspapers, but at a faster rate in the tabloids. In New Zealand, rates of determiner deletion prove to be a good predictor of Anglophone or pro-American tendencies, which in turn relate to the social mix of different audiences.

In the context of New Zealand radio, certain linguistic features (e.g. con-sonant clusters) vary with the prestige of the medium, and with whether the medium is national or local. In other words, perceptions of the social class or other audience characteristics influence specific linguistic features of those media. Some newscasters vary their style to suit the medium they are working for: they converge to a station style, and that style represents an attempt to converge with a perception of the speech style with which a given population is considered likely to feel comfortable.

Bell introduces the concept of *referee design* 'in relation to the study of how media language either responds to audience styles, or diverges from them. Regular listeners can be addressed in a style normally reserved for strangers or vice versa. In this case speakers diverge from the style appro-priate to their addressee and more towards that of a third party — the referee. Such shifts are functional. In the case of *in-group referees* the speaker shifts to an extreme version of the style for his own in-group, and he may do this when the addressee is a member of an out-group or when the addressee is a member of the in-group. Such strategies are typically actions of rejection of an out-group and of solidarity with the in-group; but they also relate to levels of formality which may vary according to topic. In the case of *out-group referee* design the speaker shifts to a speech and identity which holds prestige for the speaker and his addressee (i.e. accommodates to the out-group): e.g. to claim authority.

News as narrative

Like van Dijk, Bell recognizes news discourse as a version of narrative but his identification of its elements are different. He contrasts news narrative with the narratives of personal experience (Labov & Waletsky, 1967). These include the elements of abstract (summary), orientation, complicating action, evaluation, resolution, coda. The different components of the schema occur in that order, except that evaluation can be dispersed across the narrative. News narratives have an abstract, an orientation (who, what, where), an evaluation (why it is significant — information typically contained in the lead), action (seldom chronological and sometimes reversed, with the end of the chronological story getting first mention — perceived news value over-turns temporal sequence and imposes an order completely at odds with the linear narrative), and a resolution (not as clear-cut as in the case of personal narrative — instead, news is more like a serial than a story), with no coda.

Both personal and news stories like to use direct quotation (providing a sense of direct involvement). Personal narratives are personal to the teller, which is generally not the case with news stories. Personal stories have one view-point, news stories use several. News stories, unlike personal stories, use numbers, statistics, and precise quantities. Personal stories are charac-terized by simple syntax while news stories are surprisingly complex (reflect-ing the requirement that lead paragraphs contain the essential news topics and summarize the contents of the whole story, sometimes providing detail that sub-editors cut from the rest of the story before going to press), with negative implications for semantic clarity and audience recall.

News stories are informed by news values: the values identified by Galtung & Ruge (1965), listed here in their original form as negativity, recency, proximity, consonance, unambiguity, superlativeness, relevance, personalization, eliteness, attribution, facticity, are complemented by Bell who proposes the following additions to the list: continuity (has the story already been reported?), competition (me too!), co-option (does it relate to some other, bigger story?), composition (does it suit the overall mix or balance of the news programme?), predictability (can the story be covered without having to go to exceptional lengths?), prefabrication (is there a ready-made text that can be used?).

Bell solicits judgements from news sources as to the accuracy of news reports in which they have figured, in a study of 'misreporting': and attri-butes much of it to the 'rhetorical strategy of factuality' to which van Dijk refers. Other factors include: over-statement in headlines and leads (annul-ment of ambiguities; narrowing of time-scale; over-emphasis of negativity). Common sources of error include misquotation; misattribution or unclear attribution; inaccurate reporting of units of measurement (but Bell observes that these quantitative inaccuracies are systematic: they nearly always move in the direction that most heightens the shock-value of a story).

The analysis of mis-editing consists of a comparison of in-coming with out-put text. Mis-editing has the following common forms: falsification; over-assertion (where the assertive strength of a statement is increased beyond what could reasonably be interpreted from the in-put copy) via intensification of expressions ('all' or 'only') or deleting linguistic hedges; refocus and addition where information is deleted or reordered so that the balance of story is no longer congruent with in-put copy.

A summary of research into non-comprehension and mis-understanding is complemented with the results of Bell's own work in this area. Essentially, levels of recall of news are generally low, and recall is frequently inaccurate or fails to grasp the main points. Factors affecting recall include the extent to which audiences are able to 'write' their own scripts around stories (drawing on cognitive schemata — formal schemata, world knowledge, knowledge about news stories); and story structure.

Conclusions

Even on the comparatively few occasions when linguistically trained scholars take an interest in the study of media they do not always exploit to the full the very tools of analysis which their training provides, but when they do, the dividends are rewarding. Scope for quantitative analysis is considerable, and the yield can be impressive when the methodology is sufficiently rigorous. More worrying are attempts to characterize texts through unsystematic sampling and analyzing of particular segments. This does not mean that the 'meaning' of a text can be accessed through the naive counting of the incidence of particular features. Equally, it cannot be accessed through the tendentious lifting of particular examples of linguistic features without explicit criteria of selection, or without reference to the interpretations of actual readers. Just as problematic is sampling which makes no attempt to relate to holistic meanings of actual texts and their historical contexts. The linguistic devices which can be discovered in texts do not in themselves determine the 'truth' or 'falsity' of texts; that is a far more complex task and requires quite different means of investigation. While none of these authors has drawn significantly from literary theory (with the notable exception of their treatment of narrative structure) van Dijk and Bell, in particular, have contributed significantly to the development of integrative frameworks for the analysis of textual production, content and comprehension or reading, which largely protects their work from the worst excesses of what I have called the 'effects fallacy', the notion that structural analysis of itself yields information about how texts are read. Perhaps the most important contribution of these authors is that they have highlighted many features of journalistic production that media scholars, even those whose interest is in the dynamics of professional practice, tend to take for granted. This focus has a very important place in our understanding of the tension between the study of the political-economy of media institutions and the study of how media texts actually 'work' in practice.

References

Alvarado, M. and Boyd-Barrett, O. (1992) *Media Education: An Introduction*. London: British Film Institute.

Bell, A. (1991) *The Language of News Media.* Oxford: Basil Blackwell.

Cook, G. (1992) *The Discourse of Advertising.* London: Routledge.

Corner, J. (1986) *Documentary and the Mass Media.* London: Edward Arnold.

Davis, H. and Walton, P. (eds) (1988) *Language, Image, Media.* Oxford: Basil Blackwell.

Fowler, R. (1991) *Language in the News.* London: Routledge.

Galtung, J. and Ruge, M. H. (1965) The structure of foreign news. *Journal of Peace Research* 2 (1), 64–91.

Hall, S. (1982) The rediscovery of ideology: Return of the repressed in media studies. In M. Gurevitch *et al.* (eds) *Culture, Society and the Media.* London: Methuen.

Hall, S., Hobson, D., Lowe, A. and Willis, P. (eds) (1980) *Culture, Media, Language.* London: Hutchinson.

Hansen, A. and Murdock, G. (1985) Constructing the crowd: Populist discourse and press presentation. In Mosco and Wasko (eds) *The Critical Communications Review* Vol. 3. Norwood, NJ: Ablex.

Labov, W. and Waletsky, J. (1967) Narrative analysis: Oral versions of personal experience. In J. Helm (ed.) *Essays on the Verbal and Visual Arts.* Proceedings of the 1966 Annual Spring Meeting of the American Ethnological Society. Seattle: University of Washington Press.

Leavis, F. R. and Thompson, D. (1948) *Culture and Environment.* London: Chatto and Windus.

McQuail, D. (1983) *Mass Communication Theory.* London: Sage.

— (1992) Media performance. *Mass Communication and the Public Interest.* London: Sage.

Morely, D. (1980) *The 'Nationwide' Audience.* London: BFI.

Scannell, P. (ed.) (1991) *Broadcast Talk.* London: Sage.

Scannell, P. and Cardiff, D. (1991) *A Social History of Broadcasting,* Vol. 1. Oxford: Blackwell.

Trudgill, P. (1983) *Sociolinguistics.* Harmondsworth: Penguin.

Turner, J. (1988) *Film as Social Practice.* London: Routledge.

van Dijk, T. A. (1988a) *News Analysis.* Hillsdale, NJ: Lawrence Erlbaum.

— (1988b) *News as Discourse.* Hillsdale, NJ: Lawrence Erlbaum.

— (1991) *Racism and the Press.* London: Routledge.

3 What is a Text?

DAVID GRADDOL

Introduction

The writers whose work is included in this volume all share an interest in
the text. This, in turn, reflects the extent to which the text has become the
focus of analysis in recent theories of human communication. It will be clear
from the title of this volume, however, that the word 'text' is being used in
ways which depart from its traditional sense. In this article I briefly discuss
the nature of the text as it has become defined in recent writing, and discuss
some of the theoretical interests which have developed around it.

In traditional usage, the word 'text' is often used to distinguish written
words from other forms of communication. The examples below, based on
usages in *The Times* and *Sunday Times* during 1992, are typical, and contrast
the written word in turn with images, music, spoken delivery (intonation,
accent), and theatrical performance.

(1) The illustrations were imaginative, but the book was badly let down by
the text.

(2) The invitation gave Handel a chance to write an oratorio on a text so
sensitive that it demanded a discreet, out of town try out.

(3) An indifferent text, delivered with passion as Neil Kinnock could do
would have worked. An intelligent text, delivered in Smith's measured
tones, would have impressed in a different way. But this was an indifferent text, delivered without passion actually just plain lazy.

(4) The power of a well written text, allied to strong theatrical images,
would seem to be the healthy trend for 1993, even though the bulk of a
week's theatre going is pantomime and Christmas shows.

What is notable about these examples is that they exclude precisely what
is included by recent theories of the text. Now, it is possible to speak of an
advert on TV as a 'media text' and refer to the whole complex sequence of
speech, image, music and sound effects. Since the exclusion of these elements seems to be central to the meaning of 'text' in its more traditional

usage, there has clearly been something of a major shift in the way a text is conceived.

A text has a concrete existence of some kind and what all definitions of text seem to share is a concern with the nature of that materiality. In its narrowest form, a text is a verbal, written entity, printed with ink on paper. This definition is narrow in several senses. It excludes the nonverbal, it excludes certain rhetorical modes of the verbal (such as spoken); and it insists on a particular physical form in which this written language will manifest itself.

This draws attention to an important ambiguity in speaking of material form. Are we talking of physical material, such as ink, paper or plastic? Or of semiotic material such as words, images, and music? I will first examine the ways in which our expectations about the physical material of texts have evolved, and then discuss what has emerged as the more important and interesting area of debate: that of the semiotic construction of texts.

The Physical Materiality of a Text

Most texts can be described as *communicative artefacts*. A great deal flows from their status as artefacts. They are commodities which can enter social and economic relations: they can be advertised, sold for profit, presented as gifts, owned as property. Their creation typically involves divisions of labour and their use involves a wide range of social, political, and cultural practices. These things are clearly true of texts like a paperback novel, but they are also true of such things as private letters or school homework.

Artefacts are the product of a technology and their material form in part reflects the nature of that technology. Early techniques of written text production involved axes and knives which were used to inscribe marks on stone, wood or clay. The style of lettering and the content and purposes of such texts in some ways reflected these technologies: such texts tended to be brief, monumental or matters of official record. Parchment and pen led to the manufacture of a very different kind of artefact (a scroll rather than a tablet of stone, for example) and different styles of handwriting. Much later, the printing press gave rise to kinds of book construction which were different again, new forms of lettering and page layout.

The traditional notion of a text also reflects traditional technologies. As is well known, newer technologies permit forms of text other than words printed with ink on paper. Libraries make extensive use of microfiche, for example, to store texts in a compact way on photographic film. Electronic mail involves the exchange of messages which are composed on a keyboard and displayed on a computer screen. The works of Shakespeare and the *Oxford English Dictionary* are available on CD-ROM — a device like an audio compact disc but which is attached to a computer. The examples taken from *The Times* (above) were found using a CD-ROM. None of these texts require paper or ink; each requires rather different knowledge and skills on the part of the user; each form of text has become associated with different communicative and social functions. The newer definitions of text embrace a variety of media and physical forms.

The Semiotic Materiality of a Text

Since the revival of semiotic theory in the mid 1960s there has been an increasing interest in the semiotic, rather than the physical, form of a text. Some readers may feel that describing the semiotic level as being a material one is stretching the concept of materiality a little. Surely, they may argue, what we are dealing with at the semiotic level is precisely the *immaterial*, it is the level not of *things* but of *meaning*. The confusion comes from the systematic ambiguity of the 'sign' in semiotic theory. A sign has two sides to it, just as — to use Saussure's own example — a piece of paper must have two sides. There is the *signifier* which must be expressed in some kind of material form, and the *signified*, which refers to the content or meaning. Semioticians tend to regard any aspect of the signifier as being a matter of materiality. Words like 'expression', 'expressive substance', and 'form' are used in connection with signifiers. Words like 'meaning' and 'content' are associated with signifieds.

The physical life of a 'W'

What then is the material existence of a signifier if it is *not* a physical one? It has to be admitted that signifiers technically do *not* require physical form at all. There exists a class of signifiers which are significant 'absences'. Perhaps the most well known example in English literature is in Conan Doyle's novel *Silver Blaze*:

> 'Is there any other point to which you would wish to draw my attention?'

> 'To the curious incident of the dog in the night-time.'

> 'The dog did nothing in the night-time.'

> 'That was the curious incident', remarked Sherlock Holmes.

We can leave aside, for the moment, the thorny problem of signifiers which, like the dog's bark, are absences since it would be difficult (but not impossible) to fabricate a text from them. The majority of semiotic material does have some form of physical expression. However, the physical form which a particular signifier takes may be diverse, even ephemeral. Its semiotic materiality transcends these various physical expressions. Take the first letter of this paragraph (an upper case 'W'). I will sketch out something of its brief life history and the myriad forms of existence it will possess before it becomes a streak of black ink on paper — the condition in which I presume you now find it.

I will regard the W — somewhat arbitrarily — as coming into physical existence in the finger movement which depressed a key on the keyboard of the word processor I am using to compose this text. At that point its physicality lies in a gesture of flesh and bone, in a particular point of space and time. The act of hitting a key sets in train a number of electronic processes which I propose to gloss over. The letter now has some kind of murky electronic existence within the computer's memory. I do not know exactly what physical form it has but I guess it must be described in terms of electric charges in semiconductor material. I know enough about computers to understand that at heart they only 'know' about numbers and that every kind of semiotic material which they manipulate must be coded and reduced to numeric form. My W becomes coded as 87 in the ASCII code almost universally used by computers for this purpose. Actually, it might be better to express the number in the binary form 01010111 since I am told that is nearer the form in which the computer stores the number.

In some mysterious way, the computer is able to display the letter on a screen and thus give it a luminescent form which is directly perceptible. This is scarcely the start of its physical life. When I have finished the text it will be transmitted via modem and telephone line from my study at home to the university's mainframe computer. During this process it will be subjected to many new recodings; it will be given temporary new numeric forms which allow the system to check for errors in transmission and increase efficiency; the modem will convert the numbers into a variety of whistling tones more suited to a line designed for voice communication; these tones will be processed by the digital exchange and turned into numbers again — though not any number which bears a direct relation to the number 87.

Let us pause for a moment to consider the form and status of the W at this moment in the process. There exists a sequence of numbers which encode (in a very complex way which I do not fully understand) the durations and pitches of some tones produced by my modem. These tones in turn encode a series of numbers. This series of numbers in turn encodes the number 87 along with neighbouring numbers in the data stream. The number 87 at last encodes the W.

At the university, all this must be electronically unravelled. Eventually, yet another series of numbers swishes around the university data networks and finds the computer at my desk. I prepare a floppy disc for the publishers (we are now in the realm of magnetic media again), which they use to prepare the layout of the page which you are now looking at. The printers in turn use the resulting disc to prepare film (metal and plastic) for the printing process (paper and ink).

This repeated and multi-layered coding of signifiers is common in human communication systems. The International Standards Organisation (ISO) describes many such layers for data links used in the telecommunications industry. Through such processes digital communication allows the entire universe of human understanding to be reduced, by layer upon layer, to the two elements of the binary code. In creating such complexity, engineers have borrowed an idea from verbal language, which allows a very large number of signifiers to be constructed from a limited number of basic building blocks. For example, the words of this text are created from an inventory which includes the letters of the alphabet and a number of punctuation characters. These characters do not mean much in themselves but they are used to construct the signifiers (words) which *can* mean something.

The various forms of recoding which I have discussed are sometimes referred to as *expression to expression* coding: a coding which gives expressive substance new form. The signifier itself transcends such changes in existence, since ultimately what is at stake is its *opposition* to other characters in the available inventory (in this case the alphabet and punctuation characters) and this oppositional contrast exists at an abstract level. There is a continuity and unity in the material existence of my W from my first keystroke to the ink on paper. Its Wness was never called into question (I hope) during this process.

Actually, even when this W emerges as ink on paper there is little interest attached to it at the textual level. As we have just seen, it is part of a further expression to expression coding system which builds words from smaller bits of material just as the computer built the W from 8 bits of binary code. It is at the level of the word that we can first develop an interest in *expression to content* coding: the point at which the signifier (semiotic material) is related to the signified (meaning).

Spoken texts

The semiotic material of texts is thus composed of signifiers. When analysis has shifted to this level it is, of course, rather difficult to exclude the spoken word from the definition of a text. The differences in the physical form of speech and writing now lacks interest. If there is an interesting difference between speech and writing it will manifest itself at a textual level, in differences in semiotic construction.

Recent theories of the text hence embrace the idea of spoken text of some kind but there is still some debate about how far to go. Some theorists, such as Michael Halliday, are willing to go the whole way in regarding spoken events as texts which can be analysed in a similar way to written material. Live speech, however, lacks the quality of *durability* which other theorists regard as an important textual characteristic. This lack usually prevents a text from fully achieving the status of an artefact. Halliday himself (this volume) admits that 'the notion of "spoken text" is still not easily accepted'. He continues with the observation that spoken events became theorised as texts only when the technology of tape-recording allowed them to become 'the object of systematic study'. Hence even if spoken events are not regarded as texts at the moment of utterance they are, in practice, textualised in various ways, and must routinely be so transformed before they can be analysed as a text.

Tape-recording has the effect of turning an ephemeral spoken event into a relatively stable object. A tape-recording of speech shares with other kinds of text certain key qualities. It can be edited, copied, and recontextualised: that is, replayed in a different context (and to a different audience) to the one in which the words were originally uttered. A simpler (technologically rather than semiotically speaking) way to textualise speech is to transcribe it — to 'reduce it to writing'. Special conventions of punctuation and layout have arisen for representing spoken language in printed form. But it is a moot theoretical point whether or not, in the process of transcription, the event has been transformed into a written text rather than into a durable record of a spoken one.

Visual and other semiotic codes

Perhaps the most important extension in meaning which the term 'text' has acquired in recent theory is the inclusion of visual elements. This broader meaning of a text reflects the extent to which, within semiotic theory, nonverbal communication has become conceptualised as being like verbal language. It is hence not merely a metaphor to call a film a text, but more strongly theoretically motivated. A good example of this theoretical approach is provided by Graeme Turner in this volume who describes the 'languages' of film. By this he means the conventions of image composition and sequencing which can be analysed in similar ways to the vocabulary and syntax of verbal language. But he also draws into the definition of 'language' sound effects, music, and indeed any other semiotic system which is employed in a structured way.

The Semiotic Construction of a Text

Texts have structure. They are not random collections of messages but orderly constructions. Within this volume, for example, Halliday considers the rhetorical structure of the clause; Hasan explores the connections between clauses; Bell discusses the larger narrative structure of news stories. Structure thus occurs at many different levels in a text. One might speak not so much of the structure of a text but of its architecture.

Architectural design, of course, is not pure genius but subject to a number of constraints and conventions. These include codes of aesthetics, the intended practical and social functions of the building, institutionally defined building codes, and the structural properties of the chosen materials. So it is with texts (indeed, some theorists would be happy to regard a building as an architectural text). The conventional form that a text takes is referred to as its *genre*. Within media studies the word genre usually implies a concern for content and the way certain themes are treated (e.g. the 'Western' film, or the 'News Bulletin'). In linguistic analysis there is a greater concern for form and function. A genre, in both areas of study, is taken to be socially constituted, representing particular institutional interests and ideological functions. In Halliday's framework — which many of the contributors to this volume explicitly or implicitly make use of — a text cannot help but encode particular social relations (between reader and writer, and between third parties), as well as communicate particular ideas.

The Semiotic Resources of a Text

Historically, our modern word 'text' derived from a Latin word meaning 'to weave'. A text was, metaphorically, a substance created by weaving many threads. Those threads were originally conceived to be ideas. More recent theories appeal to a similar metaphor, conceptualising a text as something which is woven from several different semiotic threads. As Anne Freadman has remarked:

> texts are the product of an interaction of a variety of 'languages', or semiotic systems, none necessarily homologous with any other . . . it is practically impossible to find a text that mobilises only one language . . . if we are to account for what it is to make a text, we are unlikely to find out a great deal from studying the properties of only one of its languages. (Freadman as cited by Threadgold, 1988: 328)

One of the problems facing a theorist who wishes to explain 'how a text works' is to understand the contributions made by these different semiotic systems, and how they interact with each other to create a complex whole.

Semiotic resources of a spoken text

Spoken language typically employs a number of semiotic devices besides verbal language, of which the most important is probably those features of intonation, stress and rhythm which together make up the *prosodic system*.

One of the main functions of prosody in speech is an organisational one: it helps 'chunk' the text and mark important structural boundaries such as those relating to clause structure; it identifies information structure by helping distinguish between 'given' and 'new'; and through emphasis can mark contrasts and deviation from expectation.

Prosody is a complex semiotic system which serves a variety of functions besides 'chunking'. It helps indicate such things as irony or sarcasm, for example, and can in various other ways modify the meaning of the verbal message. In some languages, like Thai or Mandarin — the so called tone languages — pitch movement also forms a part of the lexical system. Hence, the system of stress and intonation is intimately connected with verbal forms: in speech, the one cannot exist without the other. Yet another function of prosody allows it to convey such things as emotion, gender identity (and sometimes other kinds of social identity), and attitude of a speaker. This is a more autonomous mechanism. Speech which has been filtered so that all the higher frequencies are removed (as happens when voices are heard through a wall) cannot be understood at the verbal level, but much of the emotional, attitude, and speaker identity information is still communicated. A listener can still typically distinguish between male and female voices, tell whether one or both parties are angry, upset and so on.

Those aspects of body movement and posture which are popularly called 'body language' are also important in signalling attitude and attention. Gesture is mainly a speaker's behaviour: many kinds of body movement are synchronised with the rhythm of speech and help indicate structural boundaries in a similar way to prosody. Gesture and eye contact can also help regulate turn taking (as is shown by Swann & Graddol, 1993, for example).

Semiotic resources of a written text

Punctuation in written text serves some similar functions to prosody in spoken text, but cannot easily represent the complexities of spoken language: it is a much cruder system, and one which does not map on easily to the phenomena of speech. A question mark, for example, does not indicate a rising 'questioning' intonation, but is used for any kind of question regardless of intonation. (Questions beginning with 'Wh-' words like 'who' regularly have a falling intonation in many varieties of English.) The subtleties of rhythm and speaking rate can hardly be represented in writing at all.

Printed texts, however, use a number of semiotic resources not available to speakers. A typeset page makes use of a typographic system, of characters in different fonts, different weights and point sizes. This system is used to indicate headings and other organising devices. The use of space on the page is itself a semiotic mechanism: the size of the page, the number of columns, the amount and arrangement of white space — all these signify to the reader things about the generic nature of the text — broadsheet or tabloid newspaper, for example.

Handwriting comes close to paralleling the accent system of speech in conveying information about speaker identity, but there is far less consensus and regularity in the social meaning of handwriting — less so now than once used to be the case.

The semiotic resources of a media text

Words and images have always been closely related in texts. Indeed, modern writing itself seems to have arisen from iconic symbols and pictograms. In the middle ages, illuminated manuscripts brought words together with image, colour, and other forms of decoration. Such nonverbal elements may themselves be regarded as conforming to generic conventions in composition and content: photographic images in the western press, for example, are often composed so that they read from left to right, top to bottom, in the same way as writing.

In TV or film texts music and sound effects can be used in a very similar range of ways to the prosodic system in spoken texts. Sound can be used to group together several shots into a single 'intonational group' and mark significant boundaries in editing. A significant beat or musical gesture can coincide with a movement or action on the screen thus giving it emphasis. Sound is also an important part of the affect system of film and TV, and helps sets mood and indicates to the viewer how to respond emotionally to images. Music also serves as an identity system, by indicating historical period, geographical and cultural location, and so on.

There have been occasional attempts to fashion a musical language which is capable of the autonomous expression of ideas. Richard Wagner, for example, attempted to create symbolic inventories through the *leitmotif* system (allowing his music to lie, or at least betray a tension between characters' words and thoughts).

In media texts especially, but also in other forms of text, the different semiotic threads may relate to each other in different ways. Does one just modulate or diffusely support another (as often occurs with music and visual narrative); are two played against each other, as when in a children's picture book the pictures tell of events in a different way to the words? The interplay between different semiotic threads is an important part of textual strategy and one in which several theorists are interested.

The History of Texts

Texts, like other artefacts, have a production history. They are created within particular historical and material circumstances by people who work in particular relations of power. The final form which a text takes will reflect in various ways the historical process of its production. Several theorists have become keenly interested in this history, partly to understand what kinds of social relations and ideological positions have become encoded in texts, partly because they consider that some of the more interesting ideological effects of a text occur during its creation, rather than its consumption.

For example, an important aspect of text production lies in the ways in which a writer is persuaded or coerced, gently or not so gently, to conform to generic conventions which may serve the interests of others. Bell (1991) describes in detail the processes of selection and editing out of which a news story emerges. A school essay is typically preceded by various forms of spoken interaction and its eventual conformity to generic requirements formally graded.

Creation is only one half of the history of a text — the remainder of its history tells of its use. The creators of a text may have difficulty in predicting how it will eventually be used. The same text can be read many times and used in many different ways by different people. Texts can be relocated, recontextualised, plagiarised. The text may already contain quotations from earlier texts and fragments from it in turn may appear in other future texts.

Take, for example, a television interview with an international politician which is sold by a news agency to the domestic television companies of many countries, who will each select different moments and set them within different stories. Within the same broadcasting company, a sound bite may become shorter and tighter in successive news bulletins and the story surrounding it may change. Later, the sequence may be used in quite a different programme as archive or library material.

And in each case, the programme will be viewed by people with different interests and experiences of the world, engaged in different social activities: eating, ironing, doing homework, avoiding doing homework, chatting, avoiding talking, dozing, trying to stay awake. For some, if not most, the meaning of the TV text becomes inseparable from their own purposes and activities. Producers of media texts have long been concerned with how audiences respond and make use of their material, and how TV programmes are located in domestic practices and timetables. This interest in the way the meaning of a text emerges from its embedding in wider social practices is one of the distinctive features of recent theory.

Texts and Literacy

Closely associated with definitions of the text are definitions of literacy. Literacy might be defined as the ability to produce, understand, and use texts in culturally appropriate ways. Hence changes in the accepted definition of text have implications for the perceived nature of literacy.

Etymologically, 'literacy' refers to the ability to read rather than write, to understand rather than to produce. The modern uses of the word literacy have never completely thrown off that asymmetry. A literate person is expected to be able to read complex printed productions, but only to produce a manuscript suitable for publication, not a finished product. The publisher or editor takes on the equivalent role of the amanuensis or scribe in relation to the selection of type faces and sizes, page layout and so on.

Literacy often implies not just the ability to read but also the knowledge which comes from reading. The kinds of texts which make a person literate are conservatively defined, however. The canonical works of literature are included; media texts, like other forms of popular culture, are typically excluded.

The modern world is perfused with texts in the wider sense. Adverts, packaging, leaflets, forms, till receipts, school timetables — all are texts each with their own conventions of design and function. And if the skills in using a book, such as how to open it and where to find an index or publisher's name are to be regarded as a component of literacy, then is not knowing which end to open a cornflakes packet also a literacy skill of some kind, requiring the user to be able to 'read' the packaging and understand cultural conventions in carton design? Such problems hint at why debates about literacy and the text have such powerful political as well as educational agendas.

References

Bell, A. (1991) *The Language of News Media*. Oxford: Blackwell.
Swann, J. and Graddol, D. (1994) Gender inequalities in classroom talk. In D. Graddol, J. Maybin and B. Stierer (eds) *Researching Language and Literacy in Social Context*. Clevedon: Multilingual Matters.
Threadgold, T. (1988) The genre debate. *Southern Review* 21, 315–29.

4 Spoken and Written Modes of Meaning

M. A. K. HALLIDAY

Spoken Language and Education

It seems to me that one of the most productive areas of discussion between linguists and educators in the past quarter century has been that of speech and the spoken language. Twenty-five years ago, when I launched the 'Linguistics and English Teaching' project in London, which produced *Breakthrough to Literacy* and *Language in Use*, it was still rare to find references to the place of spoken language in school, or to the need for children to be articulate as well as literate. Dell Hymes had not yet introduced 'communicative competence'; the words *oracy* and *orality* had not yet entered the field (Andrew Wilkinson's *Some Aspects of Oracy* appeared in 1967); David Abercrombie (1963/1965) had only just published his 'Conversation and Spoken Prose'. Language, in school, as in the community at large, meant written language.

The word *language* itself was hardly used in educational contexts. In the primary school, there was reading and writing; in the secondary school there was English, which meant literature and composition. Not that a classroom was a temple of silence; but the kind of spoken language that had a place, once a pupil had got beyond the infant school, was prepared speech: reading aloud, drama, debating — language that was written in order to be spoken, or at least was closely monitored in the course of its production. Spoken language in its natural form, spontaneous and unselfconscious, was not taken seriously as a medium of learning.

Among linguists, by contrast, the spoken language had pride of place. One learnt in the first year of a linguistics course that speech was logically and historically prior to writing. The somewhat aggressive tone with which linguists often proclaimed this commitment did not endear them to educators, who sensed that it undermined their authority as guardians of literacy and felt threatened by a scale of values they did not understand, according to which English spelling was out of harmony with the facts of the

English language — whereas for them it was the pronunciation that was out of step, being a distorted reflection of the reality that lay in writing.

The linguists' professional commitment to the primacy of speech did not, however, arise from or carry with it an awareness of the properties of spoken discourse. It arose from the two sources of diachronic phonology (the study of sound change) and articulatory phonetics (the study of speech production), which came together in twentieth century phonological theory. This was an interpretation of the system of speech sounds and of the phonological properties of the stream of speech; it did not involve any attempt to study the grammar and semantics of spoken as distinct from written language. As early as 1911, in his discussion of functional variation in language, Mathesius (1911/1964) was referring to 'how the styles of speech are manifested in the pronunciation of language, in the stock of words, and in syntax' (p. 23), and to 'the influence of functional styles on the lexical and semantic aspects of speech' (p. 24); and it is clear that 'speech' for him (*parole*) did encompass both spoken and written varieties. But it was not until the 1950s, with the appearance of tape recorders, that natural speech could become the object of systematic study. The notion of 'spoken text' is still not easily accepted, as can be seen from the confusion that prevails when spontaneous speech is reduced to writing in order to be analysed.

Spoken language came to figure in educational discussions in the context of language in the classroom: the language used by teachers to structure, direct and monitor their students' progress through the lesson. But the emphasis was on verbal strategies rather than on the text as a document; the investigators of the fifties and early sixties were not concerned with the particular place of spoken language in the learning process. It was assumed, of course, that students learnt by listening; but the expository aspects of the teacher's language were given little attention, while the notion that a student might be using his own talk as a means of learning was nowhere part of the picture. Probably it would have been felt that the principal means of learning through the spoken language was by asking questions; but studies of the early seventies revealed that students seldom do ask questions — not, that is, while they are occupying their role (i.e. in class). It is the teachers that ask the questions; and when they do so, both question and answer may be somewhat removed from the patterns of natural dialogue.

Complexity of Natural Speech

Already half a century earlier Franz Boas (1911/1963) had stressed the unconscious character of language, unique (as he saw it) among the phenomena of human culture. Boas' observation was to be understood in its contemporary context as a characterization of the language system (*langue*);

not that, writing in 1911, he could have read Saussure's *Course in General Linguistics*, any more than Mathesius could have done; but the unconscious was in the air, so to speak, and playing a critical role in the conception of systems as regularities underlying human behaviour. But Boas may also have had in mind the unconsciousness of the behaviour itself: the act of speaking (*act de parole*) as an unconscious act. The lack of conscious awareness of the underlying SYSTEM, and the difficulty that people have in bringing it to consciousness, are things which language shares with other semiotic systems — for example, social systems like that of kinship; what is unusual about language is the extent to which even the MANIFESTATION of the system, the actual process of meaning, remains hidden from observation, by performer and receiver alike. In that respect talking is more like dancing, or even running, than it is like playing chess. Speaker and listeners are of course aware that the speaker is speaking; but they are typically not aware of what he is saying, and if asked to recall it, not only the listeners but also the speaker will ordinarily offer a paraphrase, something that is true to the meaning but not by any means true to the wording. To focus attention on the wording of language is something that has to be learnt — for example if you are studying linguistics; it can be a difficult and somewhat threatening task.

About 30 years ago, as a result of being asked to teach English intonation to foreign students, I began observing natural spontaneous discourse in English; and from the start I was struck by a curious fact. Not only were people unconscious of what they themselves were saying; they would often deny, not just that they HAD said something I had observed them to say, but also that they ever COULD say it. For example, I noticed the utterance *it'll've been going to've been being tested every day for the past fortnight soon*, where the verbal group *will have been going to have been being tested* makes five serial tense choices, present in past in future in past in future, and is also passive. This passed quite unnoticed by both the speaker and the person it was addressed to; yet at the time it was being seriously questioned whether a simple verb form like *has been being tested,* which one can hear about once a week, could ever occur in English. Five-term tense forms are, predictably, very rare — one can in fact make a reasonable guess as to how rare, on the basis of observed frequencies of two- and three-term tense forms together with the constraints of the tense system; but they are provided for within the resources of the spoken language. Another instance I observed was *they said they'd been going to've been paying me all this time, only the funds just kept on not coming through.*

Other things I noted regularly included present in present participial nonfinites like *being cooking* in *I never heard you come in — it must have been with being cooking*; marked thematic elements with reprise pronoun, as in *that poor child I couldn't get him out of my mind*; and relatives reaching into dependent clauses, such as *that's the noise which when you say it to a horse the horse goes faster.* These are all systematic features that people are unaware that they incorporate in their speech, and often deny having said even when they are pointed out; or at least reject as unsystematic — after 'I didn't say it', the next line of defence is 'well it was a mistake'. But of course it was not a mistake; it was a regular product of the system of spoken English.

But perhaps the most unexpected feature of those early observations was the complexity of some of the sentence structures. Here are two examples from recordings made at the time:

(1) It's very interesting, because it fairly soon is established when you're meeting with somebody what kind of conversation you're having: for example, you may know and tune in pretty quickly to the fact that you're there as the support, perhaps, in the listening capacity — that you're there, in fact, to help the other person sort their ideas; and therefore your remarks, in that particular type of conversation, are aimed at drawing out the other person, or in some way assisting them, by reflecting them, to draw their ideas out, and you may tune in to this, or you may be given this role and refuse it, refuse to accept it, which may again alter the nature of your conversation.

(2) The other man who kicks is the full-back, who usually receives the ball way behind the rest of his team, either near his line or when somebody's done what the stand-off in the first example was doing, kicked over the defenders; the full-back should be able then to pick it up, and his job is usually to kick for touch — nearly always for touch because he's miles behind the rest of his side, and before he can do anything else with the ball he's got to run up into them, before he can pass it, because he can't pass the ball forward, and if he kicks it forward to another of his side the other man's automatically off-side.

And you get a penalty for that, do you, the other side?

Depending on whether it's kicking or passing forward. Passing forward — no, it's a scrum. If you kick it forward and somebody else picks it up that will be a penalty.

And if not, if the other side picks —

If the other side picks it up that's all right; but the trouble is this is in fact tactics again, because you don't want to put the ball into the hands of the other side if you can avoid it because it's the side that has possession, as in most games of course, is at an advantage.

Examples such as these were noteworthy in two respects. One was they they embodied patterns of parataxis (combining with equal status) and hypotaxis (combining with unequal status) between clauses which could run to considerable length and depth. The other was that they were remarkably well formed: although the speaker seemed to be running through a maze, he did not get lost, but emerged at the end with all brackets closed and all structural promises fulfilled. And this drew attention to a third property which I found interesting: that while the listeners had absorbed these passages quite unconsciously and without effort, they were difficult to follow in writing.

Lexical density

These two examples have been around for a long time; so let me turn to some recent specimens taken from recordings made by Guenter Plum to whom I am indebted for drawing them to my attention. In these spontaneous narratives Plum regularly finds sequences such as the following:

1A I had to wait, I had to wait till it was born and till it got to about eight or ten weeks of age, then I bought my first dachshund, a black-and-tan bitch puppy, as they told me I should have bought a bitch puppy to start off with, because if she wasn't a hundred percent good I could choose a top champion dog to mate her to, and then produce something that was good, which would be in my own kennel prefix.

This displays the same kind of mobility that the earlier observations had suggested was typically associated with natural, unselfconscious speech — which is what it was. I asked myself how I would have expressed this in writing, and came up with two rewordings; the first (1B) was fairly informal, as I might have told it in a letter to a friend:

1B I had to wait till it was born and had got to about eight or ten weeks of age; that was when I bought my first dachshund, a black-and-tan bitch puppy. By all accounts I should have bought a bitch puppy at the start, because if she wasn't a hundred percent good I could mate her with a top champion dog and produce a good offspring — which would carry my own kennel prefix.

My second rewording (1C) was a more formal written variant.

IC Some eight or ten weeks after the birth saw my first acquisition of a dachshund, a black-and-tan bitch puppy. It seems that a bitch puppy would have been the appropriate initial purchase, because of the possibility of mating an imperfect specimen with a top champion dog, the improved offspring then carrying my own kennel prefix.

The aim was to produce a set of related passages of text differing along this one dimension, which could be recognized as going from 'most likely to be spoken' to 'most likely to be written'. How such variation actually correlates with difference in the medium is of course problematic; the relationship is a complicated one, both because written/spoken is not a simple dichotomy

— there are many mixed and intermediate types — and because the whole space taken up by such variation is by now highly coded: in any given instance the wording used is as much the product of stylistic conventions in the language as of choices made by individual speakers and writers. Here I am simply moving along a continuum which anyone familiar with English usage can readily interpret in terms of 'spoken' and 'written' poles.

The kind of difference that we find among these three variants is one that is often referred to as a difference of 'texture', and this familiar rhetorical metaphor is a very appropriate one: it is as if they were the product of a different weave, with fibres of a different yarn. But when we look behind these traditional metaphors, at the forms of language they are describing, we find that much of the difference can be accounted for as the effect of two related lexicosyntactic variables. The written version has a much higher lexical density; at the same time, it has a much simpler sentential structure. Let us examine these concepts in turn.

The *lexical density* is the proportion of lexical items (content words) to the total discourse. It can be measured in various ways: the ratio of lexical items either to total running words or to some higher grammatical unit, most obviously the clause; with or without weighting for relative frequency (in the language) of the lexical items themselves. Here we will ignore the relative frequency of the lexical items and refer simply to the total number in each case, providing two measures (Table 1): the number of lexical items (1) as a proportion of the number of running words, and (2) as a proportion of the number of clauses. Only non-embedded clauses have been counted (if embedded clauses are also counted, then each lexical item occurring in them is counted twice, since it figures in both the embedded and the matrix clause — i.e. both in the PART, and in the WHOLE of which it is a part). The figures are given to the nearest decimal.

Table 1 Lexical density of texts 1A, 1B and 1C

	(1) Lexical items	(2) Running words	(1:2)	(3) Clauses	(1:3)
1A	23	83	1:3.6	13	1.8:1
1B	26	68	1:2.6	8	3.3:1
1C	25	55	1:2.2	4	6.3:1

As Jean Ure showed in 1969 (Ure, 1971), the lexical density of a text is a function of its place on a register scale which she characterized as running from most active to most reflective: the nearer to the 'language-in-action' end of the scale, the lower the lexical density. Since written language is characteristically reflective rather than active, in a written text the lexical density tends to be higher; and it increases as the text becomes further away from spontaneous speech.

Jean Ure measured lexical density as a proportion of running words; but as is suggested by the figures given above, if it is calculated with reference to the number of clauses the discrepancy stands out more sharply. Thus in the example given above, while the number of lexical items remained fairly constant and the number of running words fell off slightly, the number of clauses fell steeply: from 13, to 8, to 4. In other words, the lexical density increases not because the number of lexical items goes up but because the number of non-lexical items — grammatical words — goes down; and the number of clauses goes down even more.

Let us attempt a similar rewording the other way round, this time beginning with a passage of formal written English taken from *Scientific American*:

2A Private civil actions at law have a special significance in that they provide an outlet for efforts by independent citizens. Such actions offer a means whereby the multiple initiatives of private citizens, individually or in groups, can be brought to bear on technology assessment, the internalization of costs and environmental protection. They constitute a channel through which the diverse interests, outlooks and moods of the general public can be given expression.

The current popular concern over the environment has stimulated private civil actions of two main types.

2B is my attempt at a somewhat less 'written' version; while 2C is another step nearer to speech:

2B Private civil actions at law are especially significant because they can be brought by independent citizens, so enabling them to find an outlet for their efforts. By bringing these actions, either as individuals or in groups, private citizens can regularly take the initiative in assessing technology, internalizing costs and protecting the environment. Through the use of these actions as a channel, the general public are able to express all their various interests, their outlooks, and their moods.

Because people are currently concerned about the environment, they have been bringing numerous private civil actions, which have been mainly of two types.

2C One thing is especially significant, and that is that people should be able to bring private civil actions at law, because by doing this independent citizens can become involved. By bringing these actions, whether they are acting as individuals or in groups, private citizens can keep on taking the initiative; they can help to assess technology, they can help to internalize costs, and they can help to protect the environment. The general public, who want all kinds of different things, and who think and feel in all kinds of different ways, can express all these wants and thoughts and feelings by bringing civil actions at law.

At present, people are concerned about the environment; so they have been bringing quite a few private civil actions, which have been mainly of two kinds.

Table 2 Lexical density of texts 2A, 2B and 2C

	(1) Lexical items	*(2)* Running words	*(1:2)*	*(3)* Clauses	*(1:3)*
2A	48	87	1:1.8	5	9.6:1
2B	48	101	1:2.1	12	4.0:1
2C	51	132	1:2.6	17	3.0:1

Table 2 shows the relative lexical density of the three variants of Text 2. Again, the number of lexical items has remained fairly constant; the variation in lexical density results from the increase in the total number of words — which means, therefore, in the number of grammatical words. This, in turn, is related to the increase in the number of clauses — where, however, the discrepancy is again much more striking.

Grammatical intricacy

We have characterized the difference in general terms by saying that written language has a higher lexical density than spoken language; this expresses it as a positive feature of written discourse and suggests that writing is more complex, since presumably lexical density is a form of complexity. Could we then turn the formulation around, and express the difference as a positive characteristic of spoken language? To say that spoken discourse has more words in it, or even more clauses, does not seem to convey anything very significant about it. We need to look at how the words and clauses are organized.

Let us consider a shorter example of a pair of texts related in the same way, one 'more written' (Text 3A), the other 'more spoken' (Text 3B). I have constructed these so that they resemble the originals of Texts 1 and 2;

Table 3 Notational conventions for the clause complex[a]

Logical-semantic relations		Interdependencies	
Category	Symbol	Category	Symbol
expansion:	elaborating = extending + enhancing x	parataxis hypotaxis[b]	1 2 3 . . . α β γ . . .
projection:	idea ' locution ''		

[a] For details of analysis see Halliday (1985: 192ff).
[b] Hypotaxis is not equivalent to embedding, which is a constituency (not a 'tactic') relation.

but they are based on a natural example occurring in two texts in which a person had described the same experience twice over, once in speech and once in writing.

More 'written':

3A Every previous visit had left me with a sense of the risk to others in further attempts at action on my part.

More 'spoken':

3B Whenever I'd visited there before I'd end up feeling that other people might get hurt if I tried to do anything more.

The first version (3A) is one sentence consisting of one clause: a 'simple sentence' in traditional grammar. The second version (3B) consists of four clauses (assuming that *ended up feeling* and *tried to do* are each single predicators); but these too have to be transcribed as one sentence, since they are related by hypotaxis — only one has independent status. These four clauses form what is called in systemic grammar a *clause complex* (for analysis and notation see Table 3):

Whenever I'd visited there before	${}^1\beta$
I'd end up feeling	α α
that other people might get hurt	α ${}'\beta$ α
if I tried to do anything more	α β ${}^1\beta$

The structural representation of this clause complex is given in Figure 1. The lower lexical density of Text 3B again appears clearly as a function of the number of clauses. But the significant factor is not that this text consists of four clauses where Text 3A consists of only one. It is that Text 3B consists of a CLAUSE COMPLEX consisting of four clauses. The clauses are not strung together as one simple sentence after another; they are syntactically related. Looked at from the point of view of the sentence structure, it is the

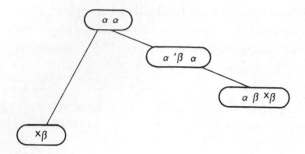

Figure 1 Structural representation of Text 3B as clause complex

spoken text that appears more complex than the written one. The spoken text has a lower degree of lexical density, but a higher degree of grammatical intricacy.

Types of complexity

Two distinct points need to be made here, and both of them run counter to received attitudes towards spoken language. One is that speech is not, in any general sense, 'simpler' than writing; if anything, it is more complex. There are, of course, many different kinds of complexity, and we have already noted one measure — lexical density — whereby speech will appear as the simpler of the two. But the patterns we have been illustrating, which are the patterns of the organization of the clause complex, referred to above as *grammatical intricacy,* would seem to be at least as central to any conception of complexity; and in this respect, speech appears as the more complex. The 'syntactic complexity expected in writing', with which Deborah Tannen (1982) introduces her discussion of oral and literate strategies, does not turn out to be a characteristic of written discourse.

Of course, there are many other variables. Some writers achieve considerable intricacy in the structure of the clause complex; it can be learnt and consciously developed as a style. Some forms of spoken discourse, on the other hand, militate against it: rapid-fire dialogue presents no scope for lengthy interdependencies — complex semantic patterns can be construed BETWEEN interactants, but usually without being realized in syntactic terms. And the categories of 'written' and 'spoken' are themselves highly indeterminate — they may refer to the medium in which a text was originally produced, or the medium for which it was intended, or in which it is performed in a particular instance; or not to the medium at all, but to other properties of a text which are seen as characteristic of the medium. So it is important to indicate specifically which variable of discourse is being referred to, when one variety is being said to display some distinctive characteristic.

Spoken and written language, then, tend to display different KINDS of complexity; each of them is more complex in its own way. Written language tends to be lexically dense, but grammatically simple; spoken language tends to be grammatically intricate, but lexically sparse. But these *buts* should really be *ands,* because the paired properties are complementary, not counterexpectative. It is hard to find a form of expression which will show them to be such; I have usually had recourse to metaphors of structure versus movement, saying for example that the complexity of written language is crystalline, whereas the complexity of spoken language is choreographic. The complexity of spoken language is in its flow, the dynamic mobility whereby each figure provides a context for the next one, not only defining its point of departure but also setting the conventions by reference to which it is to be interpreted.

With the sentence of written language, there is solidarity among its parts such that each equally prehends and is prehended by all the others. It is a structure, and is not essentially violated by being represented synoptically, as a structural unit. With the clause complex, of spoken language, there is no such solidarity, no mutual prehension among all its parts. Its mode of being is as process, not as product. But since the study of grammar grew out of writing — it is when language comes to be written down that it becomes an object of study, not before — our grammars are grammars of the written language. We have not yet learnt to write choreographic grammars; so we look at spoken language through the lens of a grammar designed for writing. Spoken discourse thus appears as a distorted variant of written discourse, and not unnaturally it is found wanting.

For example, Chafe (1982) identifies a number of regular differences between speech and writing; writing is marked by more nominalization, more genitive subjects and objects, more participles, more attributive adjectives, more conjoined, serial and sequenced phrases, more complement clauses, and more relative clauses; all of which he summarizes by saying, 'Written language tends to have an "integrated" quality which contrasts with the fragmented quality of spoken language' (p. 38).

The general picture is that of written language as richly endowed, while speech is a poor man's assemblage of shreds and patches. But Chafe has described both speech and writing using a grammar of writing; so it is inevitable that writing comes out with positive checks all round. Not that he has no pluses on the spoken side: speech is said to have more first person references, more speaker mental processes, more *I means* and *you knows,* more emphatic particles, more vagueness like *sort of,* and more direct quotes — all the outward signs of language as interpersonal action. Chafe summarizes them as features of 'involvement' as opposed to 'detachment'; but they are items of low generality, and negative rather than positive in their social value.

This leads me to the second point that, as I remarked above, runs counter to our received attitudes towards speech. It is not only that speech allows for such a considerable degree of intricacy; when speakers exploit this potential, they seem very rarely to flounder or get lost in it. In the great majority of instances, expectations are met, dependencies resolved, and there are no loose ends. The intricacy of the spoken language is matched by the orderliness of spoken discourse.

The Myth of Structureless Speech

Why then are we led to believe that spoken discourse is a disorganized array of featureless fragments? Here it is not just the lack of an interpretative grammar for spoken language, but the convention of observing spoken discourse that we need to take into account.

Speech, we are told, is marked by hesitations, false starts, anacolutha, slips and trips of the tongue, and a formidable paraphernalia of so-called performance errors; these are regularly, more or less ritually, cited as its main distinguishing feature. There is no disputing the fact that these things occur, although they are much less prevalent than we are asked to believe. They are characteristic of the rather self-conscious, closely self-monitored speech that goes, for example, with academic seminars, where I suspect much of the observation and recording has taken place. If you are consciously planning your speech as it goes along and listening to check the outcome, then you naturally tend to lose your way: to hesitate, back up, cross out, and stumble over the words. But these things are not a particular feature of natural spontaneous discourse, which tends to be fluent, highly organized and grammatically well formed. If you are interacting spontaneously and without self-consciousness, then the clause complexes tend to flow smoothly without you falling down or changing direction in the middle, and neither speaker nor listener is at all aware of what is happening. I recorded this kind of casual discourse many years ago when studying the language spoken to and in the presence of a small child, and was struck by its fluency, well formedness, and richness of grammatical pattern. Interestingly, the same feature is apparent at the phonological level: spontaneous discourse is typically more regular in its patterns of rhythm.

However, while the myth of the scrappiness of speech may have arisen at the start from the kind of discourse that was first recorded, it has been perpetuated in a different way — by the conventions with which it is presented and discussed. Consider, for example, Beattie (1983: 33):

Spontaneous speech is unlike written text. It contains many mistakes, sentences are usually brief and indeed the whole fabric of verbal expression is riddled with hesitations and silences. To take a very simple example: in a seminar which I recorded, an articulate (and well-known) linguist was attempting to say the following:

> No, I'm coming back to the judgements question. Indeterminacy appears to be rife. I don't think it is, if one sorts out which are counterexamples to judgement.

But what he actually said was:

> No *I'm saying* I'm coming back to the judgements question (267) *you know there appear to* (200) *ah* indeterminacy (1467) appears to be rife. I don't think it is (200) *if one* (267) if one sorts out which one counterexamples (267) to judgement, I mean observing.

Here, the brief silences (unfilled pauses) have been measured in milliseconds and marked (these are numbers in brackets) and all other types of hesitation — false starts, repetitions, filled pauses and parenthetic remarks put in italics. It is these hesitations (both filled and unfilled) which dominate spontaneous speech and give it its distinctive structure and feeling.

In other words: when you speak, you cannot destroy your earlier drafts. If we were to represent written language in a way that is comparable to such representations of spoken language, we should be including in the text every preliminary scrap of manuscript or typescript, with all the crossings out, misspellings, redraftings and periods of silent thought; this would then tell us what the writer actually wrote. Figure 2 is a specimen.

Now, there are undoubtedly research purposes for which it is important to show the planning, trial and error, and revision work that has gone into the production of a piece of discourse: it can have both educational and clinical applications. This is as true of writing as it is of speech: written material of this kind has been used in neuropsychiatry for most of a century. But for many purposes the discarded first attempts are merely trivial; they clutter up the text, making it hard to read, and impart to it a spurious air of quaintness. What is much more serious, however, is that transcribing spoken discourse in this way gives a false account of what it is really like. It may seem a harmless piece of self-gratification for a few academics to present spoken language as a pathological phenomenon; one might argue that they deceive nobody but themselves. But unfortunately this is not the way. Just when we are seeing real collaboration between linguists and educators, and the conception of 'language in education' is at last gaining ground as a field of training and research, it seems we are determined to put the clock back to a time when spoken language was not to be taken seriously and could have no place in the theory and practice of education.

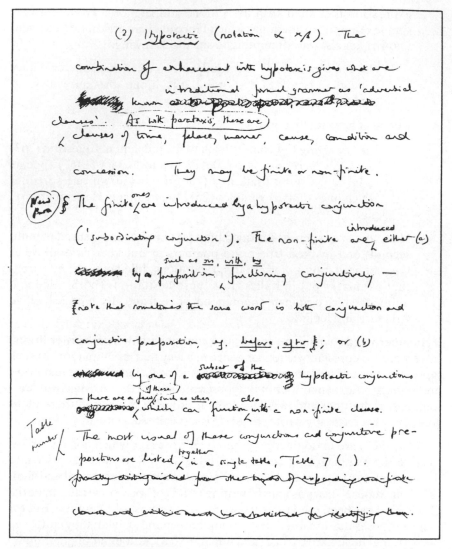

Figure 2 Written discourse

Let us recapitulate the argument. Speech and writing as forms of discourse are typically associated with the two modal points on the continuum from most spontaneous to most self-monitored language: spontaneous discourse is usually spoken, self-monitored discourse is usually written. We can therefore conveniently label these two modal points 'spoken' and 'written' language. Spoken and written language do not differ in their systematicity: each is equally highly organized, regular, and productive of coherent discourse. (This is clearly implied once we recognize them both as 'language'.)

Discourse in either medium can be characterized by hesitation, revision, change of direction, and other similar features; these tend to arise when attention is being paid to the process of text production. Since highly monitored discourse is typically written, these features are actually more characteristic of writing than of speech; but because most written text becomes public only in its final, edited form, the hesitations and discards are lost and the reader is shielded from seeing the process at work. Where they are likely to remain in is precisely where they occur least, in the more spontaneous kinds of writing such as personal letters. (Not all discourse features that are regarded as pathological, or assigned negative value, are of this self-monitoring kind. One form of discourse that has received a lot of critical attention is casual conversation, where the well-recognized characteristics are those of turn-taking, such as interruptions and overlaps. But the strictly LINGUISTIC 'deviations' of casual conversation are mainly systematic features that would not seem deviant if we had a grammar that took into account the specifically 'spoken' resources of the linguistic system.)

Spoken and written language do differ, however, in their preferred patterns of lexicogrammatical organization. Neither is more organized than the other, but they are organized in different ways. We have already identified the principal variable. Spoken language tends to accommodate more clauses in the syntagm (to favour greater 'grammatical intricacy'), with fewer lexical items in the clause. Written language tends to accommodate more lexical items in the clause (to favour greater 'lexical density'), with fewer clauses in the syntagm. (This does not imply, of course, that the AVERAGE number of clauses per clause complex will be greater in spoken language, because there may also be a tendency towards very short ones, especially in dialogue. It would be better to say that the greater the intricacy of a clause complex the more likely it is to be a product of spontaneous speech.)

Written language represents phenomena as if they were products. Spoken language represents phenomena as if they were processes (see the discussion in Martin, 1984).

In other words: speaking and writing — each one makes the world look like itself. A written text is an object; so what is represented in writing tends to be given the form of an object. But when one talks, one is doing; so when one talks about something, one tends to say that it happened or was done. So, in Text 3 above, the written variant tells the story in nouns: *visit, sense, risk, attempt, action*; whereas the spoken version tells it in verbs: *visited, ended up feeling, might get hurt, tried to do*.

This is to look at it from the point of view of the writer or speaker. For reader or listener, there is a corresponding difference in the way the discourse is received. To the reader, the text is presented synoptically: it exists, spread out on the page. So the reader is predisposed to take a synoptic view of what it means; behind it is a tableau — like the pictures from which writing originally evolved. But when one is listening, the text reaches one dynamically: it happens, by travelling through the air. So the listener is predisposed to take a dynamic view of what it means; behind it is a film, not a picture.

Grammatical Metaphor

Where then in the linguistic system do spoken and written discourse diverge? A language, if it is not written down, consists of three interrelated subsystems: a semantic system (meanings), coded into a lexicogrammatical system (wordings), recoded into a phonological system (sounds). A language that has a writing system has an alternative form of expression: visual symbols as well as sounds. In such a language, a written text could, in principle, be a spoken text that has been written down ('transcribed'); here the written version is a transcoding of something that has already been coded in sound. Most writing is not like this. Secondly, a written text could be an alternative EXPRESSION of a given wording: in this case meanings are coded as words and structures ('wordings'), which are then expressed EITHER in sound OR in writing. If this was the norm, there would be no systematic difference between spoken and written texts; the medium would not be a significant register variable. But there are such differences; so, to some extent at least, spoken and written discourse must represent alternative WORD-INGS. In this case, meanings are coded either as 'speakable wordings' or as 'writeable wordings', the former appropriate to the dynamic nature of the text process, the latter appropriate to the synoptic nature of the text product. This is the sort of interpretation we have been offering.

But is it the whole story? There is still a fourth possibility — that speech and writing can diverge already at the semantic level, so that spoken and written discourse embody different meanings. Is there any sign that this can happen? It would of course be only a very partial effect; no one has suggested that the two derive from different semantic systems (or even two different lexicogrammatical systems, for that matter). But we should consider the possibility that there is some flowback into the meaning.

Consider the last sentence of Text 2, in its original written form (2A):

The current popular concern over the environment has stimulated private civil actions of two main types.

We 'translated' it into something more speechlike as:

At present, people are concerned about the environment; so they have been bringing quite a few private civil actions, which have been mainly of two kinds.

But this could be wrong; it may have meant:

> At present, people are concerned about the environment; so there have been mainly two kinds of action being brought by private citizens.

There is no way of deciding: BY REFERENCE TO THE SPOKEN VERSION, the written version is simply ambiguous. Compare the following also from a written text:

> A further complication was the 650-ton creeper cranes poised above the end of each 825-foot arm.

Does this mean

> Above the end of each 825-foot arm there were poised 650-ton creeper cranes, and they made the work more complicated.

or does it mean

> . . . and this made the work more complicated.

(i.e. not the cranes, but the fact that they were poised where they were)? Another example is

> Slavish imitation of models is nowhere implied.

This could be reworded either as *it is nowhere implied that models have been slavishly imitated,* or as . . . *that models should be slavishly imitated.*

Examples of this kind could be added to indefinitely; they arise because nominal constructions fail to make explicit many of the semantic relations that are made explicit in clause structure. Written discourse conceals many local ambiguities of this kind, which are revealed when one attempts a more 'spoken' paraphrase.

But the final sentence of Text 2 illustrates another significant feature of written language, which can be seen in the wording *popular concern over the environment has stimulated private civil actions.* We reworded this as *people are concerned about the environment, so they have been bringing private civil actions.* The original is one clause with the verb *stimulate* representing the Process; in other words, the thesis is encoded as a single happening, and what happened was that A brought about B. But A and B are themselves nominalized processes. The meaning of *stimulate* here is as in *pruning stimulates growth.* The spoken version represents the thesis as two distinct processes, linked by a relation of cause; cf. *if the tree is pruned, it will grow.*

Here one kind of process has been dressed up by the grammar to look like a process of a different kind — or, in this instance, two processes, one mental and one material, have been dressed up as one which is neither. This coding of a semantic relation BETWEEN two processes as if it was THE single process

is very common in writing; the sentence immediately preceding Text 2A
contained another example of the same thing, here with the verb *leads to*:

> A successful court action leads to a judgement of damages or an injunc-
> tion against the defendant company.

But this is just one type of a more general phenomenon, something that
I call *grammatical metaphor* (Halliday, 1985, chap. 10). Written language
tends to display a high degree of grammatical metaphor, and this is perhaps
its single most distinctive characteristic.

Here are three further examples of grammatical metaphor taken from
various written sources, together with suggested rewordings which are less
metaphorical:

> Issue of the specially-coded credit cards will be subject to normal credit
> checking procedures.
>
> > 'Credit cards have been specially coded and will be issued only
> > when credit has been checked in the normal way.'

> Strong Christmas sales were vital to the health of the retail industry,
> particularly in the present depressed climate.
>
> > 'Unless many goods were sold at Christmas the retail industry
> > would not be healthy, particularly when the economy is
> > depressed as it is now.'

> He also credits his former big size with much of his career success.
>
> > 'He also believes that he was successful in his career mainly
> > because he used to be big.'

In all these examples **nominalization** plays a significant part, as it does in
many types of grammatical metaphor; so it is perhaps worth stressing that
nominalization is well motivated in English. It is not simply a ritual feature
that has evolved to make written language more ambiguous or obscure; like
the passive, which is another feature whose functions are widely misunder-
stood, nominalization is an important resource for organizing information.
Take the example *youth protest mounted,* which is not a headline but a complete sentence from a feature article. We might reword this as *more and
more young people protested,* or *young people protested more and more;* but
the only way to get the combination of *youth* and *protest* as the Theme of the
clause is by means of a nominalization (not necessarily such a laconic one; it
might have been *the protests of the young people,* but this is still a nominaliz-
ing of the process). So while there is a price to be paid, in that the information being conveyed may become mildly (and sometimes severely) ambiguous, there is also a payoff: more choice of status in the discourse. In terms
of systemic theory, there is a loss of ideational information, but a gain in

textual information. This of course favours the specialist: you need to know the register. If you do not know the register you may misinterpret the thesis, so the fact that it is highly coded as a message is not very helpful to you; but if you do know it you will select the right interpretation automatically, and the additional 'functional sentence perspective' is all tax-free profit.

Some nominalizations of course cannot be denominalized, like *private civil actions at law* or *an injunction against the defendant company*. These are abstractions that can enter into the structure of a clause — civil actions can be brought, an injunction can be issued — but cannot themselves be coded as finite verbs. Much of our environment today consists of such abstract entities and institutions; their representation in nominal form is no longer metaphorical — if it ever was — and they have become part of our ideology, our way of knowing about the world we live in. Patterns of this kind invade the spoken language and then act as infiltrators, providing cover for other metaphorical nominalizations — which are still functional in speech, but considerably less so, because spoken language has other resources for structuring the message, such as intonation and rhythm.

Grammatical metaphor is not confined to written language: quite apart from its tendency to be borrowed from speech into writing, there are specific instances of it which seem clearly to have originated in speech — most notably the pattern of lexically empty verb with the process expressed as 'cognate object' (Range) as in *make a mistake* 'err', *have a bath* 'bathe', *give a smile* 'smile'. But in its principal manifestations it is typically a feature of writing. Writing — that is, using the written medium — puts distance between the act of meaning and its counterpart in the real world; so writing — that is, the written language — achieves this distance symbolically by the use of grammatical metaphor. It is often said that written discourse is not dependent on its environment; but it would be more accurate to say that it creates an environment for itself and this is where it depends on its metaphorical quality. If I say *technology has improved,* this is presented as a message; it is part of what I am telling you. If I say *improvements in technology,* I present it as something I expect you to take for granted. By objectifying it, treating it as if it was a thing, I have backgrounded it; the message is contained in what follows (e.g. . . . *are speeding up the writing of business programmes*). Grammatical metaphor performs for the written language a function that is the opposite of foregrounding; it backgrounds, using discourse to create the context for itself. This is why in the world of writing it often happens that all the ideational content is objectified, as background, and the only traces of process are the relations that are set up between these taken-for-granted objects. I recall a sentence from the O.S.T.I. Programme in the Linguistic Properties of Scientific English (Huddleston, Hudson, Winter & Henrici, 1968) which used to typify for us the structures found in scientific writing:

The conversion of hydrogen to helium in the interiors of stars is the source of energy for their immense output of light and heat.

Ways of Knowing and Learning

In calling the written mode metaphorical we are of course making an assumption; in fact each mode is metaphorical from the standpoint of the other, and the fact that the spoken is developmentally prior — the individual listens and speaks before he reads and writes — while it means that the language of 'process' is LEARNT first, does not guarantee that it is in any sense 'closer to reality'. It might be a hangover from an earlier stage of evolution, like the protolanguage that precedes the mother tongue. But personally I do not think so. I am inclined to think the written language of the future will go back (or rather forward) to being more processlike; not only because the traditional objectlike nature of written discourse is itself changing — our reading matter is typed into a memory and fed to us in a continuous flow as the lines follow each other up the screen — but also because our understanding of the physical world has been moving in that direction, ever since Einstein substituted space-time for space and time. As Bertrand Russell expounded it in 1925 (1977: 54).

> We are concerned with *events,* rather than with *bodies.* In the old theory, it was possible to consider a number of bodies all at the same instant, and since the time was the same for all of them it could be ignored. But now we cannot do that if we are to obtain an objective account of physical occurrences. We must mention the date at which a body is to be considered, and thus we arrive at an *'event',* that is to say, something which happens at a given time.

Meanwhile, grammatical analysis shows spoken and written English to be systematically distinct: distinct, that is, in respect of a number of related tendencies, all of which combine to form a single package. But it turns out to be a semantic package: the different features that combine to distinguish spoken and written discourse can be shown to be related and encompassed within a single generalization, only when we express this generalization in semantic terms — or at least in terms of a functional, meaning-oriented interpretation of grammar. Speech and writing will appear, then, as different ways of meaning: speech as spun out, flowing, choreographic, oriented towards events (doing, happening, sensing, saying, being), processlike, intricate, with meanings related serially; writing as dense, structured, crystalline, oriented towards things (entities, objectified processes), productlike, tight, with meanings related as components.

In their discussion of the comprehension and memory of discourse, Hildyard & Olson (1982: 20) suggested that meaning is PRESERVED in different ways by speakers and listeners:

> Readers and listeners may tend to extract different kinds of information from oral and written statements. Listeners may tend to recall more of the gist of the story and readers may recall more of the surface structure or verbatim features of the story.

In other words, the listener processes text largely at the level of meaning, the reader more, or at least as much, at the level of wording. But this is specifically a function of the medium in which the text is received rather than of the linguistic features of the code that lies behind it. The notion of different ways of meaning implies, rather, that there are different ways of knowing, and of learning. Spoken and written language serve as complementary resources for acquiring and organizing knowledge; hence they have different places in the educational process. Teachers often know, by a combination of intuition and experience, that some things are more effectively learnt through talk and others through writing. Official policy usually equates educational knowledge with the written mode and commonsense knowledge with the spoken; but teachers' actual practice goes deeper — educational knowledge demands both, the two often relating to different aspects of the same phenomenon. For example: definitions, and structural relations, are probably best presented in writing; demonstrations of how things work may be more easily followed through speech. The two favourite strategies for describing the layout of an apartment, reported in the well-known study by Linde & Labov (1975), would seem to exemplify spoken and written modes of symbolic exploration. We may assume that speech and writing play different and complementary parts in the construction of ideologies (Hasan, 1986), since each offers a different way of knowing and of reflecting on experience.

Considerations of this kind are an essential element in any linguistic theory of learning. The development of such a theory is perhaps the most urgent task of educational linguistics; and certain components of it can already be recognized: (1) the child's construction of language, from pre-symbolic communication through protolanguage to the mother tongue; (2) the processing of new meanings into the system; (3) the interaction between learning elements that are ready coded and learning the principles of coding; (4) the relation between system and process in language; (5) the unconscious nature of linguistic categories; (6) the social construction of reality through conversation; (7) linguistic strategies used in learning; (8) the development of functional variation, or registers; (9) the relation between everyday language and technical language; and (10) the development of generalization, abstraction, and metaphor. The absence of any general theory of learning based on language has been a significant gap in educational thinking and practice. This provides an important context for our current concern, since the complementarity of spoken and written language will certainly be a central issue in any learning theory which has language as its primary focus.

References

Abercrombie, D. (1963) Conversation and spoken prose. *English Language Teaching* 18 (1).

Beattie, G. (1983) *Talk: An Analysis of Speech and Non-Verbal Behaviour in Conversation*. Milton Keynes: Open University Press.

Boas, F. (1911) *Introduction to the Handbook of American Indian Languages*. Washington, DC: Smithsonian Institution.

Chafe, W. L. (1982) Integration and involvement in speaking, writing and oral literature. In D. Tannen (ed.) *Spoken and Written Language: Exploring Orality and Literacy*. Norwood, NJ: Ablex.

Doughty, P. S., Pearce, J. J. and Thornton, G. M. (1971) *Language in Use*. London: Arnold.

Halliday, M. A. K. (1985) *Introduction to Functional Grammar*. London: Arnold.

Hasan, R. (1986) The ontogenesis of ideology: An interpretation of mother–child talk. In T. Threadgold *et al.* (eds) *Semiotics, Ideology, Language*. Sydney: Sydney Association for Studies in Society and Culture.

Hildyard, A. and Olsen, D. R. (1982) On the comprehension and memory of oral vs. written discourse. In D. Tannen (ed.) *Spoken and Written Language: Exploring Orality and Literacy*. Norwood, NJ: Ablex.

Huddleston, R. D., Hudson, R. A., Winter, E. O. and Henrici, A. (1968) *Sentence and Clause in Scientific English* (O.S.T.I. Programme in the Linguistic Properties of Scientific English, Final Report). London: University College, Communication Research Centre.

Hymes, D. H. (1971) Competence and performance in linguistic theory. In R. Huxley and E. Ingram (eds) *Language Acquisition: Models and Methods*. London & New York: Academic Press.

Linde, C. and Labov, W. (1975) Spatial networks as a site for the study of language and thought. *Language* 51, 924–39.

Mackay, D., Thompson, B. and Schaub, P. (1970) *Breakthrough to Literacy*. London: Longman.

Martin, J. R. (1984) Process and text: Two aspects of human semiosis. In J. D. Benson and W. S. Greaves (eds) *Systemic Perspectives on Discourse: Selected Theoretical Papers from the Ninth International Systemic Workshop*. Norwood, NJ: Ablex.

Mathesius, V. (1911) O potenciálnosti jevů jazykových [On the potentiality of the phenomena of language]. *Proceedings of the Czech Academy of Sciences, Philosophy and History Section*. (English trans. in J. Vachek (ed.) *A Prague School Reader in Linguistics*. Bloomington, IN: Indiana University Press, 1964.)

Russell, B. (1925) *ABC of Relativity*. London: Allen & Unwin.

Smart, N. (1968) *Secular Education and the Logic of Religion*. London: Faber & Faber.

Tannen, D. (1982) Oral and literate strategies in spoken and written narrative. *Language* 58, 1–21.

Ure, J. N. (1971) Lexical density and register differentiation. In G. E. Perren and J. L. M. Trim (eds) *Applications of Linguistics: Selected Papers of the Second World Congress of Applied Linguistics, Cambridge, 1969.* London: Cambridge University Press.

Wilkinson, A. M. (ed.) (1966) *Some Aspects of Oracy.* London: National Association for the Teaching of English.

5 The Texture of a Text

RUQAIYA HASAN

What is Texture?

Let me begin by a brief discussion of two examples (Examples 1 and 2).

Example 1

Once upon a time there was a little girl
and she went out for a walk
and she saw a lovely little teddybear
and so she took it home
and when she got home she washed it.

Example 2

He got up on the buffalo
I have booked a seat
I have put it away in the cupboard
I have not eaten it.

Faced with these two examples, any natural speaker of English is bound to say that Example 1 displays certain continuities that are lacking in Example 2. One of these continuities is, of course, describable in terms of generic structure. Although the first passage is incomplete, it is a clear instance of a familiar genre; we have no difficulty in recognising it as an unfinished story. It is, however, doubtful if Example 2 will be seen as representative of a genre quite so readily, though many of us who have taught a foreign language might not be surprised to find that the four sentences of Example 2 have been lifted from a foreign language teaching exercise. Now, even if we were to accept that a foreign language teaching exercise represents a genre, it appears undeniable that such a genre would not possess structure in quite the same sense as is usually understood. For one thing, there is no discernible beginning, middle, and end in such exercises. In fact, due to deplorable misconceptions about language, the continuities in a language teaching exercise are normally strictly meta-textual; there is a purely formal reason for grouping the sentences of Example 2 together, which has very little to do with language as used in everyday life.

But structural continuity is not the only kind of continuity; Examples 1 and 2 differ in another important respect; I would talk of this difference in terms of texture. Thus I would claim that the first of these examples possesses the attribute of texture, and that this attribute is lacking in the second.

Texture, Cohesive Ties and Cohesive Devices

The exaggerated difference between Examples 1 and 2 might lead one to suppose that coherence is an all-or-none phenomenon. This is decidedly not true, as a reading of Texts 1 and 2 will demonstrate.

Text 1
- (1) once upon a time there was a little girl
- (2) and she went out for a walk
- (3) and she saw a lovely little teddybear
- (4) and so she took it home
- (5) and when she got home she washed it
- (6) and when she took it to bed with her she cuddled it
- (7) and she fell straight to sleep
- (8) and when she got up and combed it with a little wirebrush the teddy-bear opened his eyes
- (9) and started to speak to her
- (10) and she had the teddybear for many many weeks and years
- (11) and so when the teddybear got dirty she used to wash it
- (12) and every time she brushed it it used to say some new words from a different country
- (13) and that's how she used to know how to speak English, Scottish, and all the rest.

Text 2
- (1) the sailor goes on the ship
- (2) and he's coming home with a dog
- (3) and the dog wants the boy and the girl
- (4) and they don't know the bear's in the chair
- (5) and the bear's coming to go to sleep in it
- (6) and they find the bear in the chair
- (7) they wake him up
- (8) and chuck him out the room
- (9) and take it to the zoo
- (10) the sailor takes his hat off
- (11) and the dog's chased the bear out the room
- (12) and the boy will sit down in their chair what the bear was sleeping in.

It would be untrue to claim that Text 2 is entirely incoherent or that it possesses no texture, though it is equally obvious that the text is less coherent than is Text 1. This raises two questions:

(1) How do Texts 1 and 2 differ in their texture, if they do?

(2) If the two vary in the degree of coherence, what, if any, patterns of language correlate with this variation.

In the sections below, I attempt to answer these questions. However, before we can examine and compare the specific texture of Texts 1 and 2, we need to be clear about the semantic and lexico-grammatical patterns essential to the creation of texture in general. I shall discuss the linguistics of texture before I return to the two questions I have raised.

Cohesive tie

In talking about texture, the concept that is most important is that of a TIE. The term itself implies a relation: you cannot have a tie without two members, and the members cannot appear in a tie unless there is a relation between them. Let us draw a picture of the tie:

If you think of a text as a continuous space in which individual messages follow each other, then the items that function as the two ends of the tie — the A and the B — are spatially separated from each other; A may be part of one message and B part of another. But there is a link between the two, depicted above by the two-headed arrow. The nature of this link is semantic: the two terms of any tie are tied together through some meaning relation. Such semantic relations form the basis for cohesion between the messages of a text. There are certain kinds of meaning relation that may obtain between the two members. For instance, take the first two lines of the rhyme in Example 3.

Example 3
I had a little nut tree
Nothing would it bear
But a silver nutmeg
And a golden pear.

Then thinking of *little nut tree* in line 1 as member A and *it* in line 2 as member B you can see that the semantic relation between the two is the identity of reference. The pronoun *it* refers to no other nut tree but the one that has already been mentioned as *a little nut tree*; the situational referents of both are the same thing. In the literature on the discussion of textual continuity, this relationship of situational identity of reference is known as CO-REFERENTIALITY.

Imagine now that we have two other sentences (see Example 4).

Example 4

I play the cello. My husband does, too.

Then following the earlier practice, we could say that *play the cello* is member A and *does* is a member B of the cohesive tie. But this time the relationship is not of referential identity. The cello playing that I do is a different situational event from the cello playing that my husband does. So the relation here is not of co-referentiality, but of the kind that could be described as CO-CLASSIFICATION. In this type of meaning relation, the things, processes, or circumstances to which A and B refer belong to an identical class, but each end of the cohesive tie refers to a distinct member of this class. Thus there is a significant difference between co-referentiality and co-classification.

A third kind of semantic relation between the two members of a tie is exemplified by *silver* and *golden* in the last two lines of Example 3. Here the relationship is neither of co-reference nor of co-classification; it is, rather, that both refer to something within the same general field of meaning. Thus both silver and gold refer to metal, and within metal to precious metal — their primary class affiliation is not identical — unlike two separate acts of playing the cello — but there is a general resemblance. For want of a better term, I refer to this kind of general meaning relation as CO-EXTENSION.

These three semantic relations of co-referentiality, co-classification, and co-extension are precisely what ties the two members of a tie, and the existence of such ties is essential to texture. The longer the text, the truer this statement.

Cohesive devices — co-reference and co-classification

These semantic relations are not independent of the lexico-grammatical patterns. It is not the case that they can be established randomly between any two types of language units; instead, there are very strong tendencies for a specific relation to be realised by a clearly definable set of items. For example, the relation of co-referentiality is typically realised by the devices of reference, such as the pronominals 'he', 'she', 'it', etc. or by the use of the definite article 'the' or that of the demonstratives 'this' or 'that'. By contrast, co-classification is normally realised either by substitution or by ellipsis. I should emphasise, perhaps, that this is a statement of what is typical; it does not describe all cases. Either of the devices can realise either of the relations,

but it is more typical for reference type devices to signify co-referentiality
and for substitution and ellipsis to signify the relation of co-classification. I
have already given an example of substitution in Example 4; an example of
ellipsis is given in the mini-dialogue Example 5.

Example 5

— 'Can I borrow your pen?'
— 'Yes, but what happened to yours?'

Here the nominal group *yours* is elliptical and its non-elliptical version
would be 'your pen'. Note that my pen and your pen are two distinct objects;
they belong to the same class, but they are two distinct members of the class.
Thus the realisation of these two semantic relations — i.e. co-referentiality
and co-classification — typically involves two distinct types of lexico-grammatical patterns.

There, is however, something in common to the lexico-grammatical
patterns that typically realised these two semantic relations: and this something that is in common can be pointed out by looking more closely into the
nature of the member B of each tie type (see Figure 5.1).

Figure 5.1

	A	B	tie type
Example 3	little nut tree	it	= co-referential
Example 4	plays the cello	does	= co-classification
Example 5	your pen	yours	= co-classification

Member B of each of these ties is an item to which we can refer as an
implicit encoding device. What this means is that the specific interpretation
of *it*, *does*, and *yours* is not possible in the same way as that of *nut tree, husband, cello,* and *pen* is. The interpretation of this latter set is possible without referring to any other item of the text; this is patently not true with such
items as *it, the, my, this, do so,* and *yours*. Their interpretation has to be
found by reference to some other source. And it is this essentially relational
nature of the implicit encoding devices that endows them with the possibility
of functioning as a COHESIVE DEVICE.

Such devices become cohesive — have a cohesive function and so are constitutive of texture — precisely if and when they can be interpreted through
their relation to some other (explicit) encoding device in the same passage. If
the source for their interpretation is located within the text, then a cohesive tie
of the type(s) discussed above is established; the establishment of such a tie
creates cohesion. In our earlier work (Halliday & Hasan, 1976) such cohesive devices have been referred to as GRAMMATICAL COHESIVE DEVICES.

Recall that we have a third type of cohesive tie — the type in which the
semantic relation is that of co-extension. Before embarking on a discussion

of the nature of the linguistic units that can act as terms in this third kind of tie, I would like to take up a question here that arises from the recognition of implicit encoding devices.

Implicit devices and their interpretation

In the above discussion, I pointed out that an implicit encoding device is essentially relational; its interpretation has to be found by reference to some other source. This raises the question of where the interpretative source is to be found, and an examination of that question will force us to revise some of the comments made earlier about the terms of the tie; at the same time it will add another parameter to our understanding of tie types.

It follows from the functional nature of language, and the close relationship that exists between context and text structure that any linguistic unit from a text that we focus on has two environments: (1) the extra-linguistic environment — the context — relevant to the total text; and (2) the linguistic environment — the co-text — the language accompanying the linguistic unit under focus. So, the source for the interpretation of the implicit encoding devices could either be co-textual or purely contextual.

The interpretation is said to be ENDOPHORIC (Halliday & Hasan, 1976) when the interpretative source of the implicit term lies within the co-text as, for example, with *she* and *little girl* or *it* and *nut tree*. It is really the endophoric ties that are crucial to the texture of a text: unless an endophoric interpretation of the implicit term can be sustained, cohesion would not be perceived. Note that in Example 2, it is impossible to sustain an endophoric interpretation of any of the implicit devices.

Given the fact that language unfolds in time, the linguistic units of a text occur in succession. This permits a further factoring of endophoric interpretation. Whatever implicit term is under focus may either follow or precede that linguistic unit by reference to which it is interpreted — i.e. its LINGUISTIC REFERENT. When it follows its linguistic referent, the label given to such a cohesive tie is ANAPHORIC (Halliday & Hasan, 1976). Every example of cohesive tie (except that between *silver* and *golden*) provided so far in this chapter has been anaphoric. When the implicit term precedes its linguistic referent, the cohesive tie thus established is known as CATAPHORIC (Halliday & Hasan, 1976). An illustration is given in Example 6.

Example 6

I shall be telling this with a sigh
Somewhere ages and ages hence:
Two roads diverged in a wood, and I —
I took the one less travelled by,
and that has made all the difference.

This is the last stanza from Robert Frost's 'The road not taken'. Here the demonstrative *this* of the first line will be interpreted by reference to lines 3–5 of the stanza. So there exists a cataphoric co-referential cohesive tie between *this* and lines 3–5.

The interpretation of an implicit device is said to be EXOPHORIC when the source for its interpretation lies outside the co-text and can only be found through an examination of the context. Imagine a situation in which a small child is hammering away at some toy, making a good deal of noise while the mother is trying to concentrate on writing a conference paper. It is highly probable that she might say to the child:

Example 7
Stop doing that here. I'm trying to work.

The first message of Example 7 is highly implicit; and none of the items *doing, that,* and *here* can be interpreted except by reference to the immediate context of situation. Exophorically interpreted implicit devices create an opaque link between the text and its context so far as speakers outside the context are concerned. The degree of opacity is obviously variable (Hasan, 1984c), but if all the implicit devices in a passage could only be interpreted exophorically, then to an outsider, the passage would appear either to lack all texture, or if it is perceived as possessing texture, it would be because of cohesive ties with the semantic relation of co-extension.

Cohesive interpretation and cohesive tie

One last point needs to be made before turning to co-extension, and this is as follows: the interpretation of the implicit term must be seen as an issue that is, in principle, separate from the kind of semantic relation between the terms of the tie. It is possible to determine the kind of semantic links between the two terms of a tie, even though the intended specific meaning of the terms might not be available. Consider Examples 8 and 9.

Example 8
They asked the sailor for some food
and he gave them a loaf of bread.

Example 9
I don't want this one
I want that one.

Most of us when faced with Example 8 will treat *them* in the second message as co-referential with *they* even though we would have no idea whether the two refer to 'two children' or 'some beggars' or whatever. Thus we would say that there is a cohesive co-referential tie between *they* and *them*, which is not a claim that could be made about *they* and *them* in Example 10.

Example 10

They asked the sailor for some food
and he found *them* in the bottom of the bag.

The reason why most speakers would not think of *them* as co-referential
with *they* in Example 10 is furnished by their understanding of English language. Turning to Example 9, we would treat *one* in the second message as
co-classificational with *one* in the first. This treatment would not be possible
if Example 9 were to be rewritten as Example 11.

Example 11

I don't want this one
so you can have it.

I have laboured this point because

(1) it throws a new light on some of the statements made in the previous
    sections 'Cohesive devices' and 'Implicit devices and their interpreta-
    tion';
(2) it raises the question of the basis of perceiving the semantic relations of
    co-reference and co-classification; and
(3) it is relevant to the role of exophoric devices in creating texture.

To take the first point first, I said earlier that cohesion is established when
an implicit device is interpreted by reference to some item of the text. This
is true so far as it goes, but Examples 8 and 9 clearly demonstrate that a
cohesive link can be established even when the specific meaning remains
unknown. This demonstrates that what is more important to texture is the
identity and/or the similarity of the semantic content rather than the content
itself. The interpretation of a term *it* by reference to another term *nut tree*
creates texture not because the interpretation has become available, but
because the interpretation clinches the fact that a particular kind of semantic
relation obtains.

So how about exophora? Are exophorically interpreted items an embarrassment to this approach to texture? Whenever scholars have attempted to
prove that it is possible to have texts without cohesion, in order to demonstrate their point they have normally created what I would describe as
'minimal texts' consisting of either a single message by one participant,
or one message per participant. Now, since the status of text as text is func-
tionally defined, in principle, it is irrelevant what number of messages a text
contains. However, in describing the attributes of a class of phenomena we
need to start with typical members; and it cannot be denied that discourse
whether spoken or written is typically productive of much larger — non-
minimal — texts, which display the full range of possibilities open to texts in
general. By contrast, taking the minimal text as typical, we would be forced

to concede many points that it would be absurd to have to concede. For example, we might have to say that texts do not have generic structure; and to concede this is quite absurd. So in order to support our statements about texts in general, we must take non-minimal texts into account, since this will permit generalisations about minimal texts as well, while the reverse is not true.

A case in point are those implicit devices — 'he', 'she', 'it', etc. — which have no specific linguistic referent within the text. When the text is minimal as in Example 7, it appears impossible to arrive at the interpretation of such devices except by reference to the context of situation. Moreover, the devices seem to enter into no cohesive relation with any other linguistic items in the text. However, if we examine longer texts, we find that both these conditions are an artefact of the size of the text. Implicit encoding devices **can** be interpreted without recourse to situational clues even in the absence of a specific linguistic referent in the text. In fact, sometimes, this is the only possibility open to us in poetic texts. Consider an extract from Tomlinson's lyric, whose title is just 'Poem' (see Example 12).

Example 12

Upended, it crouches on broken limbs
About to run forward. No longer threatened
But surprised into this vigilance
It gapes enmity from its hollowed core.

Moist woodflesh, softened to a paste
Of marl and white splinter, dangles
Where overhead the torn root
Casts up its wounds in a ragged orchis.

Throughout this poem, the word 'tree' never appears, yet a practised reader is bound to interpret *it* (line 1) and *its* (line 4) as tree. Since, in the case of literary texts, appeal to the immediate situation is patently impossible, it follows that the interpretation has been arrived at due to some feature(s) of 'Poem'. And here the importance of such expressions as *hollowed core, woodflesh, splinter,* and *torn root* cannot be denied. Note also that the reader will perceive the semantic relation of co-referentiality between *it* (line 1), *it* and *its* (line 4). One might claim that these items are, after all, not exophoric, since their referent is determined text-internally; however, there is no specific linguistic referent of *it* present in the entire text. Even conceding that the pronominals are exophoric does not force us to accept that they are irrelevant to texture. In the following poem, 'A slumber did my spirit seal', by Wordsworth, *she* is definitely exophoric, but the relations between the three instances of *she* are still cohesive (see Example 13).

Example 13

A slumber did my spirit seal;
I had no human fears:
She seemed a thing that could not feel
The touch of earthly years.

No motion has she now, no force;
She neither hears nor sees;
Rolled round in earth's diurnal course,
With rocks, and stones, and trees.

As in the case of Tomlinson's stanza, so here it can hardly be denied that the perception of continuity presupposes the perception of a relation of co-reference between the pronominals. I want to put forward the hypothesis that the interpretation of items in the absence of a linguistic referent and/or any situational clues as well as the perception of semantic relation between un-interpreted implicit devices is made possible because of the third type of tie — that which is based on co-extension. Where such ties do not exist, the relation of co-reference and co-classification are at least problematic if not impossible to establish. This brings us to the discussion of the nature of the linguistic units that can act as the terms of a co-extensional tie.

Cohesive devices — co-extension

Let us go back to Example 3.

Figure 5.2

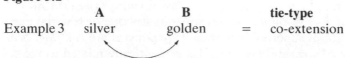

	A	B	tie-type
Example 3	silver	golden	= co-extension

Compare the tie in Figure 5.2 with the three ties laid out in Figure 5.1. You will immediately note an important difference: neither of the terms in this tie is implicit; we do not need to refer to anything else in order to interpret the terms *silver* and *golden* — we only need to know the language. The two terms of a co-extensional tie are typically linguistic units that we refer to as 'content words' or 'lexical items'. The relation of co-extension, described earlier, naturally does not exist between any two randomly co-occurring lexical items. So we need to state under what conditions such a relation comes about. 'The same general field of meaning' is a vague expression. And if we leave the expression unelaborated, then any kind of meaning association could be taken as constituting a relation. We could end up with a chain in which the members of the tie were as follows: flower, petal, stem, stalk, twig, branch, trunk, tree, wood, log, faggot, tinder, fire, flame. In this list we have ended up grouping items such as 'flower' and 'flame', between which it is not very easy to say what kind of general meaning relation obtains. But if we examine the list, we would find that in this collection there is no point at which we could stop on the ground that the members of the pair are not related meaning-wise. The members of each consecutive pair such as, say, 'flower' and 'petal', 'petal' and 'stem', and 'stem' and 'stalk' show a close meaning relation, but the further apart the items are the more difficult it is to relate them to each other semantically; for instance, consider 'flower' and 'faggot'. So obviously what we have to do is to delimit the notion 'general field of meaning'.

To achieve this end, I have used the traditional concept of sense relation with certain additions. The three sense relations generally recognised in the literature on semantics are those of SYNONYMY, ANTONYMY, and HYPONYMY. Whenever two lexical expressions stand in any of these relations, a cohesive tie is established.

In SYNONYMY, the experiential meaning of the two lexical items is identical; this does not mean that there is a total overlap of meanings, simply that so far as one kind of meaning goes, they 'mean the same'. The standard literature in semantics, for example, mentions such pairs as 'woman' and 'lady', 'buy' and 'purchase', and 'smile' and 'grin', etc.

ANTONYMY can be described as the oppositeness of experiential meaning; the members of our co-extensional tie *silver* and *golden* are an example of this kind of meaning relation.

HYPONYMY is a relation that holds between a general class and its subclasses. The item referring to the general class is called SUPERORDINATE; those referring to its sub-classes are known as its HYPONYM. If we take *animal* as an example of superordinate then its hyponyms are *cat, dog, bear,* etc. Note that *cat, dog,* and *bear* are also semantically related as the cohyponyms of the superordinate *animal*.

The lexicon of a language is organised into a hyponymic hierarchy, so that we have differing degrees of generality. For example, in English, the most general and therefore the superordinate *par excellence* is the item 'thing', which can be used to refer to almost anything. Consider also the gradation of generality in *food, fruit, berry, blueberry*. At this point let me draw attention to the fact that when we have a relation of co-hyponymy, as for example, between *cat* and *dog*, we can also think of the relation as that of weak antonymy. The distinction between a certain kind of antonymy and cohyponymy is not easy to draw. On the other hand, this matters little for our immediate purposes, since whether the two items are related as antonyms or as co-hyponyms, the relation will contribute to cohesion in either case.

To these generally recognised sense relations, I would add that of MERONYMY: the term refers to a part — whole relation as in the case of *tree, limb,* and *root,* where *limb* and *root* are co-meronyms, naming parts of the superordinate *tree.* While meronymy is very much like a sense relation, there is another kind of lexical patterning that contributes to texture but, strictly speaking, is not recognised as a kind of sense relation. I have in mind the REPETITION of the same lexical unit. The repetition of the same lexical unit creates a relation simply because a largely similar experiential meaning is encoded in each repeated occurrence of the lexical unit as in Example 14.

Example 14

There were children everywhere.
There were children on the swings, children on the slides, and children on the merry-go-round.

It is also possible to have repetition where the morphologically distinct forms of the same lexical unit occur. In Example 15, the items *suggested* and *suggestion* are really two distinct morphological forms of the same lexical unit and can be treated as a case of repetition.

Example 15

The committee suggested that all sexist language be removed from the regulations. If this suggestion is adopted, we shall have to avoid 'he', 'his', etc.

Table 5.1 summarises the devices discussed.

Table 5.1 Summary of cohesive devices

		COMPONENTIAL RELATIONS		ORGANIC RELATIONS
		Device	Typical tie relation	
GRAMMATICAL COHESIVE DEVICES	A:	**Reference** 1. Pronominals 2. Demonstratives 3. Definite article 4. Comparatives	co-reference	A: **Conjunctives** e.g. causal tie concession tie . . .
	B:	**Substitution & Ellipsis** 1. Nominal 2. Verbal 3. Clausal	co-classification	B: **Adjacency pairs** e.g. Question (followed by) answer; offer (followed by) acceptance; order (followed by compliance . . .
LEXICAL COHESIVE DEVICES	A:	**General** 1. Repetition 2. Synonymy 3. Antonymy 4. Meronymy	co-classification or co-extension	**Continuatives** (e.g. still, already . . .)
	B:	**Instantial** 1. Equivalence 2. Naming 3. Semblance	co-reference or co-classification	

The interdependence of grammatical and lexical cohesion

I suggested before that even if two implicit terms remain un-interpreted, as in Examples 8 and 9, it is still possible to perceive relations of co-reference and co-classification between them. With Example 12 I drew attention to the fact that even in the absence of both a specific linguistic referent and any situational clues, there are occasions when it is possible to provide an interpretation of the implicit device. I went on to suggest that both these things happen largely because of the semantic relations maintained through lexical ties. In a text of non-minimal size, there normally occur many such threads of semantic relation, and their simultaneous operation is important in the resolution of both the above problems. The moral from this is easy to draw: to be effective, grammatical cohesion requires the support of lexical cohesion.

However, the relationship is not so one-sided: to be effective, lexical cohesion, in its turn, requires the support of grammatical cohesion. The reciprocity of these two kinds of cohesion is essential, as can be seen from Examples 16 and 17.

Example 16

John gets up early. We bought him a tie. He loves peaches.
My house is next to his.

Example 17

A cat is sitting on a fence. A fence is often made of wood. Carpenters work with wood. Wood planks can be bought from a lumber store.

In Example 16 there is no grammatical reason that would prevent *he, him,* and *his* from referring back to *John*. But if I say that *him* in the second sentence of this example should be interpreted as *John*, you just have to take it on faith; there is nothing in the text that points you in the direction of that particular interpretation. Why? Because grammatical cohesion is not supported here by lexical cohesion; the relations discussed under 'Co-extension' do not tie any two lexical items of Example 16. By itself, grammatical cohesion does not work. On the other hand, lexical cohesion does not work by itself either. In Example 17, we find only lexical cohesive relations: of reiteration, synonymy, and hyponymy. Thus we have *fence* and *wood* reiterated, and we have *lumber* and *wood planks*. None the less, it is an odd kind of text, if text it is. In comparison with Example 16, we may perhaps be willing to think of it as more of a text, but by no stretch of the imagination could we think of it as a typical one.

In a typical text, grammatical and lexical cohesion move hand in hand, the one supporting the other. The many differing kinds of semantic relations operate at one and the same time through sizeable portions of a text. To demonstrate this point, let me examine in some detail the first five clauses of Text 1. In Figure 5.3 each rectangle stands for one clause. Within each of these clauses there are components that enter into a grammatical or lexical cohesive relation. There are four such threads of continuity:

(1) the first, with the first element *girl* in clause 1;

(2) the second, with *went* in clause 2;

(3) the third, with *teddybear* in clause 3; and

(4) the fourth, with *home* in clause 4.

Figure 5.3

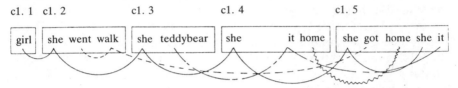

Each of these form part of a CHAIN in which the members are related to each other in specific ways. To indicate the movement of the chain, I will connect the members of the first chain with a solid line; those of the second with dots; those of the third with dots and dashes, while the links in the fourth chain will be indicated with a wavy line. Each rectangle contains only those components of the clause that function as elements or links in the chain. Figure 5.3 demonstrates the appropriateness of the metaphor 'threads of continuity running throughout the text' to describe the simultaneous operation of many cohesive chains, each of which supports and refines the domain of meaning for the others. This is one reason why, in natural uses of language, we hardly ever notice ambiguities.

A technical term that has appeared in this discussion is COHESIVE CHAIN. What is a cohesive chain? As the analysis provided in Figure 5.3 shows, a chain is formed by a set of items each of which is related to the others by the semantic relation of co-reference, co-classification, and/or co-extension. Taking the type of relation into account, we can sub-categorise chains into two types: IDENTITY CHAINS and SIMILARITY CHAINS. Again, both of these are exemplified in Figure 5.3. Thus chain 1 with *girl, she,* etc. is an identity chain. The relation between the members of an identity chain is that of co-reference: every member of the chain refers to the same thing, event, or whatever, as in this chain, where each item refers to the same girl. This particular identity chain is text-exhaustive, i.e. it runs from the beginning to the end of the text. This, I would suggest tentatively, is a characteristic of short narratives: texts of this category normally contain at least one text-exhaustive identity chain.

Now, turning to similarity chains, an example of which is provided by chain 2 in Figure 5.3 with *went, walk,* etc.: the members of a similarity chain are related to each other either by co-classification or co-extension. Each such chain is made up of items that refer to non-identical members of the same class of things, events, etc., or to members of non-identical but related classes of things, events, etc.

The distinction between identity and similarity chains is important, relating both to the notion of text and of context. Let us take the identity chain first. Each item in an identity chain refers to the same 'thing' (where the word 'thing' should be interpreted as covering any class of referent). Paradoxically, however, the extra-linguistic identity of the thing is immaterial to texture. Let me develop this point a little. While writing this chapter I have used such items as *I, me, my.* These make an identity chain, each item in the chain referring to the same extra-linguistic thing: Ruqaiya Hasan. Now, independent of this text, Ruqaiya Hasan is the same person who will be talking to students at Macquarie University in a few weeks' time. I find that it is not possible to give talks without such expressions as 'I find . . . ', 'let me show . . .', and 'in my opinion . . .'. These expressions were present in my earlier talks, they are present today, and they will most probably be present in future talks as well. I am sure that you can anticipate what I am about to say: if we take the criterion of 'referring to the same extra-linguistic thing' literally, then all of these variants of the first person singular pronoun will form but one identity chain. Such an identity chain may definitely have uses in the construction of biographies and case histories, but it is quite useless so far as notions of textual unity and textual identity are concerned. So we come up with the rather interesting conclusion that the notion 'the same extra-linguistic thing' must be modified by the expression 'within the context of this specific text', rather than being taken as a text-independent entity.

The members of a similarity chain are related by co-classification and/or co-extension. In Figure 5.3, a similarity chain occurs with members *went, walk,* and *got* (i.e. reached); the relationship between these items is not identity of reference but similarity of reference, so that the referents lie within the same general field of meaning. For example, walking is a kind of going, and going is an important part of getting anywhere.

There is one rather significant difference between similarity and identity chains. If two texts embedded in the same contextual configuration are compared, we are highly likely to find a considerable degree of overlap in at least some of the similarity chains found in them. This is not an accident. The items in a similarity chain belong to the same general field of meaning, referring to (related/similar) actions, events, and objects and their attributes. The lexical items in a general field of meaning form a semantic grouping that represents the potential for the formation of similarity chains. This semantic grouping is genre-specific and to the extent that similarity chains are really a part of the total semantic grouping, they too are genre-specific. The implication is that if we know the specific social process — the field of discourse — relevant to an interaction, it will be possible to predict that some selection from this or that semantic grouping will appear in the shape of similarity chains in the text generated; equally, selections from given semantic groupings are constitutive of the field of discourse. So semantic groupings are logically related to specific contextual configurations, though how much of such a grouping will appear in the shape of similarity chains in a particular text of a given genre is open to variation.

By contrast, identity chains, particularly when their terms refer to some specific individual — person(s) or object(s) — rather than to a whole class as such, are essentially accidental from the point of view of the contextual configuration. So far as appointment making is concerned, it matters little whether the patient is Smith or Wilson, whether the receptionist is Glen or Anderson. This does not imply that identity chains are unimportant; in fact, in certain genres, they appear to be rather closely related to the overall structural shape of a text.

References

Halliday, M. A. K. and Hasan, R. (1976) *Cohesion in English*. London: Longman.
Hasan, R. (1984) Ways of saying and ways of learning. In R. Fawcett, M. A. K. Halliday, A. Makkai and S. M. Lamb (eds) *The Semiotics of Culture and Language*. London: Pinter.

6 Hysterical Style in the Press

ROGER FOWLER

Press Hysteria

In the winter of 1988–9, for roughly the three months from late November to early March, an hysterical episode of massive proportions built up in the British media. There was a panic about food poisoning, and specifically about two types of bacterial poisoning the incidence of which allegedly had been increasing alarmingly: salmonella poisoning caused by the strain *Salmonella enteritidis* phage type 4, apparently newly discovered to be present in eggs (as opposed to poultry meat); and listeriosis, a flu-like illness caused by *Listeria monocytogenes*, a bacterium occurring widely in the environment and now found in pre-cooked and chilled food, and some cheeses. Food poisoning 'cases' and 'out-breaks' had apparently increased substantially in numbers over recent years and months; and during the panic of that winter, a few deaths and stillbirths specifically linked to salmonella and listeria occurred or were reported.

To have doubt cast on eggs and cheese, staple foods in Britain and inexpensive sources of protein, was alarming enough. The Press kept these products in high focus throughout the period, reporting all statements by politicians and experts, giving statistics, dispensing advice, investigating producers and retail outlets, commenting on the responsibilities and short-comings of the government departments involved (Health and Agriculture). But the panic went far beyond eggs and cheese: it collected all kinds of problems in a wide range of areas, some quite unrelated to the two bacteria and their effects. In the sphere of food, other dangerous organisms or substances were identified (e.g. aluminium coating on sweets, pesticide residues in cereal products); there was a general concern with hygiene in shops, restaurants and kitchens, with adulteration and with the production of food (the use of animal remains in animal feed, milk hormone, high-technology practices in food production generally). The concern broadened to include other kinds of 'poisoning' and 'infection' (hepatitis, legionnaires' disease). Widening further, it included contamination of water supplies, highlighted by illnesses caused in an area of North Cornwall by the accidental dumping of aluminium sulphate in the main supply; the concern with water was sustained by parliamentary and public discussion of the privatization of the water industry. Numerous other specific environmental hazards were reported (radon gas, methane in rubbish tips), often in articles placed adjacent to reports of the latest on the salmonella scare. By February 1989 the context was global; copious discussion in the Press of such matters as the destruction of the Amazonian rain forests, breaches in the ozone layer caused by the use of CFCs, acid rain, an oil spillage in the Antarctic and the 'greenhouse effect' gave salmonella and listeria a heightened, universal significance. They were by now instances of 'The poisoning of our world' (*Daily Express*, 13 February 1989).

I would like to explain carefully what I mean by 'hysteria'. We are told that the bacteria concerned are dangerous. For example, Dr Barbara Lund of the Institute of Food Research in Norwich was quoted by the *Eastern Evening News* on 24 February 1989:

(1) I feel that listeria presents a health risk to the public. Listeria is life-threatening, causing quite a variety of symptoms.

   In pregnant women it tends to give a generalized infection like flu. This can result in the foetus being aborted, or birth of an infected baby which is very seriously diseased.

In using the word 'hysterical', I do not wish to suggest that salmonella and listeria poisoning are insignificant or illusory. Nor am I in a position to claim that the level of public alarm was out of proportion to the level of medical risk and actual illness ('the risks are exaggerated', as some contributors to the debate, notably government spokesmen, alleged): the facts about 'infection' are themselves controversial or inaccessible, so I cannot easily say that the public response was excessive. Certainly, people have died from these causes. Without meaning to contrast the facts and the newspapers' response to them, one can assert that this response was hysterical in terms of its high emotive content, the massive scale of Press reporting and its extraordinary generalization to 'the poisoning of our world'.

Hysteria is not simply behaviour which is in excess of the events which provoked it; it is also behaviour which attains autonomy, which sustains itself as an expressive performance, independent of its causes. People behaving hysterically 'go on and on' (sustain) and 'shout and scream' (excess, express). Hysteria requires an expressive system, a mode of discourse, and, established, exists within that mode of discourse independent of empirical reality. Since expressive systems are shared among members of a community, hysteria can be intersubjective: mass hysteria. Such was the status of listeria hysteria/the great egg scare: once established in the discourse of the media, it persisted autonomously within that discourse, going on and on at an increasing pitch independent of the factual unfolding of the matter. The great egg scare was not a medical phenomenon, not an epidemic; it was a construct of discourse, a formation and transformation of ideas in the public language of the newspapers and television. I am speaking then of hysteria *in the Press*.

Some Aspects of Hysterical Style

The following extracts illustrate a range of styles of writing about the salmonella affair and its satellite topics:

(2) **Cooked food hazard 'is unchecked'**

Supermarkets are free to keep cook–chill foods in conditions which allow an astronomical increase in listeria bacteria, even though the Government has been warned of the danger by its own public health officials.

Evidence from independent sources emerged yesterday which supports claims by Professor Richard Lacey, the Leeds microbiologist, that listeria food poisoning is a serious and previously hidden health hazard which causes meningitis, still birth, and the death of up to 200 vulnerable people a year.

Supermarkets typically sell cook–chill foods which have been stored for a week or more at temperatures at over 7°C.

But these breeding conditions allow a sudden and exponential leap in the number of bacteria in infected food, according to figures from Dr Richard Gilbert, director of food hygiene at the Public Health Laboratory Service.

They show that listeria will stay virtually dormant for five days after contamination even if the food is stored at 7.5°C. But then reproduction suddenly erupts.

(*Guardian*, 24 January 1989)

(3) **Ministry knew of health risk from eggs a year ago**

The Ministry of Agriculture knew of the salmonella epidemic a year ago but was unable to persuade egg producers of the seriousness of the problem and failed to warn the public, according to confidential reports which have reached *The Independent*.

The ministry had reports 12 months ago showing that in 1987 more than 100 egg and broiler farms were infected by *Salmonella enteritidis* — a threefold increase in the number of infections over the previous year. The link between home and farm was clear because the same type 4 *enteritidis* was involved in both places. But the egg industry would not accept the evidence produced by the Public Health Laboratory . . .

The Department of Health wanted to tell the public that salmonella infection could be carried in raw egg and was not just the result of poor hygiene. But egg industry representatives wanted to put the responsibility for egg poisoning back on to the consumer by emphasizing the need for good hygiene and avoidance of cracked eggs.

So the industry decided to construct a defence that infection within eggs was a near-hypothetical risk. Later this stance was to be translated into the suggestion that the likelihood of egg poisoning was as remote as being struck by a meteorite.

(Independent, 2 February)

(4) **Don't delay on new food law**

Agriculture Secretary John MacGregor moves to allay public anxiety about the quality and safety of the food we eat as the 'blacklist' mounts alarmingly.

After a weekend of growing confusion he says, comfortingly, that a Food Act is being drawn up seeking to update old laws which have not kept pace with modern food production.

That's the good news. The bad news is that Mr MacGregor does not have a parliamentary slot. 'It is not for me' he says, meekly. And when it is suggested that perhaps Mr MacGregor *ought* to make it a matter for him, one of his aides replies haughtily 'We don't do things that way in Agriculture.'

The new proposals, perhaps the most urgent facing the Government, must be given top priority.

(Express, 13 February)

(5) **The chilling facts of safe home cooking**

Checklist of simple dos and don'ts, compiled with the help of David Edwards of the Food Hygiene Bureau:

- Don't buy cooked–chilled food outside the 'sell-by' date, and eat it by the 'use-by' date.
- Buy cooked–chilled food from reputable shops which show an awareness of hygiene.
- Buy chilled foods at the end of shopping expeditions and get them home to the fridge as soon as possible, particularly in summer.
- Check that your fridge is working properly.
- Follow the cooking instructions and ensure your reheating is thorough.

(Sunday Times, 22 January)

(6) **Have a heart for housewives**

What tough days these are for the poor housewife.

When she goes shopping for her family, she must feel as if she is entering a minefield about which foods are safe and which potentially dangerous.

If, in her dilemma, she is angry with the Government, who can blame her? . . .

Since Edwina Currie's famous warning about eggs it has been speaking with two voices — and sometimes with no voice at all — on matters vital to the nation's health.

Agriculture Minister John MacGregor's flirtation with a ban on non-pasteurized cheese is the latest example of fumbling indecisiveness.

He does not exactly say he will forbid imports.

And he does not exactly explain why these products have suddenly become suspect.

(*Sun*, 13 February)

(7) **Currie really got it right**

. . . It was Mrs Currie who recognized this and became the first politician, let alone government minister, to articulate it. In this she was assisted by her remarkable ability to strike a popular chord, catch the public eye and hit the headlines. For this she has been criticized frequently, and wrongly.

It is an important quality of political leadership.

What is certainly true is that in launching her attacks on northern eating habits and calling on old people to wear warm clothes, she emphasized personal responsibility while wrongly and patronizingly ignoring the impact of material deprivation. In this she was a true Thatcherite.

But she was none the less right about the importance of individual responsibility.

(*Sunday Times*, 29 January)

(8) **You damage the earth just by living on it**

You burn fossil fuels — petrol, oil, coal — and huge amounts more are burnt by those who supply you with goods and services.

You create waste, which has to be buried, burnt or discharged into the sea.

You accept the profits of investments which are trading on Third World poverty and putting further strain on already over-stretched resources.

You buy goods from farms and factories whose ill-effects from chemical waste range all the way from dead fish to dead people.

You are a polluter. But you are also a conservationist.

(*Sunday Times* Magazine, 26 February)

Some brief, informal notes on the style of hysteria in these extracts. (2) and (3) highlight a vocabulary of 'hazard' and 'risk'. Note also the indications of large-scale growth: 'astronomical increase', 'increase'. Extract (3) is a typical narrative of secret dealings between government departments, and between government departments and industry; (4) and (6) are unusual in attempting to lay the blame on an individual. (4) speaks of 'public anxiety' and 'growing confusion'; cf. 'dilemma' in (7). Extract (5) encodes a strategy of educating (and therefore blaming) 'the poor housewife' (cf. (6)): (5) employs the rhetoric of *command*, also dominating extract (8). These rhetorics are distinctive, tailored for the job and linguistically specifiable. Extract (7) comes from a long article praising Mrs Currie in a style of unusual optimism and vivacity; other politicians and organizations are generally dealt with in a tone of tetchy gloom. Finally, extract (8) is an ecological tirade, raised to an apocalyptic pitch as the *Sunday Times* had by now globalized the agenda and the guilt.

Let us look in more detail at some aspects of hysterical style, and how a high level of intensity, an excess of negative feeling is expressed.

The most obvious source of stridency in the discourse is its permeation by terms denoting emotive reactions, always negative, clustering around the concepts of fear and confusion. The most common one is 'scare' (at least 27 times), also 'confusion' (10 times), 'anxiety' (6 times) and a number of related terms.

Another prominent vocabulary set stresses 'danger', 'risk', 'hazard'; it includes words which connote deliberateness or malevolence such as 'threat', 'menace'.

There is, particularly in the 'serious' papers, a multiplicity of technical and medical terms, terms of a kind which people find difficult, unfamiliar, frightening:

- *types of bacteria, viruses,* etc.: rota virus, Norwalk virus, *Escherichia coli, Salmonella typhimurium, Salmonella enteritidis* phage type 4, *Listeria monocytogenes*, legionella bacterium, cryptosporidium, staphyloccus, campylobacter;

- *infections and diseases:* Alzheimer's disease, cholera, typhoid fever, campylobacteriosis, septicaemia, giardisis, listeriosis, hepatitis, legionnaires' disease, pneumonia, bovine spongiform encephalopathy or 'BSE' (a horrible-sounding cattle disease);

- *chemicals, minerals,* etc.: bovine somatropin ('BST'), aluminium, aluminium sulphate, lead, nitrates, chlorofluorocarbons ('CFCs'), tri-chloroethylene, cytotoxic drugs, radon, methane.

This technical and medical jargon is alienating and disturbing.

The salmonella and, particularly, listeria bacteria are treated to a rhetoric of animation: they are 'germs' or, worse, 'bugs' which can be presented as deliberately harmful. The *Sun's* melodramatic phrase 'the killer bug listeria' (28 February) captures well this aspect of the presentation of the food poisoning affair. Elsewhere we find metaphors of 'war' and 'battle' in the kitchen against 'a billion bugs'; cf. 'minefield' in extract (6). There are also formulations like 'keep the salmonella or listeria at bay' (*The Times*, 2 February), 'Cooked food hazard "is unchecked"' (*Guardian*, 24 January), connoting a struggle against wild animals threatening to go out of control.

But the language does not have to be particularly melodramatic or ominously metaphoric to suggest that we are threatened by a very powerful and virulent enemy. In the nature of the case, explanations of the bacteriological processes involved were provided for readers who, like the journalists, had never heard of listeria. In the extracts below, I have italicized words and phrases which animate and activate the bacteria:

(9) [L]isteria will stay virtually *dormant* for five days after contamination even if the food is stored at 7.5°C. But then *reproduction suddenly erupts* . . . listeria, unlike most bacteria, *gets even more virulent when it is threatened* by extremes of temperature.

(Guardian, 24 January)

(10) The bacteria produces an enzyme, listeriolysin, which damages human cells, allowing bacteria to *invade and multiply* inside the cells.

(Independent, 23 January)

(11) Campylobacters and salmonellas become much more *dangerous* when, like listeria, they are *invasive, penetrate* the gut wall and *enter* the bloodstream, *causing* septicaemia.

(Letter in *Independent*, 26 January)

Animacy is also enhanced by the use of phrases such as 'breeding ground' and 'breeding conditions' which occur frequently but happen not to appear in the above three extracts. And note that it is transitivity as well as vocabulary which assists the effect of animate and deliberate activity: noun phrases designating the 'bugs' occupy the agent role in many clauses, coupled with verbs which designate actions having consequences for other organisms.

The meanings of the metaphor of a battle against the bugs are available to readers by intertextuality. Horror movies and stories, and science fantasies, supply antecedent paradigms of invasion by little creatures, germ warfare, uncontrollably multiplying chemical and botanical threats, assault by plagues of birds and insects. But the central meanings of this discourse of billions of hostile bugs are recognized only when we notice that it intersects with a discourse specifically aimed at 'the housewife': extract (6) above makes the link absolutely clear. Women are supposed to be afraid of 'bugs' or 'creepy-crawlies' like spiders and ants; they are supposed to go hysterical in fear of such; and their fears are supposed to be sexual: cf. expressions like 'reproduction suddenly erupts', 'penetrate', 'invade', in extracts (9)–(11); other connotations of sexual assault may be found in a further set of hysterical terms, to be discussed in a moment (see list (15) below). Furthermore, the intertext is not merely the cultural stereotype of the woman in a fright because a spider might run up her skirt. The cartoon animation of bugs and germs, and the threat they present, is a common strategy in the television advertising of disinfectants, toilet cleaners, and so on; these advertisements are aimed at women, and they articulate an important part of the culture's housewifely image.

Finally, a different discursive strategy for intensifying hysteria is the rhetoric of quantification; and this is really the dominant stylistic feature of the discourse. Throughout the three months' hysterical episode, there were many things to be counted, phenomena to be given statistical tags; the data I collected contain hundreds of numerical expressions, most of them indicating very large quantities indeed, and also expressions of quantitative increase. The basic proposition being debated was that Britain was experiencing '"a new salmonella epidemic of considerable proportions", possibly affecting up to 2m people a year' (*Sunday Times*, 22 January). The dramatic figure is of course a statistical extrapolation from the numbers of reported cases, but the claimed number was so large as to make an alarming impact on public consciousness anyway, whatever the facts of the matter; and the speculation was repeated over and over again in the Press. Also mentioned many times was the number of 'reported cases' of either 'food poisoning' or 'salmonella poisoning'; the following statement is typical:

(12) More than half of salmonella isolations by the Public Health Laboratory, 24,123 in 1988, are now *salmonella enteritidis*. The increase in this species of salmonella accounts largely for the great increase in salmonella infections which began in 1986. Total cases of salmonella are now twice what they were in 1986.

The latest figures show there were 12,553 isolations of *salmonella enteritidis* phage type 4 last year, compared with 4,962 isolations in 1987 . . .

Campylobacter is the commonest single cause of food poisoning, responsible for 28,714 cases last year. (*Independent*, 23 January)

(13) [T]he number of cases [of campylobacteriosis] in England and Wales had risen from 12,822 in 1982 to 28,174 [*sic*] in 1988, as against 24,123 due to salmonella. (Letter in *Independent*, 26 January)

Such figures are very difficult for newspaper readers to take in and retain, especially as they refer to counts of different entities (food poisoning, salmonella poisoning, *Salmonella enteritidis* poisoning, campylobacter poisoning, etc.), or refer to different periods: 39,000, 28,196, 24,123, and so on. The quantities diverge — 28,174 or 28,714? — or are silently rounded: 23,000, 25,000 a year. Inevitably the figures blur, becoming impressions rather than facts, but what remains is the repeated mention of large quantities in the 20,000 to 30,000 range, usually associated with 1988, and this seems, subjectively, an alarmingly substantial number and a solid basis for the statistic extrapolation:

(14) Last November Mr Lacey said the number of people who fell ill with salmonella poisoning in 1988 was 24,500, but because not all cases were reported the actual number was probably 250,000, of which 150,000 were due to eggs.

The total figure could be as high as 2,500,000.

. . . A spokeswoman for the Health Department . . . said that the Government report, which said there may be as many as two million salmonella poisoning cases a year, was based on an estimate that the actual number of cases was 100 times the number of cases reported . . . 'Other suggestions are that the factor might be only 10. The fact is that nobody knows for certain.'

(*Telegraph*, 10 February)

The reader is bombarded with lots of very high numbers, and will certainly remember the 2,000,000, however sceptical s/he is about it.

Large numbers are mentioned throughout the discourse, because things other than 'salmonella infections' had to be counted, calculated, reported. Calculating the chances of someone eating an 'infected egg' produced astronomical figures: 10 billion eggs eaten per year, 30 million eggs a day. Then there were 400 million eggs and 4 million hens to be destroyed under the compensation scheme, but 'only 62 of the 40,000 egg producers in the UK, offered £1.50 per bird, had sent a total of 786,000 laying hens for slaughter' (*Guardian*, 11 January). Figures are also given for listeria infections and for the proliferation of listeria bacteria at different temperatures and in different conditions: up to 'a billion bugs'. Elsewhere, 50,000 families at risk from radon gas, 600,000 people in Oxfordshire advised to boil their drinking water, 18 million tons of rubbish dumped each year, 240,000 and 360,000 cans of reject French food, Britain producing 105,000 tonnes of CFCs each year and exporting 48,000. In addition to numerical counts, percentages are also cited: 40 per cent increase in food poisoning, 50 per cent drop in egg consumption; also doublings, treblings and even a million-fold decrease in listeria bacteria after microwaving.

There is a group of recurrent predicates — verbs, or nouns derived from verbs — designating changes in numbers:

(15) increase, rise, grow, spread, mount, expand, jump, leap, multiply, proliferation, escalation.

Some, such as 'increase' and 'rise', occur so extremely frequently that they are part of the constant background (but presumably cumulatively present to readers in a subliminal way). Others are found in dramatic, metaphoric contexts, immediately striking:

(16) astronomical increase, large and accelerating rise, rampant rise, sudden and exponential leap.

They are related to other dramatic expressions such as 'reproduction suddenly erupts' noticed earlier.

These predicates are interesting because they are multipurpose: they can go with different phenomena being quantified — cases of food poisoning, or bacteria, or types of food problem, or public fears, can all increase; different things can mount, or multiply, or proliferate, and so on. As a result, ambiguous phrases appear many times: 'the growth of listeria', 'increase in salmonella', and so on. The result is a blurring, a diminution in analytic precision; an impressionist style comes over, especially in conjunction with the ubiquitous mentions of large but constantly shifting numbers. The discourse is constantly alarming and hyperbolic, but in an obscure way: a problem of considerable proportions is always being alleged; we are bound to be concerned about it, but its outlines are indistinct, like some huge threatening shape on the horizon in a bad horror movie.

7 Telling Stories

ALLAN BELL

Journalists do not write articles. They write stories. A story has structure, direction, point, viewpoint. An article may lack these. Stories come in many kinds and are known in all cultures of the world. They include fairy tales, fables, parables, gospels, legends, epics, and sagas. Stories are embedded in all sorts of language use, from face-to-face conversation to public addresses. The role of the story-teller is a significant one both in language behaviour and in society at large. Much of humanity's most important experience has been embodied in stories.

Journalists are professional story-tellers of our age. The fairy tale starts: 'Once upon a time.' The news story begins: 'Fifteen people were injured today when a bus plunged . . .' The journalist's work is focused on the getting and writing of stories. This is reflected in the snatches of phrases in which newsroom business is conducted. A good journalist 'gets good stories' or 'knows a good story'. A critical news editor asks: 'Is this really a story?' 'Where's the story in this?'

Stories can be divided into hard news and soft. The features are soft news, licensed to deviate from the structures of hard news (Cappon, 1982: 111). Hard news is news as we all recognize it, and at its core is spot news — tales of accidents, disasters, crimes, the 'coups and earthquakes' of Rosenblum's title (1979). Journalists recognize the common threads in these kinds of stories, and may label any spot news 'a fire story' (Tuchman, 1978: 102). A second major category of hard news covers politics or diplomacy: news of elections, government announcements, international negotiations, party politics. These two central kinds of hard news, as written by the international news agencies provide our main examples as we analyse the structures of news.

News Stories and Personal Narratives

As a first approach to the nature of the news story, I will compare news with another kind of story which has been researched in recent decades:

narratives of personal experience told in face-to-face conversation. The similarities and differences between these two kinds of stories will illuminate what news has in common with other storytelling, and where it differs. Labov & Waletzky (1967) and Labov (1972) have analysed the structure of such narratives into six elements:

(1) The Abstract summarizes the central action and main point of the narrative. A story-teller uses it at the outset to pre-empt the questions, what is this about, why is this story being told?

(2) The Orientation sets the scene: the who, when, where, and initial situation or activity of the story.

(3) The Complicating Action is the central part of the story proper, answering the question, what happened (then)?

(4) The Evaluation addresses the question, so what? A directionless sequence of clauses is not a narrative. Narrative has point, and it is narrators' prime intention to justify the value of the story they are telling, to demonstrate why these events are reportable.

(5) The Resolution is what finally happened to conclude the sequence of events.

(6) Finally, many narratives end with a Coda — 'and that was that'. This wraps up the action, and returns the conversation from the time of the narrative to the present.

These six elements occur in the above order, although evaluation can be dispersed throughout the other elements. Only the complicating action, and some degree of evaluation, are obligatory components of the personal narrative. To what extent do news stories follow this pattern, and where do they depart from it? In applying this framework, we will see how it needs modification to cope with news and the ways in which news stories differ from personal narratives.

Most of the examples I use in this paper are from the press. Because press stories are generally longer and carry much more detail than broadcast news, the structure of press stories is more complex. A framework which handles press news is likely to be adequate for the text of broadcast stories. Even long broadcast stories such as those carried by Britain's *Channel Four News* or *World at One,* with their multiple inputs, are shorter and less complex than many press stories. The use of the newsmaker's actual voice in broadcast news is in principle no different from direct quotation in printed news. For television news one would require additional apparatus to relate voiceover commentary to the visuals. This is less of a problem than it seems. The Glasgow University Media Group's analysis (see, for instance, 1976:

STORY STRUCTURE   US troops   TIME STRUCTURE
                       ambushed
                       in Honduras

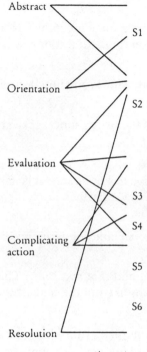

Abstract

                                    TEGUCIGALPA
                    S1   UNITED STATES troops in Hon-
                         duras were put on high alert af-
                         ter at least six American sol-   Time 7
                         diers were wounded, two ser-
                         iously, in a suspected leftist
                         guerrilla ambush yesterday,   Time 5
Orientation   United States officials said.
                    S2   Six or seven soldiers were
                         wounded when at least three
                         men, believed to be leftist guer-   Time 5
                         rillas, used high-powered weap-
                         ons in an ambush of a bus carry-
                         ing 28 passengers 20 kilometres   Time 4
Evaluation   north of the capital Tegucigalpa,   Time 3
                         United States embassy spokes-
                         man Terry Kneebone said.
                    S3   The bus was carrying the
                         soldiers from a pleasure trip at
                         a beach on the Atlantic Coast.   Time 2
                    S4   "It was a surprise attack,"
Complicating   Southern Command spokesman
action   Captain Art Haubold said in
                         Panama City.   Time 8a
                    S5   "The US forces did not return
                         fire. They kept going to get out
                         of the area as quickly as
                         possible."   Time 6
                    S6   A Tegucigalpa radio station
                         said an unidentified caller said   Time 1, 8b
Resolution   the leftist group Morazanista
                         Patriotic Liberation Front
                         claimed responsibility for the at-
                         tack. — NZPA-Reuter

Figure 7.1 Narrative structure and time structure of international spot news story (*The Dominion,* Wellington, 2 April 1990)

125) indicates that despite television newsworkers' efforts and beliefs to the contrary, the written text remains paramount and the visual subsidiary. In practice, news pictures are often tangential to the spoken text of a story, because it is impossible for cameras to be regularly in the right place at the right time. There are differences between printed and broadcast news styles, which we will touch on below, but the differences are less than the similarities.

Figure 7.1 displays a hard news story typical of those which appear daily on the international pages of any newspaper. The international news agencies are the chief suppliers of hard news and custodians of its style (as, for example, in Cappon's *Associated Press Guide to Good News Writing,* 1982). We can expect such stories to embody the core components of news discourse. Our example story contains some but not all of the elements of the personal narrative, and their order and importance are different.

Abstract

The lead or first paragraph has precisely the same function in news as the abstract in personal narrative. It summarizes the central action and establishes the point of the story. For major news stories, the lead paragraph is often set off from the remainder of the story in larger type or across several columns of the body copy.

In Figure 7.1, the first paragraph presents two main actions — the wounding of the US soldiers, and the consequent alert for US troops in Honduras. The story has a double abstract, a feature which can also occur in personal narratives. The consequence is treated as the prior point, with the violent incident second. The lead as summary or abstract is obligatory in hard news, where in personal narrative it remains optional. The lead is the device by which copy editor or audience can get the main point of a story from reading a single opening sentence, and on that basis decide whether to continue.

Press news has headlines as well as lead paragraphs. The headline is an abstract of the abstract. The lead pares the story back to its essential point, and the headline abstracts the lead itself. In Figure 7.1, the headline highlights the ambush, even though the lead begins with the consequent military alert. The lead paragraph is the journalist's primary abstract of a story. While to the reader the headline appears as first abstract in the printed story, in fact headlines are absent from broadcast news and even in press news are a last-minute addition. Broadcast news has no headlines, except in so far as stories are summarized at the beginning and/or end of a news bulletin. There are no headlines in news agency copy, from which most published news derives. Nor do journalists put headlines on their own stories: that is the work of subeditors. For journalists and news agencies, stories are identified by the ultimate in abstracts — a one-word catchline or slugline, unique to the story.

Orientation

In personal narrative, orientation sets the scene: who are the actors, where and when did the events take place, what is the initial situation? In news stories such orientation is obligatory. For journalists *who, what, when* and *where* are the basic facts which concentrate at the beginning of a story, but may be expanded further down. The lead in Figure 7.1 crams in no less than five sets of people: United States troops in Honduras, the six wounded soldiers, the two seriously wounded, leftist guerrillas, and US officials.

International agency stories as received off the wire are 'datelined' at the top for time and place origin, with the deictics *here* and *today,* used in the lead paragraph. In this story the time of the ambush is given as *yesterday.* The time of the alert is unspecified (but in fact was also *yesterday* because this was published in a morning paper, and Honduras is some 18 hours behind New Zealand time). The dateline specifies the location from which the journalist 'filed' the story to the news agency. Here as in many news-papers, the dateline is carried below the headline and above the lead. The lead paragraph names Honduras, the second sentence (S2) specifies the exact site of the ambush and identifies the capital city, a necessary detail for news about a country whose geography will not be well known to the read-ers. Further detail of place is given in S3. In S4 there is a change of country with a regional command spokesperson outside Honduras quoted. This may indicate that the story has been combined by agency copy editors from separate despatches from both Tegucigalpa and Panama City.

Evaluation

Evaluation is the means by which the significance of a story is established. In personal narrative, evaluation is what distinguishes a directionless sequence of sentences from a story with point and meaning (Labov, 1972: 367). In the case of the fight stories studied by Labov, the point is often the self-aggrandizement of the narrator. Evaluation pre-empts the question, so what? It gives the reason why the narrator is claiming the floor and the audi-ence's attention.

News stories also require evaluation, and in their case its function is iden-tical to that in personal narrative: to establish the significance of what is being told, to focus the events, and to justify claiming the audience's atten-tion. The story in Figure 7.1, stresses repeatedly the importance of what has happened. *High alert, at least six* wounded, *two seriously* in the lead paragraph all stake claims on the reader to take these events, quite literally, seriously. The claims continue in the remaining paragraphs, but with diminishing fre-quency and force: *at least three men, high-powered weapons* (S2), *surprise attack* (S4), *as quickly as possible* (S5).

The lead paragraph is a nucleus of evaluation, because the function of the lead is not merely to summarize the main action. The lead focuses the story in a particular direction. It forms the lens through which the remainder of the story is viewed. This function is even more obvious for the headline, especially when it appears to pick up on a minor point of the story. Focusing a story is a prime preoccupation of the journalist. Until a journalist finds what to lead a story with, the story remains unfocused. It is an article but not a story, and may be rejected or rewritten by editors on those grounds. On the other hand, once the journalist decides what the lead is, the rest of the story often falls into place below it. If no good lead can be found, the material may be rejected altogether as a non-story.

In personal narrative, evaluative devices may occur throughout the nar-rative but are typically concentrated near the end, just before the resolution of the events. In the news story, evaluation focuses in the lead. Its function is to make the contents of the story sound *as X as possible,* where *X* is big, recent, important, unusual, new; in a word — newsworthy. The events and news actors will be given the maximum status for the sake of the story. In the same fashion, narrators of fight stories are at pains to enhance the scale of their adversary — 'the baddest girl in the neighborhood' — and hence the magnitude of their own eventual victory (Labov, 1972: 364).

Action

At the heart of a personal narrative is the sequence of events which occurred. In Labov's analysis, a defining characteristic of narrative as a form is the temporal sequence of its sentences. That is, the action is invariably told in the order in which it happened. News stories, by contrast, are seldom if ever told in chronological order. Even within the lead paragraph of Figure 7.1, result (the military alert) precedes cause (the ambush). Down in the story proper, the time sequence is also reversed. The sequence of events as one of the participants might have told it is:

> About 30 of us went by bus for a day at the beach.
> On the way back we got to 20 kilometres north of Tegucigalpa.
> There some guerrillas ambushed us and shot up the bus with high powered rifles.
> They wounded six or seven of the soldiers.

Figure 7.1 shows the time structure of events in the story. S2 and S3 of the news story run these events in precisely the reverse order to which they happened. The result is placed before the action which caused it. This is a common principle of news writing, that it is not the action or the process which takes priority but the outcome. Indeed, it is this principle which enables news stories to be updated day after a day or hour by hour. If there is a new outcome to lead with, the previous action can drop down in the story. Our example shows traces of just such an origin in the dual abstract of its lead paragraph, which reads like an updating story from the international wires. A previous story probably carried news of the ambush, and Figure 7.1 is a follow-up which leads with the more recent information of the military alert.

The time structure of the story is very complex. In S1 the latest occurring event is presented first, followed by its antecedent. S2 and S3 pick up the action at that antecedent point in time and trace it backwards as described above. S4 shifts the story into another setting and time frame for commentary on what happened, and S5 describes the final action of the main incident, namely the bus's escape from the ambush. The last paragraph moves into a third setting and presents what is in fact temporally the beginning of the events, the group (possibly) responsible for the ambush.

Where chronological order defines the structure of personal narrative, a completely different force is driving the presentation of the news story. Perceived news value overturns temporal sequence and imposes an order completely at odds with the linear narrative point. It moves backwards and forwards in time, picking out different actions on each cycle. In one case, at the start of S2, it even repeats an action — *six or seven soldiers were wounded* — from the previous sentence. This wilful violation of our expectations that narratives usually proceed in temporal succession is distinctive of news stories. It may also have repercussions for how well audiences understand news stories.

Resolution

The personal narrative moves to a resolution: the fight is won, the accident survived. News stories often do not present such clearcut results. When they do, as noted above, the result will be in the lead rather than at the end of the story. In Figure 7.1, the nearest thing to a resolution is the general military alert. But this, of course, is only the latest step in a continuing saga. The news is more like a serial than a short story. The criminal was arrested, but the trial is in the future. The accident occurred, but the victims are still in hospital. One kind of news does follow the chronology of the personal narrative more closely: sports reporting. Sport makes good news just because there is always a result. A sports story will lead in standard news fashion with the result of the game and a few notable incidents, but then settle down to chronological reporting of the course of the game.

News stories are not rounded off. They finish in mid-air. The news story consists of instalments of information of perceived decreasing importance. It is not temporally structured, or turned in a finished fashion. One very good reason for this is that the journalist does not know how much of her story will be retained by copy editors for publication. Stories are regularly cut from the bottom up, which is a great incentive to get what you believe to be the main points in early.

Coda

Nor is there a coda to the news story. The reason lies in the function which the coda performs in personal narrative. It serves as an optional conclusion to the story, to mark its finish, to return the floor to other conversational partners, and to return the tense from narrative time to the present. None of these functions is necessary in the newspaper, where the floor is not open, and where the next contribution is another story. But the coda does have some parallel in broadcast news. The end of a news bulletin or programme — but not of individual news stories — will usually be explicitly signalled by 'that is the end of the news' or a similar formula. Between broadcast stories there is no discourse marker to mark one off from the other, although intonation or (on television) visual means will be used to flag the change of topic.

Conclusion

Our first approach to the structure of news stories indicates interesting similarities and difference to personal narrative. In news, the abstract is obligatory not optional. Orientating and evaluative material occurs in a similar fashion to personal narratives, but tends to concentrate in the first sentence. The central action of the news story is told in non-chronological order, with result presented first followed by a complex recycling through various time zones down through the story. One characteristic which news and personal narrative share is a penchant for direct quotation. The flavour of the eye-witness and colour of direct involvement is important to both forms.

The Honduras example story also points up four features which are typical of news stories but alien to the face-to-face narrative. First, the personal narrative is just that — *personal*. It relates the narrator's own experience, while the news story reports on others' experiences. The reporter has usually not witnessed these, and first person presentation is conventionally excluded from standard news reporting. Secondly, and consequently, where the personal narrative is told from one viewpoint — the narrator's — in news a range of sources is often cited. In Figure 7.1 at least four separate sources are named in the space of six paragraphs. Thirdly, the news revels in giving numbers with a precision which is foreign to conversational stories. In the Honduras story, six sets of figures counting the guerrillas, passengers, casualties, and distance to the location occur in the first two paragraphs. Fourth, the syntax of personal narratives is simple, with mostly main clauses and little subordination. The syntax of news stories can be complex, as S1 and S2 show (although these are unusually long sentences for hard news).

The Structure of News Stories

Analysing a story's structure

In Figure 7.1 we looked at a spot news story from the international news agencies. Figure 7.2 displays a typical example of the other predominant product of the same agencies, diplomatic and political news. The possible component categories of the story's structure are annotated alongside the copy. In Figure 7.3, that linear structure is redisplayed as a tree diagram, which reunites the components of different events from where they are scattered throughout the story. The structure as diagrammed in Figure 7.3 looks complex, and so it is, but in fact I have here telescoped levels and omitted nodes in order to simplify the presentation as much as possible. The complexity is a true reflection of the structure of such international diplomatic/political stories.

Troops take over Lithuanian office

HEADLINE

Event 1

ATTRIBUTION

Place

LEAD

Evaluation S1

Event 1

Event 2

EVENT 3 S2

Previous episodes S3

EVENT 1 S4

EVENT 4 S5

Action S6

EVENT 1

Context S7

Previous episodes S8

Context

Reaction S9

S10

MOSCOW

S1 STEPPING up the pressure on rebel Lithuania. Soviet troops seized a government office in the capital — and neighbouring Byelorussia threatened to claim a slice of the republic if it secedes from the Soviet Union.

S2 The parliament in Lithuania's sister Baltic republic of Estonia. meanwhile, announced yesterday it wanted to break with Moscow too. declaring the beginning of a transitional period that would end in full independence.

S3 Moscow has refused to recognise Lithuania's March 11 declaration of independence.

S4 Instead it has waged what Lithuanians call a war of nerves, with soldiers occupying public buildings and arresting Lithuanian military deserters.

S5 United States President George Bush sent Soviet President Mikhail Gorbachev a note urging peaceful settlement of the dispute.

S6 A few hours later, Interior Ministry troops moved into the public prosecutor's office in the Lithuanian capital Vilnius.

S7 It was the first Lithuanian building to be occupied by Soviet troops since Wednesday. when the Communist Party headquarters was seized.

S8 It was also the first to be taken over from the government as opposed to the party.

S9 Lithuanian President Vytautas Landsbergis went on television yesterday to denounce the move. saying it would bring shame on Moscow.

S10 "We have endured all these years...we will this time as

well." he said.

S11 "What the USSR is doing now will bring only shame in the eyes of all the world."

S12 Earlier yesterday, deputy Soviet prosecutor Alexei Vasilyev told staff at the prosecutor's office that Moscow had relieved their boss, Alturas Paulauskas, from his post.

S13 In his place Mr Vasilyev announced Moscow had appointed Antanas Petrauskas. who quickly told journalists he did not recognise Lithuanian independence.

S14 Control of the prosecutor's office is considered crucial for Moscow to enforce Soviet law which it says still holds sway in Lithuania. including penalties for army desertion.

S15 Vilnius Radio said Interior Ministry troops had also taken over the history institute of the Lithuanian Communist Party.

S16 Chief military prosecutor Alexander Katusev said yesterday a defence ministry amnesty announced on Friday for any Lithuanian deserters who returned to their units was invalid.

S17 They would be considered on a case-by-case basis, he said.

S18 Lithuania was also set upon by its neighbour Byelorussia, where the parliamentary leadership said it would lay claim to Vilnius and six other districts if Lithuania seceded.

S19 "We shall be obliged to insist on the return of Byelorussian land to the Byelorussian Soviet Socialist Republic," the presidium of the republic's Supreme Soviet. or parliament said. according to the official news agency Tass. — NZPA-Reuter

S11

S12 Action

S13

Action

S14 Evaluation

Attribution
S15 EVENT 5

S16 EVENT 6

S17

S18

EVENT 2

S19

Attribution

ATTRIBUTION

Figure 7.2 Components of an international news agency story, *Dominion Sunday Times,* Wellington, 1 April 1990 (CAPITALS represent major categories, lower-case labels are subordinate categories)

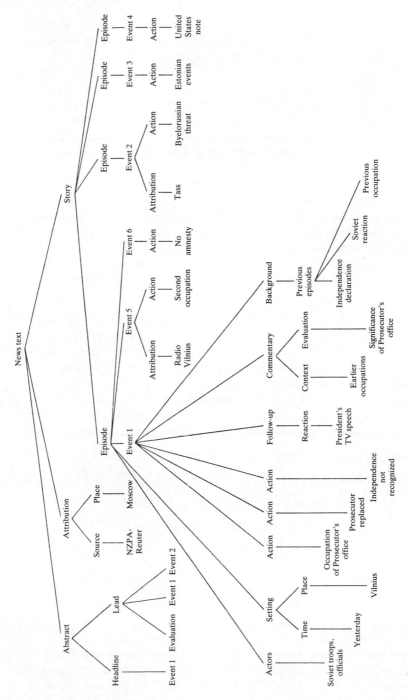

Figure 7.3 Structure of Lithuania story from Figure 7.2

The news text consists of abstract, attribution and the story proper (Figure 7.3). The attribution is outside the body copy of the story, and indicates place at the top (*Moscow,* Figure 7.2) and source at the bottom (*NZPA-Reuter*). In many papers all three constituents of the attribution would conventionally be presented at the start of the lead paragraph: *Moscow, 31 March, NZPA-Reuter.* Here the time is not stated in attribution, headline or lead, but is explicit within the story — *yesterday* (S2, S12). The NZPA-Reuter attribution means that the story originates from one of the principal international agencies, channelled through London, New York or Paris, and finally Sydney and Wellington. Although most of the action takes place in Lithuania, the story is datelined Moscow. This may indicate a reporter working from Lithuania through a Moscow office. More likely the reporting is in fact being done from Moscow itself. Such off-the-spot reporting is completely standard in international news. Within the story other media are named as sources of specific information — Vilnius radio (S15) and Tass (S19) for Events 5 and 2 respectively. Unusually, and in contrast to the Honduras story, no non-media sources of information are credited.

The abstract breaks down into headline and lead. The headline covers only Event 1, the occupation — the subeditor gratefully picking out the only hard action from a generally verbal story. The lead covers the occupation plus Event 2, the Byelorussian threat, as well as evaluating their effect on the situation. The evaluative clause *stepping up the pressure on rebel Lithuania* generalizes on the significance of the two separate events reported in the lead. This kind of explicit evaluation is a common device for drawing together the often disparate threads of such a story. There is no expansion or justification of the evaluation within the body of the story.

The story itself covers no fewer than six events:

(1) Occupation of the prosecutor's office (S1, S3–4, S6–14);

(2) Byelorussian threat to claim territory (S1, S18–19);

(3) Estonia's announcement of desired independence (S2);

(4) Bush's note to Gorbachev (S5);

(5) Occupation of the Communist Party history institute (S15);

(6) Withdrawal of deserter amnesty (S16–17).

In Figure 7.3, I subsume Events 1, 5 and 6 under a single episode. They share a common setting of place (Vilnius) as well as principal actors (Soviet troops and officials). However, it is not clear from the story how related these happenings are, and further information might lead us to treat them as separate episodes. Events 2 and 4 are related to the main episode only through the general theme of the Lithuanian independence issue. Event 3 is even more remote, drawing parallels between happenings in Estonia and Lithuania. The story as published bears all the hallmarks of a shotgun marriage by the news agency of up to four originally separate stories covering the occupation, the Byelorussian threat, Bush's note, and the Estonian situation.

Events 3–6 are picked up and dropped within a paragraph or so each (Figure 7.2). In the diagram I have not specified all the categories required in the analysis. For example, each event implies actors and setting as well as action. Although Events 1 and 2 are treated at greater length, they are delivered by instalments in a manner characteristic of news narrative. A number of devices are used to bring cohesion out of these diverse components. The inclusion of Event 3 is justified (S2) by describing Estonia as *Lithuania's sister Baltic republic,* together with the use of *meanwhile* a sure signal that a journalist is about to draw a tenuous connection between disparate events (cf. Glasgsow University Media Group, 1976: 118). Event 4, Bush's note, is said to deal with *the dispute* (S5), the label under which everything is here subsumed. (In fact, the Bush note was covered in an adjacent story in the newspaper.) A time relationship is specified (S6), linking Bush's note with the occupation which occurred *a few hours later.* The juxtaposition seems to imply not just a temporal but a causal or at least concessive relationship. The occupation is interpreted as taking place in disregard of Bush's plea for a peaceful settlement. *Also* is used both to tie Event 5 in the main occupation (S15), and when Event 2 — mentioned in the lead then dropped — reappears in S18.

The actors, time and place structure are as complicated as the action. News narrative, as Manoff (1987) notes, is a means of knitting diverse events together. The story ranges across several locations. Each event belongs to a different place, principally the Lithuanian capital Vilnius (several sites), Byelorussia, Estonia, Washington and Moscow. As well as the complex interleaving of other events between the two main events, the time structure of the main events themselves is presented non-chronologically. Event 2 is included in the lead by the rather clumsy punctuation device of the dash, and surfaces again only at the end of the story. Event 1 consists of three actions (Figure 7.3), plus follow-up, commentary and background. The event moves from the occupation itself (S1), back in time to previous episodes which form the broad background to it (S3–4). It then presents detail about the occupation (S6) plus background about previous occupation events (S7–8), moves forward in time to Lithuanian verbal reaction to the occupation (S9–11), and returns to the occupation again (S12–13) plus evaluative background on its significance (S14). Such a to-and-fro time structure is completely standard for this kind of story — which does not make it any easier for the reader to keep track of. As van Dijk (1988b: 65) says, getting coherence out of the discontinuous nature of news can be a demanding comprehension task. The analysis of a standard fire story from the *Baltimore Sun* undertaken by Pollard-Gott *et al.* (1979) shows how the same kind of non-chronological presentation, cycling through different actions, consequences and causes, occurs in a local spot news item.

Such is the outline structure of this one story. Finally, we look briefly at how news values as discussed more fully in Bell (1991) have moulded that structure. In the midst of a highly diffuse and confused situation, the journalist goes unerringly for the unambiguous 'fact' to lead with — the troops' occupation of the prosecutor's office. This action also has the value that conflict is made more overt than the exchange of words which occurs in the rest of the story. The action is described in increasing factual detail, from the lead, where the prosecutor's office is not specified, through the place detail of S6, to the description in S13–14 of what ensued. The story cycles round the action, returning for more detail on each circuit, and interspersing background and other events. The technique moves like a downward spiral through the available information. This is in fact described by journalists as the 'inverted pyramid' style — gathering all the main points at the beginning and progressing through decreasingly important information.

Spreading the scope of events as wide as possible in the shortest space, Byelorussia, Estonia and the United States are all called up in the first five paragraphs. The reference to the United States is of marginal relevance to the central action of the story, particularly since there is a detailed story about the Bush note alongside. But the news value of elite nations and persons — world powers and their presidents — leads to the events in Lithuania being cast in the light of superpower relations. The consonance of this story with Western news stereotypes of Soviet methods is seen in how the occupation is framed in contrast to Bush's urging for peace. We can also see the news value of co-option hard at work, bringing diffuse events and locations under the umbrella of one story. The push for the superlative is clear in the lexicon selected, especially in the succession of forceful words in the lead: *stepping up, pressure, rebel, seized, threatened, secedes.*

The Generalized Structure of News Stories

We are now in a position to draw some general conclusions about the categories and structure of news stories. A news text will normally consist of an abstract, attribution and the story proper (Figure 7.4). Attribution of where the story came from is not always explicit. It can include agency credit and/or journalist's byline, optionally plus place and time. The abstract consists of the lead and, for press news, a headline. The lead will include the main event, and possibly a second event. This necessarily entails giving some information on actors and setting involved in the event. The lead may also incorporate attribution (as in the Honduras story), and supplementary categories such as evaluation (see the Lithuania story).

A story consists of one or more episodes, which in turn consist of one or more events. Events must contain actors and action, usually express setting, and may have explicit attribution. The categories of attribution, actors and setting (time and place) need to be recognized as part of the structure of news stories. They perform the orientation which Labov (1972) found in narratives, as well as embedding all or part of a story as information given by a particular source. These are also part of the journalist's mental analysis of what goes in a story: who, when, where, who said?

As well as those elements which present the central action, we recognize three additional categories that can contribute to an event: follow-up, commentary and background (Figure 7.4). The Lithuanian story contained all three of these, and all but three of the lower categories of which they can be composed: consequences, expectations, and history.

FOLLOW-UP covers any action subsequent to the main action of an event. It can include verbal reaction, as in the Lithuania story, or non-verbal consequences — for example, if the upshot of the occupation had been demonstrations in Vilnius instead of a presidential speech. Because it covers action occurring after what a story has treated as the main action, follow-up is a prime source of subsequent updating stories — themselves called 'follow-ups'. We can easily imagine a subsequent story where the lead reads *Lithuanian President Vytautas Landsbergis has gone on television to condemn Soviet occupation of* . . . If the follow-up action had in fact been a demonstration, that would certainly have claimed the lead on a later agency story.

COMMENTARY provides the journalist's or news actors' observations on the action. It may be represented by context, such as the S7–8 information comparing this occupation with previous ones. It may be by explicit evaluation, as in the S14 presentation of the significance of occupying the prosecutor's office. Thirdly, and not exemplified in the Lithuania story, it may express expectations held by the journalist or a news actor on how the situation could develop next.

The category of BACKGROUND covers any events prior to the current action. These are classed as 'previous episodes' if they are comparatively recent. They probably figure as news stories in their own right at an earlier stage of the situation. If the background goes beyond the near past, it is classed as 'history'. Information on the relationship of Lithuania to the Soviet Union during the Second World War was included in stories on other events around this time.

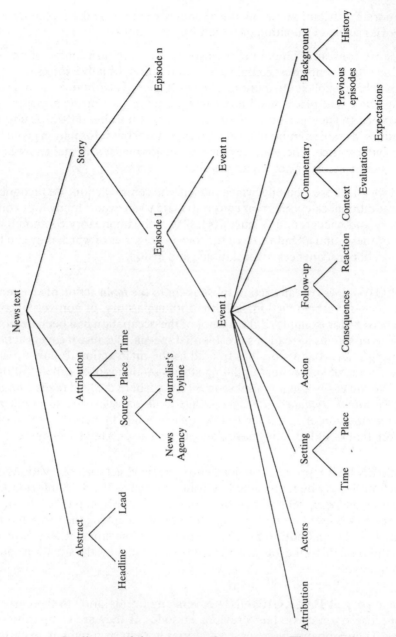

Figure 7.4 Outline model structure of news texts. There can be a number of Events or Episodes. Follow-up and Background categories can have Episodes embedded into them. Headline and Lead pick up components from the Story itself. Categories such as Attribution or Setting can be components of either an Event or an Episode.

Follow-up and background can have the character of episodes in their own right. That is, episode is a recursive category and can be embedded under consequences, reaction, history or background. If the previous episodes outlined in S3–4 of the Lithuanian story had been more fully expanded, they could easily have incorporated the apparatus of a full episode within them, including categories such as context or evaluation. Similarly, follow-up reaction or consequences can be complex. These are by nature categories which were full stories in their own right at a previous time, or may become so tomorrow.

It can be unclear where elements such as attribution, setting, previous episodes, context or evaluation belong in a particular story's structure. Do they relate to a specific event mentioned in the previous paragraph or to the whole story? The background in the Lithuania story (S3–4) could reasonably be regarded as applying to virtually the whole story rather than just Event 1, and we would then elevate it in the diagram. The unclarity over structure often represents a genuine unclarity in the story itself. The original may be deliberately equivocal about what material is attributed to whom, at what point the location actually shifted, or whether the evaluation applies to one event or a whole complex episode. This confusion results from the fragmented structure of news writing. The ideal news story is one which could be cut to end at any paragraph. It is thus common for cohesion between paragraphs to be unclear or non-existent, even when a journalist tries to enforce it using devices such as *also* noted earlier for the Lithuania story.

Probably the most striking characteristics of news discourse come from the non-chronological order of its elements: the nature of the lead, time structure, and what van Dijk has called the instalment method (1988b: 43), by which an event is introduced then returned to in more detail two or more times. Even information about actors and setting — orientation, in Labov's terms — is delivered not in separate descriptive sentences but as part of the narration of events. The complex time structure — so at odds with the chronological norms of other types of narrative — is a consequence of news obeying news values rather than ordinary narrative norms. The time structure of news stories can make the shape of a difficult film or novel look straightforward by comparison. While the reader has to decode this structure, recall that the journalist had to encode it in the first place. From notes from an interview which covered events basically in chronological order, the journalist has extracted bits of information and reassembled them in newsworthy order. So information from one part of her notes may feed into several widely separated paragraphs of the story. And when a text is assembled from many sources, the process is all the more complex.

In personal narrative, if you change the order of clauses you change the order of events (Labov, 1972: 360). In news, order is everything but chronology is nothing. As news consumers we are so accustomed to this approach that we forget how deviant it is compared both with other narrative genres and with earlier norms of news reporting. Schudson's research on news narrative styles shows that the inverted pyramid structure was a development of American journalism in the late nineteenth century. In the 1880s stories covering presidential State of the Union addresses did not summarize the key points at the beginning, but by 1910 the lead as summary was standard. This marks the movement of journalists from being stenographers recording events to interpreters.

Figure 7.5 reprints a story from the *Washington Chronicle* of 10 December 1876. It was a year when — as the centennial issue of the *Washington Post* narrates — 'General Custer was wiped out at Little Big Horn . . . Wild Bill Hickok shot from behind, . . . and the James gang ambushed'. This clip is a typical spot news story which could run in any local paper today. But it is narrated in absolute chronological order. Where the modern lead would run *A drunken man survived a jump from*

**A Man Jumps From a
Lighting Express, but Lights on his
Head and is Not Hurt**

(From the Cleveland Herald.)

On Monday night a man named Schwartz took passage at Cincinnati for New York. To all appearances he was under the influence of liquor, but got on well enough until the train arrived at a point a short distance below Galion, when Schwartz was noticed to get up from his seat in a hurry and make his way to the platform, from which he jumped while the train was running at full speed.

The alarm was quickly given, the train stopped and backed up, and Schwartz, apparently lifeless, was pulled out of the mud where he had fallen on his head and shoulders and taken on board the train, which again started on its course. In the meantime those in charge of the train began to search for anything that might show his identity, when Schwartz, without having shown any signs of life save that he breathed heavily, politely cautioned them "to let up on that."

He was brought as far as Galion, where he was left in charge until his friends were informed of his condition.

—Washington Chronicle, December 10, 1876

Figure 7.5 The way it was: story from *Washington Chronicle*, 1876

the Cincinnati–New York express . . ., the reporter of a century ago begins at the beginning and goes to the end. Even the headline tells a chronological tale. According to Schudson (1978) reporters moved from being recorders or stenographers to interpreters about the turn of the century.

Story grammarians have concluded that the minimal well-formed narrative must contain setting and action (Pollard-Gott *et al.,* 1979). What constitutes the minimal, well-formed, modern news text? The answer is straightforward: a one-sentence story. Many newspapers publish one-paragraph stories, to fill odd corners or assembled in a column of news briefs. In some broadcast news, many stories may consist of only a single sentence. Because the story is encapsulated in the lead, the lead is a story in microcosm. If we were to analyse the first sentence of the Lithuania story, we would need to specify all the basic structure of Events 1 and 2. This is not surprising. If a lead summarizes a story, we expect it to contain the principal elements of that story. Our process of analysing a news text into its constituent structure produces a summary much like that which the journalist arrives at in writing a lead. The lead-as-complete-story consists minimally of the actors, action and place which constitute a single event. Attributions, abstract, time, and the supplementary categories of follow-up, commentary and background are unnecessary.

The categories I have outlined for describing story structure, drawn from van Dijk, Labov, other story researchers, and my own work, seem to have a high degree of generality and validity. They apply in languages and cultures other than English. Van Dijk's analysis of newspaper stories in many languages (1988a) found few significant differences in news values or structure. In a comparison of different treatments of the assassination of Lebanese President-elect Gemayel in 1982, he found stories in Spanish, Chinese and Swedish all followed a similar pattern to English-language news. There were some differences between papers in the 'First' and 'Third' Worlds. But the greatest differences were between 'quality' and 'popular' papers, for instance within West Germany and the United Kingdom. The popular *Bild Zeitung* (literally 'picture paper') used a more chronological news order for dramatic effect. Burger also notes the distinctiveness of this section of the press (1984: 99), as well as the similarity of broadcast news between countries (p. 105). The reason for the similarities is clear but beyond our scope here: news norms worldwide are patterned on Western, and particularly Anglo-American, models.

References

Bell, A. (1991) *The Language of News Media*. Oxford: Blackwell.
Burger, H. (1984) *Sprache des Massenmedien* (Language of the Mass Media). Berlin: Walter de Gruyter.

Cappon, R. J. (1982) *The Word: An Associated Press Guide to Good News Writing*. New York: Associated Press.
Glasgow University Media Group (1976) *Bad News*. London: Routledge and Kegan Paul.
Labov, W. (1972) The transformation of experience in narrative syntax. In W. Labov (ed.) *Language in the Inner City*. Philadelphia: University of Pennsylvania Press.
Labov, W. and Waletzky, J. (1967) Narrative analysis: Oral versions of personal experience. In J. Helm (ed.) *Essays on the Verbal and Visual Arts (Proceedings of the 1966 Annual Spring Meeting of the American Ethnological Society)*. Seattle: University of Washington Press.
Manoff, R. K. (1987) Writing the news (by telling the 'story'). In R. K. Manoff and M. Schudson (eds) *Reading the News*. New York: Pantheon.
Pollard-Gott, L., McCloskey, M. and Todres, A. K. (1979) Subjective story structure. *Discourse Processes* 2(4), 251–81.
Rosenblum, M. (1979) *Coups and Earthquakes*. New York: Harper and Row.
Schudson, M. (1978) *Discovering the News: A Social History of American Newspapers*. New York: Basic Books.
Tuchman, G. (1978) *Making News: A Study in the Construction of Reality*. New York: Free Press.
van Dijk, T. A. (1988a) *News Analysis: Case Studies of International and National News in the Press*. Hillsdale, NJ: Lawrence Erlbaum.
— (1988b) *Making News: A Study in the Construction of Reality*. New York: Free Press.

8 Film Languages

GRAEME TURNER

The title of this paper may require explanation. Film is not, of course, a language but it does generate its meanings through systems (cinematography, sound editing, and so on) which work like languages. To understand how this idea might help in our analysis of films, and to understand the limits of this idea, we need to go back to some very basic principles. The first step is to see film as communication. The second step is to place film communication within a wider system for generating meaning — that of the culture itself.

Culture and Language

Notoriously difficult to define neatly, culture, as I wish to discuss it here, is a dynamic process which produces the behaviours, the practices, the institutions, and the meanings which constitute our social existence. Culture comprises the processes of making sense of our way of life. Cultural studies theorists, drawing particularly on semiotics, have argued that language is the major mechanism through which culture produces and reproduces social meanings. The definition of language developed in this tradition of thought goes well beyond that of the normal definition of verbal or written language. For semioticians such as Roland Barthes (1973), 'language' includes all those systems from which we can select and combine elements in order to communicate. So dress can be a language; by changing our fashions (selecting and combining our garments and thus the meanings that culture attributes to them) we can change what our clothes 'say' about us and our place within the culture.

Ferdinand de Saussure is commonly held to be the founder of European semiotics. He argued that language is not, as is commonly thought, a system of nomenclature. We do not simply invent names for things as they are encountered or invented; thus the Bible story of Adam naming the objects in Eden cannot be an accurate account of how language works (whatever else it might be). If language simply named things, there would be no

119

difficulty in translating from one language to another. But there is difficulty, because cultures share some concepts and objects but not others. The Eskimos have many words for snow, since it has great significance within their physical and social worlds; Australian Aboriginal languages have no word for money as the function that money serves does not exist within their original cultures; and every viewer of westerns will know that American Indians were supposed to be unable to comprehend the concept of lying (i.e. their language did not enable them to 'think it' or 'talk it'): hence the formula 'white man speak with forked tongue'. Even cultures which share the same language are not made up of precisely the same components, and so Australians, Americans and Britons will attribute significance to the components of their worlds in different ways. The language system of a culture carries that culture's system of priorities, its specific set of values, its specific composition of the physical and social world.

What language does is to construct, not label, reality for us. We cannot think without language, so it is difficult to imagine 'thinking' things for which we have no language. We become members of our culture through language, we acquire our sense of personal identity through language, and we internalize the value systems which structure our lives through language. We cannot step 'outside' language in order to produce a set of our own meanings which are totally independent of the cultural system.

Nevertheless, it is possible to use our language to say new things, to articulate new concepts, to incorporate new objects. But we do this through existing terms and meanings, through the existing vocabularies of words and ideas in our language. A new object might be defined by connecting it with existing analogous objects — as is clear in the word 'typewriter' — or new ideas will interpellate themselves by trying to redefine current terms and usage — as feminism has done in its attack on sexist usage. Individual utterances are thus both unique *and* culturally determined. This apparent contradiction is explained by Saussure's useful distinction between the *langue* of the culture (the potential for individual utterances within a language system), and the *parole* (the individual utterance composed by choices from the *langue*). The distinction roughly corresponds to that between language and speech, and it reminds us that, although there are vast possibilities for originality in the *langue,* there are also things we cannot say, meanings that cannot be produced within any one specific language system.

All of the above is as true of film 'languages' as it is of verbal language, although the connection to film may seem a little distant at the moment. The operation of language, however, provides us with a central model of the way culture produces meaning, regardless of the medium of communication.

Language constructs meanings in two ways. The literal or denotative meaning of a word is attached to it by usage. It is a dictionary style of meaning where the relation between the word and the object it refers to is relatively fixed. The word 'table' is widely understood to refer to a flat object on (usually) four legs upon which we might rest our dinner, books, or a vase, and which has variants such as the coffee table and the dinner table. The denotative meaning is not its only meaning (in fact, it is doubtful that anything is understood purely literally). Words, and the things to which they refer accrue associations, connotations, and social meanings, as they are used. The word 'politician', for instance, is not a neutral word in most western cultures. It can be used as a term of abuse or criticism, or even as a sly compliment to someone who is not actually a politician but who manipulates people with sufficient subtlety to invite the comparison. The word can have specifically negative connotations because it can mobilize the negative associations attached to politicians. This second kind of meaning, the connotative, is interpretative and depends upon the user's cultural experience rather than on a dictionary. It is in connotation that we find the social dimension of language.

Images, as well as words, carry connotations. A filmed image of a man will have a denotative dimension — it will refer to the mental concept of 'man'. But images are culturally charged; the camera angle employed, his position within the frame, the use of lighting to highlight certain aspects, any effect achieved by colour, tinting, or processing would all have the potential for social meaning. When we deal with images it is especially apparent that we are not only dealing with the object or the concept they represent, but we are also dealing with *the way in which they are represented*. There is a 'language' for visual representation, too, sets of codes and conventions used by the audience to make sense of what they see. Images reach us as already 'encoded' messages, already represented as meaningful in particular ways. One of the tasks of film analysis is to discover how this is done, both in particular films and in general.

We need to understand how this language-like system works. Methodologies which only deal with verbal or written language are not entirely appropriate. So it is useful to employ a system of analysis which began with verbal language but which has broadened out to include those other activities which produce social meaning. The work of all these activities is called signification — the making of significance — and the methodology is called semiotics. Once we understand the basic premises of semiotics we can apply them to the particular 'signifying practices' of film: the various media and technologies through which film's meanings are produced.

Semiotics sees social meaning as the product of the relationships constructed between 'signs'. The 'sign' is the basic unit of communication and it can be a photograph, a traffic signal, a word, a sound, an object, a smell, whatever the culture finds significant. In film, we could talk of the signature tune of the shark in *Jaws* or the face of Woody Allen as a sign. They signify, respectively, a particular version of 'shark-ness' (those meanings constructed around the shark in *Jaws*) and 'Woody Allen-ness' (again, the mental concepts and meanings, both from within and outside a specific film, which are constructed around Woody Allen). We can also talk of the way different signifying systems (sound, image) work to combine their signs into a more complicated message; the helicopter attack, musically accompanied by 'The March of the Valkyries', in *Apocalypse Now!* is such a case.

Theoretically, the sign can be broken down into two parts. The *signifier* is the physical form of the sign: the image, or word, or photograph. The *signified* is the mental concept referred to. Together they form the sign. A photographic image of a tree is a signifier. It becomes a sign when we connect it with its signified — the mental concept of what a tree is. The structure of the sign can be represented diagrammatically like this.

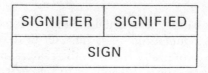

To extend this, let us refer back to our earlier example, of fashion as a language. When we change our garments to change our 'look', what we are doing is changing the signifiers through which we represent ourselves. We change our fashions (signifiers) to change what we mean to others (the signified). Our social identities are signs, too.

Signifiers carry connotations. Semiotics has enquired into advertising to show how the selection of signifiers with positive connotations (waterskiing, relaxing by a pool) is used to transpose these associations on to an accompanying advertised product, such as cigarettes. Signifieds, too, accrue social meanings. You will react to a picture of President Marcos in terms of opinions you already hold about his controversial political career. Such a picture mobilizes a second, less literal, chain of cultural meanings through the specific signifiers used, and the ideas we already have of Marcos himself.

It is this second level of meaning we will be most concerned with in this book, because it is where the work of signification takes place in film: in the organizing of representation to make a specific sense for a specific audience. Semiotics offers us access to such activity because it allows us to separate ideas from their representation (at least, theoretically) in order to see how our view of the world, or a film, is constructed. It does this by closely analysing a film (or a view of the world) as a 'text', a set of forms, relationships, and meanings. Those wishing to follow semiotic theory a little further can find a good introduction in Fiske (1982) but for the moment a definition of the three terms, signifier, signified, and sign, is all that is necessary to understand the following application of semiotics to film.

Film narratives have developed their own signifying systems. Film has its own 'codes', shorthand methods of establishing social or narrative meanings; and its own conventions — sets of rules which audiences agree to observe and which, for example, allow us to overlook the lack of realism in a typical musical sequence. (When a singer is accompanied by an orchestra, we do not expect to find it in the frame just because it is on the soundtrack.) At the level of the signifier, film has developed a rich set of codes and conventions. When the camera moves to a close-up, this indicates strong emotion or crisis. At the end of love scenes we might see a slow fade, or a slow loss of focus, or a modest pan upwards from the lovers' bodies — all coy imitations of the audience averting their eyes but all signifying the continuation and completion of the act. The shot–reverse shot system is a convention for representing conversation. The use of music to signify emotion is conventional too, as there is no real reason why the orchestra should build up to a crescendo during a clinch. Slow-motion sequences are usually used to aestheticize — to make beautiful and instil significance into their subjects. Slow-motion death scenes were in vogue during the late 1960s and early 1970s in films such as *Bonnie and Clyde* and *The Wild Bunch*; the aim was not simply to glamorize death but to mythologize these particular deaths — injecting them with added significance and power. Slow-motion love scenes both aestheticize and eroticize.

Genres are composed from sets of narrative and representational conventions. To understand them, audiences must, in a sense, bring the set of rules with them into the cinema, in the form of the cultural knowledge of what a western or a musical is. The role of the audience in determining meaning cannot be overestimated.

Shot 1 Shot 2

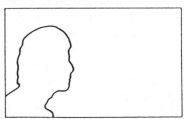 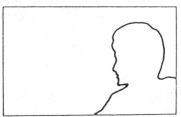

The spatial relations are reversed in the successive shots, as if to 'extend the boundaries' of the frame to include both parties to the conversation. The alternation of shots tells us they are speaking to each other.

The shot–reverse shot system for representing conversation

Film as a Signifying Practice

Film is not one discrete system of signification, as writing is. Film incorporates the separate technologies and discourses of the camera, lighting, editing, set design, and sound — all contributing to the meaning. Mary Tyler Moore's repressed domesticity in *Ordinary People* is represented through the signifiers of her heavily made-up face, the decor of the house, or the combination of visual and aural signs in the editing together of shots of her tightly clenched jaw and the chomping of the in-sink kitchen garbage disposal unit. No one system for producing meanings operates alone in film. The rebel hero in *Mad Max II* (*Road Warrior* in the USA) is constructed through (at least) the portentous sound-track, the choice of camera angles (Mel Gibson is consistently shot from below, exaggerating his power), the epic dimensions of the art direction, and inter-relationships between all of these.

It is now time to qualify the analogy I have so far drawn between film and language. Written and spoken languages have a grammar, formally taught and recognized systems which determine the selection and combination of words into utterances, regulating the generation of meanings. There is no such system in film. Film has no equivalent to syntax — no ordering system which would determine how shots should be combined in sequence. Nor is there a parallel between the function of a single shot in a film and that of a word or sentence in written or verbal communication. A single shot can last minutes. In it, dialogue can be uttered, characters' movements and thus relationships can be manipulated, and a physical or historical setting outlined. This may be equivalent to a whole chapter in a novel.

If there is a grammar of film, it is minimal and it works like this. Firstly, each shot is related to those adjacent to it. As we watch a film we often defer our understanding of one shot until we see the next. When we see a character addressing another off-screen, our view of the significance of those words may have to wait until we see the following shot, depicting the person being addressed. Secondly, unlike the grammar of written language which is to a large degree explicitly culturally regulated, relationships between shots in a film have to be constructed through less stable sets of conventions. Much depends not only on the audience's 'competencies' (their experience of, or skill at, reading film), but also on the film-maker's ability to construct any relationships which are not governed by convention.

The construction of a relationship between shots can be the first moment in understanding a narrative film. But the process is not as simple as it sounds. There exists a major theoretical argument about exactly how this process works — through constructing relationships between shots (montage) or through constructing relationships within shots (*mise-en-scène*). We know that these are not mutually exclusive and that both kinds of relationships are constructed by film-makers and interpreted by audiences. Both terms occur later in this paper as we move to a survey of the basic signifying practices employed in film production.

The Signifying Systems

The following survey will not be a full taxonomy (I do not talk about titles or special effects, for instance) but it will provide a basis for work now and further reading later.

The camera

Probably the most complex set of practices in film production involves the manipulation of the camera itself. The film stock used, the angle of the camera, the depth of its field of focus, the format of screen size (for example, Cinemascope or widescreen), movement, and framing all serve specific functions in particular films and all require some degree of explanation and attention.

Different 'meanings' have attached to colour and black and white film during the slow establishment of colour processing as the norm for feature film production. We can generalize from this to point out that different kinds of film stock with their differing chemical attributes and consequent visual effects are enclosed within different sets of conventions. Often black and white film stock is used to signify the past; it has been used to simulate the documentary in the Australian film *Newsfront* and to offer a nostalgic tribute to the past in Woody Allen's *Manhattan*. At the moment, black and white is sufficiently unusual to have some power as a special effect; music videos currently make great use of the process. Film stock which is particularly fast — that is, it can shoot in conditions where there is little light — tends to be grainy or of poor definition (slightly blurred), and thus reminds us of newsreel or old documentary footage. Most films try not to look like this. The aim now is to capitalize on the vast superiority of film's clarity of definition when compared to that of domestic video tape or broadcast television. Developments in film stock have had a significant impact on cinema history. The celebrated *Citizen Kane* achieved revolutionary clarity and depth of field (the whole image, from the foreground to the far background, was sharply in focus) by pushing the film stock to its limit and by experimenting with lighting methods. The Australian revival of the 1970s was assisted by Kodak's development of a new film stock which produced sharp definition in the harsh sunlight as well as in deep shadow.

The positioning of the camera is possibly the most apparent of the practices and technologies which contribute to the making of a film. The use of overhead shots or crane shots can turn film into a performance art, exhilarating in the perspectives it offers the audience. Less dramatic manipulation of camera angles also has an effect on the experience and meaning of a film. The camera can be directed either squarely or obliquely towards its subject, with rotation of the camera possible along its vertical axis (panning), its horizontal axis (tilting), or its transverse axis (rolling). If a camera is, as it were, looking down on its subject, its position is one of power. In *Citizen Kane*, a confrontation between Kane and his second wife Susan is played in a shot–reverse shot pattern which has Susan (or the camera) looking up to address Kane in one shot and Kane (or the camera) looking down to address Susan in the next shot. Susan is oppressed and diminished by the camera angle while Kane's stature is magnified. In this sequence, the manipulation of camera angles is the major means by which the audience is informed about the changing relationship between the two characters.

Camera angles can identify a shot with a character's point of view by taking a position which corresponds to that which we imagine the particular character would be occupying. We see what the character would be seeing. An extreme example is Hitchcock's *Spellbound*, where the camera adopts the point of view of a character who is about to shoot himself; when the gun fires, the screen goes blank. Point-of-view shots are important for motivation and also for controlling aspects of the audience's identification with the characters. The fact that the audience is under pressure to 'see' from the point of view of the camera has been exploited in varied ways. In *Jaws*, we are given numerous shots of the victims from the underwater point of view of the shark. The confusion caused by our resistance to this alignment, and our privileged knowledge of the shark's proximity to the victim, exacerbates the tension and the impression of impotence felt by the audience and enhances our sense of the vulnerability of the victims. The height of the camera and its distance from its subject can also have an effect on the meaning of a shot. A conventional means of narrative closure is to slowly pull the camera back so that the subject disappears into its surroundings. This can enhance the ambiguity of emotional response, or invite the audience to project their own emotions on to the scene. It does this because it signifies the withdrawal of our close attention — the end of the narrative.

Panning the camera along the horizontal axis imitates the movement of the spectators' eyes as they survey the scene around them. Very often such a movement is connected with the point of view of a character. The prelude to the gunfight in a western is often a slow pan around the streets to check for hidden gunmen, or to register the cowardly townsfolk's withdrawal, as well as to prolong the suspense and maximize our sense of the hero's isolation and vulnerability.

Rolling the camera gives the illusion of the world, either actually or metaphorically, being tipped on its side. This is sometimes done as a point-of-view shot, to indicate that the character is falling, or drugged, or sick, or otherwise likely to see the world oddly. It is also used in stunt and special-effect photography and occasionally for comic effect. It can be extremely sinister and unsettling, as in the slight degree of roll in the initial sequences of *The Third Man* where the first pieces of the puzzle of Harry Lime are introduced. Camera roll most clearly indicates a world out of kilter in one way or another.

The apparent movement of the camera, as in a close-up, can be accomplished through the manipulation of particular telephoto lenses, or what is commonly called the zoom lens. The actual forward or lateral movement of the camera apparatus is referred to as tracking or dollying, and it is often used in action sequences or as a point-of-view shot — the gunfighter walking down the empty street, for instance. As a point-of-view shot it can be very effective in enhancing audience identification with a character's experiences. A chase scene through a city street shot in this way can have a physical effect; it reproduces many of the perceptual activities involved in the experience and is thus convincingly 'real'. Alterations in focus have a signifying function. Most films aim at a very deep field of focus in which everything from the foreground to the far background is clear and sharp. Variations from this can have specific objectives. A soft focus on a character or background may pursue a romantic or lyrical effect, such as that achieved in Bo Widerberg's *Elvira Madigan*. A halo around a star's face, created through the manipulation of focus or lighting, or by placing vaseline or gauze on the lens, gives an exaggeratedly glamorous and dreamlike effect. 'Rack' focus is used to direct the audience's attention from one character to another. This is accomplished by having one face in focus while the other is blurred, and using the switch in focus from one to the other for dramatic or symbolic effect.

The composition of images within the physical boundaries of the shot, the frame, requires close attention, and the function of the frame in either enclosing or opening out space around the images on the screen is also important. Figures and other elements can be moved around within the frame to great effect. As Charles Foster Kane moves towards Susan in their argument at Xanadu, his shadow falls over her, signifying domination. In another scene in *Citizen Kane*, Kane is defeated but the audience gradually apprehends the strength of his resistance as he moves from the background to the centre of the foreground, dominating those on either side of him. At times, the frame takes part in, rather than simply contains, the narrative. In the opening sequence of *The Searchers,* the titles and credits give way to an apparently black screen over which appears the title, 'Texas, 1868'. Then the image changes as a door opens to reveal that the black screen was a dark interior, the homestead, and through its door we look out on to the desert. The juxtaposition of an image of the wilderness with the enclosed, domestic world of the homestead initiates a chain of contrasts which are thematically and structurally central to the film. The frame is used to symbolic effect in *The Chant of Jimmie Blacksmith* where a tableau of the half-caste Aboriginal boy eating his meal with his white mentor, a minister of religion, is serially framed by, first, one doorway, then another, and then by the image's frame. The effect is appropriately claustrophobic.

Lighting

It could be said that there are two main objectives to film lighting; the first is expressive — setting a mood, giving the film a 'look' (as in Zeffirelli's Titian-coloured *Taming of the Shrew* or Hugh Hudson's hazy *Chariots of Fire*), or contributing to narrative details such as character or motivation. In *The Searchers*, again, there is a moment when John Wayne's Ethan Edwards turns to the camera and reveals the degree of his obsessions; the shadow of his hat has obscured his face with the exception of one shaft of light reflecting from his eye. The effect is sinister and alarming. A whole film can be lit in an expressive way. The gloomy darkness of *Blade Runner* is an index of its moral and spiritual decay and the uncertainties which dog its plot line (which characters are the replicants?). The blue/grey of gleaming technology and electric light is the dominant tone, only alleviated by the sickly pink of flesh tones and the bright red of lipstick. When the hero and heroine escape into the open country the sudden rush of natural colours is important in overwhelming the audience's understandable scepticism about their future. This film owes a lot to expressionist films shot in black and white (such as *Metropolis*), as well as to the Sam Spade *films noirs* of the 1940s where a similar chiaroscuro lighting was used as an index of hidden, dark motives at work within the characters.

Realism is lighting's second objective. This is by far the most common and least apparent aim of film lighting. If it is successful, the figures are lit so naturally and unobtrusively that the audience do not notice lighting as a separate technology.

The basic equipment used to light sound stages or film sets includes a main light (the key light) which is usually set slightly to one side of the camera and directed at the figure to be lit; the fill lights, which remove the shadows caused by the key light and mould the figure being lit in order to add detail and realism; and the back light which defines the figure's outline and separates him or her from the background, thus enhancing the illusion of a three-dimensional image. In conventional high-key lighting, we view a brightly lit scene with few shadow areas, as the fill lights mop up any shadows left by the key light. Much expressive lighting, however, aims at exploiting

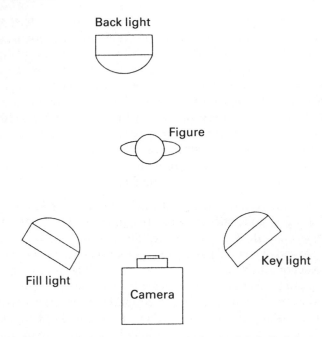

A conventional three point set-up for high key lighting

shadows, and at lighting only part of the screen to give a sense of ambiguity or threat. This is called low-key lighting; it makes much less use of fill lights, and thus has sharp, deep shadows. Low-key lighting will often move the key light from its conventional position and move it to one side of the figure so that only half the face is visible, or increase the angle so that the face is lit from below and acquires a distorted, threatening aspect.

In general, high-key lighting is realist, while low-key lighting is expressive. These are only conventions, which only work because we let them. But they are important constituents of the meaning of a shot and in many cases of an entire film. It is worth noting how lighting picks out and emphasizes elements within the frame, and how this appears to be a natural means of directing the audience's attention to one feature of the frame while obscuring others. This is particularly so during long takes, where a character can move in and out of shadow, into dominant or dominated positions, simply by moving from one regime of lighting to another.

Sound

Surprisingly little attention is given to the role of sound in the cinema. Dialogue can seem less important than the image, and in many cases seems to be used to 'fix' the meaning of the image rather than to motivate the image itself. Yet sound is important. It can serve a narrative function (as does the tune played by the spaceship in *Close Encounters of the Third Kind*); it is the basis of the musical; and it can provide powerful emotional accompaniment to a film's high points. Most importantly, if most obviously, it enhances realism by reproducing the sounds one would normally associate with the actions and events depicted visually. Music was the first form of sound to be introduced into the cinema, rather than a 'diegetic' use (that is, use of sounds motivated by actions or events contained within the narrative) although this is the most basic application now. We expect to hear the sound of breaking glass when we see a window smash on screen and we expect the words uttered by the actors to synchronize with the movement of their lips. The illusion of realism is dependent upon the diegetic use of sound.

Sound has other functions, too. It can be used as a transitional device. *Citizen Kane* often concludes a speech begun in one scene after the visuals have taken us on to the following scene. The overlapping sound binds what is an episodic and disjointed narrative together. David Lean has used sound cleverly to accomplish the transition from one location to the next; in *A Passage to India* he uses the sound of a medical instrument being thrown into a steel bowl as the cue for a cut to the coupling of two train carriages. The sounds of the clashing metal bind together as one sound which welds the two shots together. Music plays an increasingly important role in sound-tracks today. It can be used as part of the construction of the world of the film, as a source of atmosphere, or as a reference point to the subcultures in the teen films of John Hughes or the more adult fare of *The Big Chill*. Unlike the realist, diegetic use of sound, however, music in films is usually non-realistic in that we rarely see its source in the frame or even within the world of the film.

Simon Frith (1986: 65) argues that the reality music 'describes/refers to is a different sort of reality than that described/referred to by visual images'. He says music amplifies the mood or atmosphere and also tries to convey the 'emotional significance' of a scene: the 'true "real" feelings of the characters involved in it'. He calls this the 'emotional reality' of film music, and its aim is to deepen the sense of the film's realism, to give it an emotional texture otherwise lacking. It is this kind of contribution that Ry Cooder's music makes to *Paris, Texas,* for instance. Further, he sees film music as assisting in the construction of the reality of time and place, the world of the film. He uses the example of the music in *Zorba the Greek*, which is responsible for much of that film's successful construction of 'Greekness'.

A further aspect of music's signifying function within film is as much a part of popular music as of film. The cultural background audiences bring to films like *Flashdance, Purple Rain,* or *Absolute Beginners* is crucial to their idea of what they see and hear. That cultural background specifies a range of musical, as well as cinematic, events. In these days of Dolby stereo and music-packed sound-tracks, music plays an important function in pulling the major segment of the audience, teenagers, into the cinema in the first place. The close relationship between the world of the music video clip (so often resembling a feature film on fast-forward in its rapid montage of narrative images) and that of the teen movie is evidence of how much of the same cultural space is occupied by music and film.

Theme songs offered at crucial moments can dominate the competition between signifying systems. The end of *An Officer and a Gentleman*, otherwise a curiously ambiguous film, derives much of its strength from the song 'Lift Us Up Where We Belong'. The nostalgia that permeates *The Big Chill* is saved from becoming cloying and sentimental by the continuous vitality of the music track. There is a slightly more playful invocation of nostalgia in *Peggy Sue Got Married*, even before we have got past the simple graphics of the title sequence, through the Buddy Holly performance of the title song. Certain instruments, too, become temporarily identified with particular effects; the synthesizer sound-track enhances the strangeness of *Blade Runner* and the same technique is used in TV's *Miami Vice*.

Frith's final point is probably his most important. Music and images have a lot in common as media of communication; they are not understood in a direct, linear way by the audience, but irrationally, emotionally, individually. Lévi-Strauss (1966) says that music is only ever understood by the receiver, and Barthes (1977) notes that it is impossible to describe music without adjectives — that is, it must be understood in terms of its subjective effect rather than through a dictionary of meanings. Correspondingly, its effect can be profoundly personal. Film music, like the image, can have physical effects: it sends shivers down the spine or makes one tap one's feet. It has been said that film music 'feels for us', by telling us when a powerful moment is happening and indicating just what we should feel about it through the mood of the music. Simon Frith describes this phenomenon more accurately and less contemptuously:

> one function of film music is to reveal our emotions as *the audience* . . . Film scores are thus important in representing *community* (via martial or nationalistic music, for example) in both film and audience. The important point here is that as spectators we are drawn to identify not with the film characters themselves but with their emotions, which are signalled pre-eminently by music which can offer us emotional experience *directly*. Music is central to the way in which the pleasure of cinema is simultaneously individualised and shared. (Frith, 1986: 68–9)

So the convention of music swelling at the point of a clinch is not manipulation but recourse to even more direct means of communicating with the audience.

Mise-en-scène

Among the confusing aspects of film theory is the use of *mise-en-scène* as a term to describe a theory about film grammar, a shooting and production style, and — as in this section — a shorthand term for 'everything that is in the frame' of a shot. We have already talked about the way in which camera contributes to the *mise-en-scène*. In this section I want to emphasize the importance of those other aspects of the image: set design, costumes, the arrangement and movement of figures, the spatial relations (who is obscured, who looks dominant, and so on), and the placement of objects which have become important within the narrative (the murderer's gun, the secret letter, the reflection in the mirror).

We learn much, unconsciously, from the *mise-en-scène*. When we recognize the interior of a dwelling as middle-class, bookish, and slightly old-fashioned, we are reading the signs of the decor in order to give them a set of social meanings. The film's construction of a social world is authenticated through the details of the *mise-en-scène*. Further, the narrative is advanced through the arrangement of elements within the frame; characters can reveal themselves to us without revealing themselves to other characters, and thus complicate and develop the story. The practice of watching a murder thriller involves the scanning of the frame to pick up the clues in the *mise-en-scène*. *Psycho* exploits this by offering us red herrings in the form of point-of-view shots which suggest that Norman's mother is still alive.

In films of epic proportions such as *Gandhi*, the plethora of information contained within the frame can itself be spectacular. The *mise-en-scène* in such cases is not necessarily narratively significant, but is rather a *performance* of cinema, a celebration of its ability to trap so much of the world in its frame. The funeral sequence at the beginning of *Gandhi* includes overhead shots of an enormous crowd. These shots display themselves, celebrating the scale of the images, the density of their detail, the impossibility of comprehending them during their time on the screen. Many historical films work like this, using their *mise-en-scène* to celebrate the power of the medium to recreate the real so overwhelmingly and thus, presumably, so authentically.

Editing

Here we move back towards the realm of montage, the construction of the relationship between shots. We should not underestimate the importance of editing. The famous Kuleshov experiments present a powerful case for its centrality. These experiments juxtaposed a single shot of an actor with a plate of soup, then a woman in a coffin, and then a girl smiling. The audiences seeing the three sequences identified the actor's expression (which never changed) as hunger, sadness, and affection, respectively. Despite this demonstration of the power of montage, it is not so widely used now. It occurs most frequently as a means of representing a mood — cuts to shots of the sea, mountains, or crowded city streets — or for narrative 'ellipsis' — where sections of the narrative need rapid summarizing rather than full dramatization. In some cases the two functions are combined. In *Butch Cassidy and the Sundance Kid*, the period between the gang's escape from the US and their arrival in South America is summarized in a series of stills depicting the group's enjoyment of the pleasures of New York City. This fills a gap in the narrative and evokes a carefree mood which is abruptly terminated by their arrival in primitive Bolivia.

As realism became the dominant mode of feature film production, editing was required to contribute to the illusion that the film was unfolding naturally, without the intervention of the film-maker. Now editing is more or less invisible, seamlessly connecting shots so as to give the illusion of continuity of time and space. There are exceptions to this — action sequences, highly dramatic moments — but in general the craft of the editor in realist films is to remain invisible and knit the shots together according to realist aesthetics. The search for realism, in fact, has produced occasional avant-garde films which do not use editing at all; some of the late Andy Warhol's films eschewed editing in order to let the cameras record reality without any mediation. Some directors claim to 'edit in the camera', that is to shoot scenes sequentially and cut the action at the appropriate moment for the transition to the next shot. This is both difficult and unusual.

There is a multitude of editing techniques. We have already mentioned two major ones — the fade-out and the dissolve. There is also 'the wipe', in which one image replaces another preceded by a demarcation line moving across the screen. The most frequent method these days is the simple cut from one shot to the next. As with most simple techniques, it requires great skill to do this well. Various transition devices can be used or invented to soften the cut and make it less sudden or disorientating: overlapping sound from one shot to the next; the use of motivations in the first shot which take us to the next (such as an action shot where the viewer wants to see its conclusion). Most realist films avoid sudden cuts unless they are to be exploited for dramatic effect. A sudden cut produces surprise, horror, and disruption, so it tends to be saved for moments when such an effect is required. The shower sequence in *Psycho* derives its effectiveness from the fracturing and prolonging of the action — a nightmare effect produced by the rapid editing together of numerous angles of perspective on to the murder. Again, in *Psycho*, when the murderer-mother is about to be revealed, the camera tracks in on the back of her chair. When the chair is spun around, revealing her skeleton, a cut is made to a close-up of the skeleton's face. The sudden cut exacerbates the audience's shock.

There are many editing conventions which assist the film-makers and the audience to make sense of the film. I have already mentioned the shot–reverse shot convention. Other conventions include the use of short establishing shots above a new location to place the narrative within a physical context; and the observation of an imaginary line across the film set which the camera never crosses so that the viewer is given a consistent representation of the spatial relations between the actors and their surroundings (this is called the 180° rule). Skilful editors can use the timing of their cuts either to enhance the energy of the action, or to slow it down. Action sequences can take on greater drama and complexity if cuts occur within moments of high action; as a car is about to crash, for instance, we might go to several successive and separate views of the same moment. Alternatively, a cut in a moment of relative stasis can slow down action, retard the narrative, and open up ambiguities. A thoughtful character, considering his or her future, may be shot from several positions in order to expand the moment and instil significance into it.

The speed, pace, or rhythm of editing is important too. Documentary film tends to use fewer edits than narrative film, and social-realist films tend to imitate this in the pacing of their editing. Many feature films pursue an identifiable rhythm throughout their length, and single scenes can be dramatically affected by the pacing and rhythm of the editing. It is easy to demonstrate this through an example. In *Mad Max II (Road Warrior)* there is a chase scene in which the hero, Max's, large tanker truck is pursued by the followers of the villain, Humungus. Max has a shotgun with two bullets and a passenger, the 'feral kid' — a wild, 10-year-old child. During a desperate battle with the arch-enemy Wes, who has climbed on to Max's truck, the shotgun bullets roll out of the broken windshild on to the bonnet. Although Wes is knocked off the truck and disappears, Max still needs those bullets. He sends the feral kid out on to the bonnet after them while the chase continues at high speed. The musical sound-track dies down to be replaced by the sound of the wind in the child's face, and a heartbeat. At regular but gradually accelerating intervals, there is a series of cuts from the bullets on the truck bonnet back to the child's face. Rhythmically we cut back and forth from the child to the bullets, from the child to the bullets, from the child to the . . . Wes's maniacal face appears over the front of the bonnet, screaming in full close-up, and the return cut to the feral kid has him screaming too: a terrifying moment. The surprise at Wes's appearance is all the greater for the expectations set up by the alternations between the shots of the child and the bullets. The combination of the alteration in sound-track and the skill of the editor has achieved this dramatic effect.

This point is important. Film is a complex of systems of signification and its meanings are the product of the combination of these systems. The combination may be achieved through systems either complementing or conflicting with each other. No one system is responsible for the total effect of a film, and all the systems we have just been surveying possess, as we have seen, their own separate sets of conventions, their own ways of representing things.

Reading the Film

The complexity of film production makes interpretation, the active reading of a film, essential. We need to, and inevitably do, scan the frame, hypothesize about the narrative development, speculate on its possible meanings, attempt to gain some mastery over the film as it unfolds. The active process of interpretation is essential to film analysis and to the pleasure that film offers.

But films are not autonomous cultural events. We understand films in terms of other films, their worlds in terms of our worlds. 'Intertextuality' is a term used to describe the way any one film text will be understood through our experience, or our awareness, of other film texts. The moment of heroism in *Silverado* when Emmet doffs his bandage and miraculously finds the strength to do battle once more is clearly parodying the suspension of realism in many previous westerns. To see *Silverado* without the knowledge which it assumes of western movie conventions would mean finding it silly and inexplicably unrealistic.

Films are also produced and seen within a social, cultural context that includes more than other film texts. Film serves a cultural function through its narratives that goes beyond the pleasure of story.

References

Barthes, R. (1973) *Mythologies*. London: Paladin.
— (1977) *Image–Music–Text*. London: Fontana.
Fiske, J. (1982) *Introduction to Communication Studies*. London: Methuen.
Frith, S. (1986) Hearing secret harmonies. In C. MacCabe (ed.) *High Theory/Low Culture: Analysing Popular Television and Film*. Manchester: University of Manchester Press.
Lévi-Strauss, C. (1966) *The Savage Mind*. London: Wiedenfeld and Nicolson.

9 The Visual Accomplishment of Factuality

DAVID GRADDOL

Introduction

The idea that television offers a 'window on the world' in which events and places 'out there' are unproblematically made available to viewers in the home has often been remarked upon. Yet everything which is seen on the TV screen arrives there only after a complex process of mediation involving many people and institutions and a great deal of technology and artifice. TV news is expected to provide a window which is more transparent than most, but it is no different from other TV genres in these respects. Its transparency and perceived factuality is a testament to the extent to which its conventions of representation have become naturalized. Understanding the semiotics of factuality is perhaps one of the most important literacy skills required by readers and viewers in the modern industrial world. But the ways in which information and entertainment have become inextricably linked in most TV genres means that the task of identifying and evaluating claims to factuality has become more complex than ever before.

The visual element in news reports has often been discounted as being less important than the words of a newsreader. Ellis (1982), for example, suggests that, in TV generally, sound is a far more important channel than vision; that pictures are illustrations to the sound, and that, in comparison to the cinema, they lack detail. 'Sound tends to anchor meaning on TV, where the image tends to anchor it with the cinema' (Ellis, 1982: 129).

On the other hand, some researchers have pointed to the cultural importance of the visual image in establishing truth. 'Seeing is believing':

> Seeing has, in our culture, become synonymous with understanding. We 'look' at a problem. We 'see' the point. We adopt a 'viewpoint'. We 'focus' on an issue. We 'see things in perspective'. The world 'as we see it' (rather than 'as we know it', and certainly not 'as we hear it', or 'as we feel it') has become the measure for what is 'real' and 'true'. (Kress & van Leeuwen, 1990: 52)

The visual element of news is perhaps the most under-theorised element of an otherwise well researched genre. Of all semiotic codes, it has been regarded as the most straightforward and transparent. The relationship between words and pictures in news reports has been regarded as a relatively simple one: the pictures may be selective in what they show but without words they cannot tell the truth, nor for that matter can they lie. Factuality is thus assumed to be accomplished by the words rather than the pictures. In this paper, I examine how factuality is also accomplished visually. I suggest that the visual modalities of TV news are more complex than they first appear.

Modality Systems

Factuality is not merely a question of truth or lies, but a more complex semiotic system which provides for varying authority, certainty and appropriateness to be allocated to particular representations of the world. This semiotic system is called the *modality* system. That which has definiteness, certainty, lack of ambiguity is said to have *high modality*. That which is less definite, possible rather than certain, is said to have *low modality*. Factuality is not quite the same as modality (you can have high modality in fiction, for example), but it is a key part of the semiotic mechanism by which factuality is accomplished.

Verbal modality

Verbal language uses of a number of devices to express modality. Modality is so central to communication that in the English language it is an integral part of the verb. Things *can* happen, *could* happen, *will* happen, *have* happened, or *happened*. It is not possible to speak of a process or action without encoding modality. But modality is also signalled in ways other than through modal auxiliaries: through 'projecting' verbs like 'think' ('I thought it happened'), or through the use of hedges like 'possibly', 'perhaps'. The evaluations of factuality are usually those of the speaker or narrator, but they can be easily attributed to others. Indeed, attribution is a key part of news reporting — the status of a fact depends largely on the authority of the source and how distant a reporter was from sources and events. In the following fragment of a news report:

The British maintain they cleaned the site up in 1957

the verb 'cleaned' is high modality (the implicit claim is that there is no argument over this point), but the evaluation of its factuality is not that of the speaker. Responsibility for the claim of factuality has been shifted to the 'British' through the verb 'maintain'. The narrator thus expresses high modality for 'maintain' (the British definitely made this claim), but distances herself and us as viewers from the factual status of the cleaning up.

Factuality depends on high modality but also on the *genre* of the text in which a claim was made. For example, the truth value of the news fragment cited above would be quite different if it were embedded in a novel rather than a news report:

> Effects of factuality or non-factualness are produced by the formal structures of genres: so, for example, the genre of the scientific paper or of a newspaper editorial produces the former, while the genre of the novel or of casual gossip produces the latter. (Kress, 1985: 143)

The verbal modality system, like other aspects of grammar, encodes social relations as well as truth value. For example, flat contradiction or even the over definite expression of ideas is, in many cultures, regarded as impolite. Modality hence expresses the power and solidarity relations between a speaker and addressee; these need to be understood to decode factuality. Also at stake is the security of the knowledge system which gives rise to the 'facts':

> Modality points to the social construction or contestation of know-ledge-systems. Agreement confers the status of 'knowledge', 'fact' on the system, or on aspects of it; lack of agreement casts that status into doubt. Of course, agreement and affinity may have been brought about by the relations of power-difference: that is, the more powerful may have been successful in enforcing their classifications on the less powerful . . . Modality is consequently one of the crucial indicators of political struggle. It is a central means of contestation, and the site of working out, whether by negotiation or imposition, of ideological systems. (Hodge & Kress, 1988: 123)

TV news is both a knowledge system and a genre. That is, the news system represents a particular way of collecting and establishing 'facts' which are different from, say, the institutions of science or the courts, and there are conventional ways of organising and presenting these facts on television. In western society the status of TV news as a knowledge system is regularly called into question. As a genre, it is also very vulnerable, and has difficulty in maintaining its generic distinctiveness from other TV genres such as faction, docu-drama, documentary, current affairs, chat shows. Fiske (1987) even describes TV news as 'a masculine soap opera'.

The authority, quality of sources and interpretations which TV news offers are thus always potentially contestable. Its audience is heterogeneous and the social relations and values which are in play are various. In order to accomplish factuality, TV news must work hard to maintain the security of its knowledge-system, must establish the distinctiveness of the genre, and must use all the resources at its disposal for achieving high modality in its presentation. The visual component of TV news provides crucial resources in all three areas.

Visual modality

Modality operates in visual representation as well as verbal, though the devices which express it are less systematic. Hodge & Kress (1988) prefer to use the term 'modality cues' in relation to visual texts. For example, in cartoons, some figures may be drawn more realistically and in greater detail than others:

> a 'dense', detailed image can stand for realism or proximity, which can stand for present time, which can stand for factuality. An image lacking in detail and denseness can stand for unreality or distance, which can stand for past time, which can stand for fictionality. (Hodge & Kress, 1988: 134)

In TV advertising such devices as soft focus and colour saturation are routinely used to indicate forms of visual idealisation and fantasy, but in such landscapes the image of the advertised product will be shown as detailed and well focused.

One problem in identifying such visual modality cues is that they are not universal but vary with genre. What expresses high modality in one genre may express low modality in another. Kress & van Leeuwen (1990) discuss how high visual modality is achieved in scientific genres. Science is concerned with the description of an objective world which exists regardless of the point of view or experience of a human agent; aspects of this world, indeed, cannot even be perceived through the normal human senses. These values form a part of the knowledge system of science, and they are reflected in visual representations in scientific genres. Since science is concerned with universal truths context is irrelevant to their description and is removed from diagrams and figures. The perceiver or experimenter is not shown in such figures. Photography is black and white which connotes high definition (high modality) and declares that it does not form a part of a pleasure system. It often requires seemingly miraculous technology to make scientific truth visible to the naked eye. In these ways, the conventions of objectivity in science are maintained at the visual (as well as verbal) level.

The modality conventions which operate in TV news are not those of science, though news reports may draw on the resources of science genres occasionally. High modality in TV news is more typically achieved by showing the context in which events occur — indeed, that is sometimes all that news images *do* show. TV news needs also to report a variety of perspectives and points of view and to evaluate these. The world which it describes is the transient world of today and what is news tonight is not news tomorrow. Above all, TV news needs to communicate immediacy, geographical and temporal location. It regularly succeeds in evoking emotional responses from its audience. Despite these subjective aspects of its reporting, it must simultaneously persuade viewers of the authority and credibility of the world which it portrays. It must present the world in a way which does not jeopardise the idea that it objectively exists, independently of partial accounts of it.

The key to understanding how TV news accomplishes factuality lies in recognising this tension between objectivity and subjectivity. It goes some way to explaining the complex and eclectic nature of the visual modality system which TV news employs.

The Realist Tradition

TV news tells stories about the world and the dominant narrative technique for such storytelling is what is called *realism*. Realism of the kind I am referring to here first arose as a literary convention. Realist novels typically employ an omniscient narrative voice, one who can see things which individual characters cannot see and who is in all places at once. A variety of narrative devices — called focalizers — allow readers to take up the point of view of different characters as the narrative unfolds. For example, in an examination of such devices in writing for children, Stephens (1992) analyses an extract from 'Drift' by William Mayne:

> The Indian girl was trying to catch a crow that had stayed in the village by the lake all winter. The girl's name was Tawena, and she lived in the tents and cabins at the end of the village.
>
> Rafe Considine watched her, sitting on a heap of hard snow. Tawena was throwing down balls of suet from a lump of fat she had in her hand. Now and then she ate some herself. She had a fatty face, Rafe thought, and brown eyes deep in the fat. He was sure she had stolen the suet. The tent and cabin people had nothing much to live on, but some of them were well covered. (Mayne, 1985: 7)

Stephens analyses this extract as beginning in the all-knowing narrator's voice — we are told about things we could not see even if we were there (the crow had been there all winter). In the third sentence, a new character is introduced which:

> now becomes the focalizer (and remains so for the next ninety pages). The shift is formally marked by 'watched'. This verb belongs to a lexical set whose node is *perceive*, and which is commonly used as an overt signal of focalization. Soon afterwards, the conceptual terms 'thought'

and 'was sure' appear, as the character formulates opinions about what he sees. Finally, the paragraph ends with an unmarked, untagged, utterance which, following so closely after the two conceptual verbs, will be understood as a thought in Rafe's mind. (Stephens, 1992: 28–9)

In this way, the reader is transferred to the point of view of 'Rafe'. Thereafter the modality associated with accounts is modified by our perception of the character's own fallibility. When Rafe 'was sure' we, as readers are not so sure. Stephens describes this technique as 'a fallible character-focalized narration, rather than the narratorial presentation of character-focalization more typical of fiction for children' (Stephens, 1992: 29). In other words, child readers are often given accounts of the fictional world through the voice of the infallible narrator: a view which always has high modality and requires less sophistication in the reader in distinguishing between points of view. Character focalization is also used in adult fiction but in a more complex fashion. The point of view can shift between different protagonists and back to the narrator more often.

Through such narrative devices realism recognises that there is an objective world 'out there', but also that its interest lies in the subjective human experience of it. Realist narrative encourages the reader to feel they know more about this objective world than any of the characters do; they also provide the means of distancing the reader from the viewpoints of certain characters and to give them low value (low modality), whilst foregrounding the views of more 'reliable' and 'sympathetic' characters (high modality). Realist narrative thus provides a modality mechanism which is additional to those I have already described. I refer to this as *narrative modality*.

The cinema adopted and adapted the realist narrative techniques of the novel. In a realist film, we see the same action from different angles and points of view as the camera moves position; we move instantly from location to location. The camera in this way provides the all-seeing narrative voice. Within this narrative structure, the camera can take up the perspective of various characters. Graeme Turner (this volume) describes some of the camera techniques which act in a similar way to focalizing devices in novels, drawing us into the action and allowing us, temporarily, to see the world from the point of view of a particular protagonist.   ˎ

The reliability of different protagonists' accounts is cued by a number of different devices in realist film. Less reliable characters might be left partly in shadow; the shots in which they appear may be shorter or less frequent; they may be shown in extreme close up, so they appear threatening; the camera may look down upon them in a way which positions them as less powerful; it may look up to them in a way which makes them appear menacing; it may show them from an oblique angle which situates them as 'other', not one of us. In addition, a character's social role in the narrative (see Bell, this volume) may indicate whether they are 'hero', 'helper', 'victim', 'villain'. None of these devices by themselves will establish the modality of a character's world view, but together they can encourage the viewer to accept that the perspective of certain characters is more authoritative than others.

As in the narration of novels, the film-goer is thus exposed to the world-views of many characters, and the reliability of each is established through visual techniques. In addition, the viewer is given the privileged knowledge provided by the omniscient camera. Any event shown by this camera is given the highest modality: it is the objective realist narrative voice. It shows the world as it appears without characters and their individual perspectives. Realism thus provides a powerful visual technology for cueing narrative modalities. The regime of camera work and editing is so naturalized that we rarely stop to think about its artifice.

Realism in News

Indeed, the realist technique is so naturalized that TV news cannot avoid drawing on its resources when telling its own narratives. Failure to use it would run the risk that its representation of the world would appear unrealistic. Realism also provides what at first glance seems a perfect resolution to the tension between objective and subjective. It allows news to encompass a variety of voices and accounts, yet maintain through the device of the omniscient camera/narrator the belief in an objective world. It provides the viewer with a privileged account of this objective world, and gives the news producer a means of steering the viewer authoritatively through the maze of partial accounts.

I will argue that at the heart of TV news there lies a realist narrative technique. But the form of realism which TV news has adopted is a hybrid one, drawing on both literary realism and realist cinema. This reflects a constant tension in TV news between verbal and visual communication which I will explore below.

Some problems with visual realism in the news

There are a number of problems associated with the adoption of realist cinema techniques which limit their use in TV news. One derives from its origins: it is a narrative technology designed to create fictional worlds rather than represent natural ones. Our experience in constructing documentary programmes with the BBC for Open University courses gives some insight into the practical difficulties and tensions involved. One programme followed the journalist Victoria Makins whilst she researched and wrote a story which appeared in the *Times Educational Supplement*. Oliver Boyd-Barrett, the academic consultant for the TV programme, later reflected on its making:

> One might conclude that, in order for television to provide viewers with a reasonably accurate impression of what 'normality' is like, it has to create conditions of considerable abnormality for the participants in order to achieve its effect . . . A number of 're-creations' of events occurred [during filming at the T.E.S.] to represent different phases of a process that in reality had occurred over several weeks: e.g. chats between Makins and the feature editor about the progress of the story and film of Makins making the initial phone-call to the head of Peers (school), which had actually taken place several weeks earlier (shots of the head 'answering' this call had already been taken during the visit to Peers!). To film all these things as they had actually happened would have been too expensive (involving taking out film crews on many more days), and very unpredictable (because real life is like that); and, strangely perhaps, the chances of the television process disrupting the normality it sets out to capture are sometimes more severe if it attempts to film things as they really happen than if participants are asked to re-live the process for the benefit of the camera. (Boyd-Barrett, 1987: 23)

So one problem arises from the way realist techniques seem to require the recreation of the world in fictional form in order to represent it realistically. Such recreations are rarely practicable when news gathering. I say practicable rather than ethical because such reconstruction does go on.

It is standard practice, for example, to edit available shots in order to create a coherent story from what otherwise might be seen as random actuality sequences. During coverage of the Gulf War, when professional news footage from within the war zone was limited, amateur footage taken with camcorders was occasionally shown on television news. Such amateur tapes often contain a time stamp in the corner of screen which makes it possible to see how the shots have been reassembled. One sequence, for example, showed a shot of a building, a close up of a missile explosion, and a third shot of the building in flames. The pictures flowed naturally — images of a fast moving piece of actuality. The time stamps showed that the close-up of the explosion had been filmed earlier than either of the other shots (and presumably occurred in a different location) whilst the two shots of the building were taken on different days. When edited together, they told a story of cause and effect, of before and after.

The editing conventions required by realist narrative provide a dilemma for TV news. In the case of the Gulf War, material could be re-ordered to satisfy the conventions of realism, but in the majority of cases the news camera arrives at a scene only in time to show effects and consequences rather than causes. Indeed, showing causes can give rise to suspicion that there has been some fiction-mongering going on, or collusion with criminals, hostile forces, or other members of the 'villainous' groups who figure in news stories.

Relation between visual and verbal

The ability to show effects and not causes creates a major weakness in the visual narratives of TV news. It partially explains a typical relationship between verbal and visual in news bulletins: the verbal channel speaks of causes whilst the visual tells of effects.

Such a relationship, however, helps resolve an intrinsic tension between the structure of verbal and visual news stories. In realist (film) narrative the action unfolds chronologically. The narrative can follow action in more than one location, and handle parallel stories, but it cannot move freely backwards and forwards in time. Special conventions are required for this — like the flashback or switch to black and white film stock. These techniques are not naturalized — they draw attention to themselves as 'literary' devices and are therefore unusable by TV news. The requirement for chronological structuring in realist narrative is at variance with the usual structure of news stories. Bell (this volume) shows how news narrative in the verbal channel is typically ordered by news values. News stories can flit backwards and forwards in time.

The dispersal of causes and effects across verbal and visual is thus one way in which this structural tension can be resolved. It is also politically pragmatic: there is usually less conflict over consequences than causes. Consequences can be shown in vision which gives them high modality in the combined semiotic of the news bulletin. Discussion of causes can be dealt with in the verbal system, which allows the exploitation of the more complex and well established modality system available there. Agency (who was responsible) can be dealt with in ways which are discreet and tentative, which respects the sensibilities and desires of powerful social interests.

This is by no means the only way in which tension between verbal and visual narrative manifests itself and is resolved. I will shortly return to this problem in connection with the analysis of a typical news report.

Naturalism in TV News

I have already argued that in TV news there exists a conflict between objective and subjective representations of reality, and that although the techniques of realist camera work offer a resolution to this tension such techniques raise other, at times insuperable, problems. Where realism falls down in this respect, TV news employs what might be called *naturalist* (as opposed to *naturalized*) narrative techniques. By naturalism I mean a representation of the world as it might be directly experienced by the viewer, drawing on modality cues which people employ in their everyday inter- actions with the world. It is the dominant form of representation in actuality sequences. Naturalist representations interpenetrate and compete with realist ones resolving some tensions yet giving rise to new ones.

From the naturalist perspective, a news report provides vicarious experi- ence, an image of the world as we might expect to experience if we were to stand where the reporter stands. Actuality sequences typically show the point of view of a stationary observer, often at roughly eye-level or from a location — such as upper floor window of a building — that a legitimate observer could find themselves. A pan shot will represent the change of view that a bystander might get by moving their head. A zoom rather than a track- ing shot is used to get closer to action. This respects the stand-point of a stationary observer rather than allowing the viewer to take up the viewpoint of a moving protagonist. The camera does not provide the omniscient realist narrator who is everywhere at once, able to give several perspectives of the same action.

One of the key differences between realism and naturalism is that the viewer is not visually introduced to the character whose perspective is shown through any of the standard devices (such as shot from behind a character showing a part of their body). Because of the lack of focalizing devices there is an ambiguity in the point of view shown: is it the point of view of the reporter, or that of ourselves. We just seem to gaze into the TV screen and out onto the world. The objective, camera/narrator's objective voice is absent. There is no visual technique in naturalism which allows us to evalu- ate the trustworthiness of the perspective we are shown. Rather, we are led to imagine the world is not just as we *would* see it, but as we *are seeing* it. As viewers we are thus directly embedded in the flow of events as a character ourselves. Naturalism is a powerful technique ideologically, and can achieve high visual modality. On the news it is always accompanied by a verbal com- mentary, thus placing overall control over modalities back into the verbal system.

Some of the effects of naturalism derive from necessities of production. News teams usually employ a single camera — often hand held — and mini- mal crew. Important people of the moment cannot normally be persuaded to repeat takes in interviews with different camera angles and shots. Certain kinds of cinematic shot are just not possible: the tracking shot requires elaborate equipment, setting up and rehearsal to accomplish.

Because naturalism always represents a subjective view of the world, at the core of its modality system is a system of trust. As viewers we must evaluate the trustworthiness of the bearers of news, and we must be given opportunities to form the necessary judgements. That includes seeing that they were really present, and looking them in the eye when they tell us so.

Nonverbal Communication in TV News

In face to face interaction, nonverbal communication of various kinds plays an important role in the way listeners make evaluations of the reliability and accuracy of a speaker's claims. A part of the naturalist technique in news reporting is its exploitation of such modality cues.

Politicians have understood for some time the importance of gazing straight to camera whilst reading their speeches. Both President Reagan and Margaret Thatcher used a 'Head Up Display Unit' — a kind of autocue known to politicians as 'the sincerity machine' (Cockerell 1988: 276). This device allowed them to make eye contact with the unseen audience and appear to be speaking without a script.

There is an important difference between cinema and TV in the use and effect of gaze. In the cinema the viewer usually looks up to a large screen. TV is typically watched at home from a comfortable seat at a height which brings the eyes of those looking out of the TV set to roughly the same level as those of the viewer. Ellis (1982: 128) suggests this 'engages the look and the glance rather than the gaze'.

Patterns of eye-contact often reflect the status and authority of participants. Vaughan (1976) suggests that this cultural knowledge is traded on in television programmes:

> If we switch on our sets and see someone addressing us directly, we know he is a narrator or presenter. If his gaze is directed slightly off-camera, we know he is an interviewee, a talking head. If he is turned away from us by an angle of more than about 15 degrees he is part of an action sequence. It is clear that there is a hierarchy of authority implicit in this code. The talking head is permitted to gaze into the sacred sector only through the priest-like intercession of the interviewer: and, if he should speak directly to the camera, he will create an impression of insolence. (Vaughan, 1976: 16, cited by Masterman, 1980: 50)

The proxemic conventions of natural conversation are also exploited in TV news. In these, physical distance is associated with social distance. Ordinary people — particularly the distressed — may be shown in close-up (or even ECU) in a way which evokes intimacy but also positions them as less powerful. Politicians and more powerful people are framed at a more respectable distance, usually within the range of formal to casual.

The News Bulletin

I have described TV news as exploiting a range of modality cues drawn from the literate conventions of verbal language, conventions of realist cinema, and conventions of informal conversational interaction. I have further argued that this eclecticism plays an essential part in how TV news resolves a conflict between objectivity and subjectivity, but that it also creates potential tensions between, for example, the visual and verbal narratives. In the remainder of this paper I want to show how this diversity of modality systems is exploited in actual news broadcasts. First I explore some of the structured diversity within the news bulletin as a whole, then I will go on to analyse a particular news report.

The news genre

One of the problems facing a broadcasting service in Britain is the maintenance of a clear distinction between 'news' and other TV genres. The integrity of the genre is crucial to the perception of factuality and often allows it to carry off what would otherwise be dubious and ambiguous practices. Keeping news distinct requires clear boundaries to be created. The openings of national news programmes, for example, are dramatic: music or sound effects — such as the chiming of Big Ben, news presenters in silhouette who are suddenly revealed as the studio lights go up, fast moving 'generic' graphic sequences. Such openings ensure that the boundary with other programmes is strongly maintained whilst simultaneously signifying drama and urgency. Closure of the bulletin is accomplished in a similar way. These boundary markers employ semiotic devices which are forbidden within the presentation of news itself: they create a space within which the business of factual reporting can be accomplished.

The studio modality system

The studio setting is important in creating a realist environment in which newsreaders can do their work. Like any office it speaks of corporate power and solidity. Studio furnishing is usually severe: large desks — usually grey — which sweep around the room. News presenters sit behind these desks in a way which mirrors the seated position of a powerful person to whose office the viewer has been summoned. A corporate logo is prominently in view in opening sequences and is usually repeated during news reports.

Although the studio must through its design connote solidity and reliability, it cannot achieve this by appealing to old fashioned values. The marble, mahogany and chandeliers of corporate banking are unsuitable here. Rather, the studio must signify its ability to handle fast moving stories and the latest communications technologies. The main news studio is therefore designed to look high-tech.

The BBC news studio is largely a visual fiction: the desks, walls and floor, and various solid looking objects within the studio are generated by computer and these graphics are overlaid on the images of the presenters. It says a great deal for the effectiveness of the studio modality system that viewers do not regard this as a betrayal of trust but accept that the studio which the newsreaders inhabit is acceptably 'real'. It is also indicative of the typical viewer's sophistication in reading the modality systems of news that they are persuaded the reports of the world which emerge from this studio are not as imaginary as the studio itself.

A variety of realist cinematic conventions are used to set this *mise-en-scène* for the newsreader. For example, studio lighting is high-key so that figures are evenly lit, no shadows are cast, and no halo effect is given by backlighting. Although such even lighting is the most 'unnatural' form and difficult to accomplish, shadows would connote a dramatic genre in which the lighting itself was an important semiotic channel. Within the realist modality system leaving the presenter's face in partial darkness would connote ambiguity, untrustworthiness and even the sinister. Above all, as in *film noir*, shadows would connote an emotional dimension and undermine the attempt to represent as dispassionate the portrayal of the world which is being offered.

The studio acts as a secure visual base from which forays into the hostile and troubled world may be made. It provides rock steady, perfectly focused and framed, high quality pictures. In the BBC news studio, the cameras are computer controlled; they trolley around the studio floor guided by bar-coded location strips on the studio walls. This allows standard distances and shots to be precisely repeated at will. The visual security of the studio provides a frame for actuality sequences from the field. Slight degradation of picture quality or sound in these will be interpreted as a signifier of the immediacy and authenticity of the report, rather than a reflection of the quality of the news channel itself.

This provides an example of how the visual modality system varies in different sections of the news bulletin. High definition indicates high modality in the studio; low definition can signal high modality in actuality film. The former modality cue is, however, the dominant one: high definition is a central feature of realism in the west and is a difficult cue for other genres to override.

The newsreader

Our faith in news rests on our trust both in the institution and in the person who reads it. The visual appearance and technical competence of the studio deal with the former. The newsreaders themselves must have a social identity and accent which makes trust socially appropriate. Only relatively recently have women been allowed to read the news. Even now, only certain regional accents are permitted in newsreaders on British national television. More subtly, only certain voice qualities are allowed: pitch of voice must be fairly low (even in women) and distinctive voice features such as too much nasality or hoarseness render a voice unusable. On British TV, the news presenters (as opposed to specialist reporters) are always located as middle class in the accent system. Dress is also middle class, and conservative. Under such bright lighting, the presenters require make-up to make their skin colour look more 'natural' and to inhibit perspiration, but the make-up must not draw attention to itself. The newsreader's identity is constructed within the objective modality system of the studio and the display of bodily imperfections and responses to immediate environment would indicate that the newsreader is a fallible human subject.

TV news trades extensively on the verbal modality devices which have emerged in the press and radio. The form of its main reports is essentially a literate one: the script read by the newsreader has been drafted by many hands and is read rather than spontaneously uttered. Its literateness makes it the most authoritative of the many voices represented in TV news. Typically it uses all the modality resources available in the verbal news system. These have been discussed extensively elsewhere (see, for example, Fowler, 1991) and since my concern is mainly with visual mechanisms I do not intend to examine them here.

The fact that script conforms to literate rather than oral conventions is not the only way in which the newsreader is rendered authoritative. The TV news bulletin as a whole can be regarded as realist narrative, in which viewers are shown a variety of characters and their views of the world. Within this realist narrative, the newsreader takes up the role of the objective, all knowing narrator. The authority of the newsreader thus also depends on our recognising the realist convention that the narrator's voice has highest modality.

As we have already seen, there is a tension between the narrative structure of verbal news reports and realist visual narrative. A further tension develops between the competition between the verbal commentary and the camera/narrator. Both can provide focalizing devices which transfer our point of view to that of another character. The newsreader/narrator usually introduces reporters and other characters who have stories to tell. By doing so, the newsreader's role as narrator is never in danger of being usurped by the camera/narrator.

The reporter plays the role of a reliable character and anything said by him or her with high verbal modality also has high narrative modality. However, the pictures accompanying such filed reports may employ realist camera techniques as well as naturalist ones. That is, a camera/narrator can appear in addition to the reporter/narrator. This triple narrator structure (newsreader/narrator, reporter/narrator, camera/narrator) is what makes the narrative modality of TV news so complex. It also introduces complexity *within* filed news reports as the two modality systems (realist and naturalist) and two narrative systems (reporter/narrator and camera/narrator) interact.

Although greatest analytical attention in the past has been given to what newsreaders do, it is in these filed news reports that some of the more interesting contradictions in visual modality is to be found. I analyse one particular report more fully below.

The Analysis of a News Report

Appendix 1 shows the shot sequence of one such report shown on the BBC1 News (this is taken from the version shown on the 9.00 pm news bulletin on Friday 18th June 1993). The item provided some of the background to a decision by the British Government to contribute substantially to the cost of a second clean up of a former nuclear test site in Australia. The report lasted almost exactly two minutes and consisted of 22 shots. The story is introduced in the conventional way by the newsreader, and then the commentary is taken up by a named reporter who talks over pictures 'from the field'.

The pictures which start the report tell a clear narrative which unfolds in time: a nuclear test creates contaminated ground; scientists establish that it is still contaminated; Aborigines who lived on the land are dispossessed and want their land back; we return to a press conference in London where Australian government ministers announce a financial deal with the British Government. I have analysed the structure of this visual narrative in the tree diagram in Figure 9.1. The structure is shown in a similar way as the structure of a sentence is typically shown, or the hierarchical structure of a verbal narrative. The end nodes, however, are shots rather than words. The structure I describe takes no account of the structure of the verbal narrative, though as might be expected it shares elements with it.

The focalizing device which transfers our point of view from the newsreader/narrator to the reporter/narrator is a caption which appears a second or so after the pictures and commentary have begun.

The nuclear test

We begin with a clip of soldiers. Using a conventional technique of realist cinema, their view of the nuclear explosion is transferred to us. We look at them, then for a moment we see what they see. We then cut in time to the near present through a stylised continuity device.

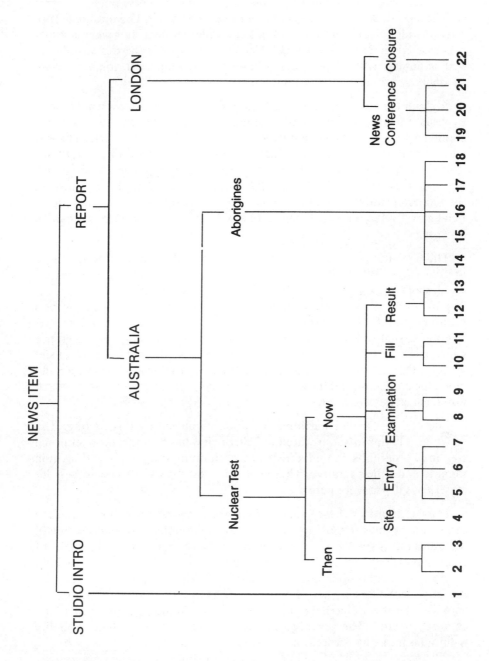

Figure 9.1 The structure of visual narrative in a BBC news report

The report continues with a coherent visual narrative. The tilt shot (4) not only provides visual continuity but also provides context. It is what is sometimes called an 'establishing shot'. The need to provide the real world context of human action belongs, as I have already suggested, to a subjective modality system rather than a scientific-objective one.

A closer examination of the next three shots (5–7) will show what I mean by visual narrative and how it is achieved. These shots are part of a narrative element which I describe in Figure 9.1 as 'entry'. We see first a pair of hands, viewed from above the left shoulder, unlocking a padlock and chain; then a shot from inside the gates which shows a man opening the gates and entering; then a scientist climbing through a strand or two of wire. In fact, the man seen entering and the scientist are two different people, but there is a superficial narrative coherence: a person opens the gate and enters the forbidden territory.

The first shot provides momentarily a certain dramatic tension. Whose are the hands? What will happen? We are expected to interpret the man we see in shot 6 as being the man whose hands were seen in the preceding shot. The hands may or may not belong to the man we see. In the same way as a pronoun can refer forwards to a noun later in a sentence and provide a cohesive tie, so such a device as hands-then-body creates a cataphoric reference which binds two shots together. In the case of these shots at the nuclear site we have the part and the whole; the outside and the inside; the before and after; the unlocking and the entering. Such pairings are the stuff from which visual narratives are built.

There is yet further narrative work accomplished by this pairing. The showing of hands intruding into the field of view has become a conventional way in photographs and advertising of positioning the viewer and inviting them to enter the narrative. These could be your hands, this could be your experience if you were here.

The continuity of these shots in cinematic terms seems natural but close inspection betrays the artifice: we are shown the unlocking and opening of the gates but it seems there is already a camera crew inside. The shift of camera position, however, obeys the conventional 180 degree rule within which shot–reverse shots are constructed. In this way we can see that the narrative technique is that of cinematic realism rather than naturalism of actuality. The event has been shown us from within the objective view of the camera/narrator. The portrayal of the event therefore has high modality within this narrative structure.

The story at this point is about contaminated ground and the scientist's examination of it. The main elements are repeatedly shown in close-up: the ground itself and feet walking over it, the probe scanning the ground, the needle on the geiger counter meter rising to maximum. There is a narrative being constructed visually which does not rely on the spoken commentary for coherence. However, we are shown these things from within the camera/ narrator's gaze. We are not, at any point, transferred to the point of view of the scientist.

Only two shots (10–11) do not properly fit this narrative. These provide cut-away shots which provide space for commentary. The work they do is not strictly narrative work and this is the first point in the report that the visual narrative gives way to the requirements of the verbal. Shot 10 shows a commemorative stone tablet engraved 'A British atomic weapon was test exploded here on 9 Oct 1957'. The shot authenticates not only the factuality of the event but also its monumental historical status and it gives precise information about the date — omitted from the spoken commentary. The camera 'voice' at this point is ambiguous. We cannot be sure whether it is the objective camera/narrator who is showing us this plaque or whether it is the scientist's view. If it is the former, then the high modality of the words on the tablet is given high narrative modality.

The sound treatment here is realist throughout — we hear chains clanging, wire twanging, footsteps, geiger counter crackle, and wind noise under the reporter's voice. The sound is raised briefly so that we hear a snatch of the scientist's voice. The synchronised sound acts more as a realist device which authenticates the images.

A visual pun over shot 9 ('foot the bill' over a shot of feet) acts as a cohesive tie which binds the spoken commentary with the visual story. Such puns are surprisingly common features of TV news, often indicating that closure is imminent.

The Aborigines

The cut to pictures of the Aborigines marks a sharp break in the visual narrative structure and we lose the camera/narrator's voice. This boundary is marked in the verbal commentary by a two second pause. The five brief shots which make up the Aboriginal sequence do not cohere: they are merely illustrations running under the commentary. The treatment of the Aborigines is in sharp contrast to earlier footage. They are represented as a people without narrative, without purpose or agency. As viewers, we are emotionally distanced from the Aborigines through camera angle and size of shot: we do not intrude upon them but maintain an impersonal distance. We see mouths move but do not hear voices. The camera is not 'respectful', that is, it does not pan, zoom, or change focus to follow their movements. The treatment in this report reflects a common social practice in the visual representation of Aborigines in Australian media (Kress & van Leeuwen, 1990). It helps distance the viewer and construct the Aborigines as 'other'.

Not only do the Aborigines lack their own narrative, they also lack a place in the larger narrative structure. If the tale were told in sequence (which the visual narrative requires), then the Aborigines belong at the very beginning. (The story chronologically would run: Aborigines cleared off, nuclear bomb tested, ground contaminated.) The verbal news story at this point follows conventional news values in relocating the Aborigines out of chronological sequence. They are regarded as tangential to the 'real story'. In the competition between verbal and visual, the verbal structuring at this point wins out. The pictures here take on the unstructured form typical of those accompanying a newsreader's commentary.

Shot 18 is a significant boundary in the visual narrative of the news report — a stylised sunset shot which provides closure to the Australian segment of the story. This and the preceding shots (14–18) are bound together by a continuous bush noise which has a sharp onset in shot 14, then is faded down during the pause in the commentary. Synchronised sound (which would allow us to hear muttering and which would show discontinuities across shots) is a requirement of realism but has been replaced by a library sound effect.

The news conference

The London news conference is portrayed in what has become a conventional order for such occasions on TV news. We see the ministers entering and sitting down at the table; a reverse shot of the press (from within the 180 degree line); and a sequence in which we hear the minister addressing the audience. The first two shots, in particular the reverse shot, are crucial in positioning the viewer. We see the press conference for what it is, a stage managed event, and we are transferred to the point of view of the press corps through the shot–reverse shot. There is no danger of the minister appearing to speak directly to the viewer and usurping the reporter's own role as narrator.

The acoustic of the commentary changes subtly at this point, becoming a little more reverberant. It is as if the reporter is speaking from an internal space herself, although the acoustic of the room in which the press conference is held sounds different in the minister's speech. The modification of the ambient acoustic — although probably created in the studio — allows the commentary to trade on the realist convention that synchronised sound is recorded at the same time as the events being shown. It adds to the impression that the reporter was present and can vouch for the authenticity of the portayal.

News reports containing interviews with sources have always posed a problem for editors. Unlke feature film production, such interviews are normally carried out with a single camera in a single take. This prevents the use of standard shot–reverse shot convention and similar realist techniques which require the editing together of film from several takes and cameras. Nor can the film simply be cut so that the interviewee appears to jump from position to position. The convention usually adopted by TV news involves a minor sleight of hand. When the interview has finished the interviewer either repeats the questions (often to an empty seat) or just nods to camera. These 'noddies' or other 'cut away shots' (of an audience or surroundings) are then inserted to cover edits in the interviewee's replies, give the sense of natural continuous speech, and replicate the shot–reverse shot technique. This particular report is unusual in that no sources were directly interviewed. This probably accounts for its brevity, but as a consequence, we have not yet seen the reporter herself.

Closure

At certain points in a reporter's narrative, there will be a cut to a direct view of the reporter speaking 'to camera'. Such a cut accomplishes several things simultaneously. It is important because the distance of the reporter from the scene of action is one of the main sources of modality coding in news reports. The brief authentication of the reporter's presence 'in the field' helps the viewer calibrate the modality of the report they have just seen. Such a sequence also allows the reporter to take up the authoritative relationship with the viewer which comes from the 'direct to camera' eye contact. But this shot of the reporter is, of course, shown within the objective camera/narrator's point of view. This may be one reason why it is commonly used, as here, as a device for achieving closure, since it helps transfer us back to the objective newsreader/narrator's voice. Other more cinematic closure devices which serve a similar function are also commonly used. For example, the camera/narrator may provide a slow zoom out showing the wider landscape and hence context of events.

Some ambiguities in the report

One of the extraordinary aspects of this otherwise routine report is that the reporter was not, in any significant sense, 'there' at all. The story could be said to be an 'Australian' one, but the reporter is shown in London standing outside Australia House. The footage from Australia has almost certainly been compiled from fragments of library film and bought in pictures. The opening sequence may even be from an old fictional or 'documentary' propaganda film (there is a faint trace of a removed music track which hints that its origins are from another genre).

A further ambiguity arises from the way the Aborigines seem to be constructed narratively as victims. Who then is the villain? The British Government's role is made highly ambiguous by being cast also as the 'rescuer' and hence hero. The low visibility of the British government is notable: we are not told which British officials met the Australians and agreed the compensation; they do not appear at any press conference; no words or views are attributed to them. Although the story is ultimately authenticated as a London one, London plays only a very shadowy role in it.

Even though the report has clearly been assembled in London from bits and pieces, it nevertheless has all the generic form of a report from the field. A variety of realist techniques have constructed for it an acceptable 'reality' and helped gloss over some of the problems and ambiguities in its account.

Conclusion

The analysis of the news report illustrates some of the various ways in which factuality is constructed generically in news bulletins. I have focused here on the visual treatment of news, showing how cinematic editing and camera techniques, sound effects, and nonverbal communication are routinely used to provide an apparent transparency to representations of the world. I am not here concerned with the accuracy or 'truth' of such representations, merely to demonstrate that factuality is (necessarily) achieved generically, and that this process includes complex conventions at the visual level. I have described the TV news genre as heterogeneous in its techniques of editing and the modality systems it employs; as suffering from several intrinsic tensions and contradictory needs — between objectivity and subjectivity; between verbal and visual narrative structure; and between literate and conversational modes of representing truth.

I have argued that two major visual modality systems are exploited in TV news — those of realism and of naturalism. In the naturalist treatment of actuality sequences the verbal commentary takes on the major role of establishing the modality of the pictures, and it is this aspect of news reports which has received most analytical attention in the past. But realist narrative techniques — with their associated technologies of visual modality — penetrate news reports more than has been acknowledged. Furthermore, the news bulletin as a whole must be seen as a realist narrative, based in the realist studio setting, with the newsreader providing the objective narrator's voice. Within such a larger frame, the introduction of filed reports from the field is a focalizing narrative device, allowing us to take up, temporarily, the subjective perspective of a reliable character who can introduce us to yet further characters who have stories to tell.

The visual accomplishment of factuality in TV news thus relies extensively on a narrative modality system which is deeply entrenched in western fiction, and relies on the cinematic techniques which provide realism in exactly those drama and entertainment programmes from which TV news seeks to distance itself.

References

Boyd-Barrett, O. (1987) Deadline midnight Wednesday. In Open University (ed.) *EH207: Communication and Education. Unit 1: How Do People Communicate?* Milton Keynes: Open University Press.

Cockerell, M. (1988) *Live from Number 10: The Inside Story of Prime Ministers and Television*. London: Faber and Faber.

Ellis, J. (1982) *Visible Fictions*. London: Routledge & Kegan Paul.

Fiske, J. (1987) *Television Culture*. London: Routledge.

Fowler, R. (1991) *Language in the News*. London: Routledge.

Hodge, R. and G. Kress (1988) *Social Semiotics*. Cambridge: Polity.

Kress, G. (1985) Socio-linguistic development and the mature language user: Different voices for different occasions. In G. Wells and J. Nicholls (eds) *Language and Learning: An Interactional Perspective*. London: Falmer Press.

Kress, G. and T. van Leeuwen (1990) *Reading Images*. Victoria: Deakin University.

Masterman, L. (1980) *Teaching About Television*. London: Macmillan.

Mayne, W. (1985) *Drift*. London: Heinemann.

Stephens, J. (1992) *Language and Ideology in Children's Fiction*. London: Longman.

Vaughan, D. (1976) *Television Documentary Usage*. London: British Film Institute Monograph 6.

Appendix 1

Commentary	Speaker	Shot description	No
Britain has offered to pay towards the cost of another clean up of its former nuclear test site at Maralinga in South Australia. The sum hasn't been disclosed, but it is thought to be more than twenty million pounds. Australia's foreign and energy ministers who had two days of talks in London will now take the offer back to their cabinet.	**News-reader**	Newsreader to camera. Still image of Aborigine sitting on ground on screen behind right shoulder.	1
Forty years ago Australians	**Reporter**	CUT TO/ oblique shot of line of soldiers, backs to camera. Sound of distant explosion. Soldiers turn 180 degrees in quick disciplined manoeuvre and shade eyes as if against glare, they look into distance.	2
welcomed Britain's choice to use part of the Great Victorian Desert		CUT TO/ mushroom cloud. Camera angle looking up.	3
in the race to develop an independent nuclear deterent but it's an invitation they now regret.		CUT TO/ sun into camera lens causing starburst effect, camera looking up. Camera tilts down to show barbed wire fence. Through fence is visible a yellow danger sign with NO ENTRY clearly marked and radiation warning symbol.	4
Eight years ago, the Australian government ordered		CUT TO/ close up of male hands and wrists undoing padlock and chain securing gates. Viewpoint is over left shoulder of unknown person. Bright sunlight casts sharp shadows of wire over skin. Sound of chain clanking.	5
an investigation into the site at Maralinga.		CUT TO/ mid shot of entrance gates from inside. Man opens gates, truck parked on outside of gates.	6

Commentary	Speaker	Shot description	No
British, Australian and American scientists discovered fragments of plutonium scattered over a far		CUT TO/ Mid shot of man in shirtsleeves carrying apparatus and ducking under a strand of wire. Desert and scrub land in background. Sound.	7
wider area than previously admitted. What you can hear is the gamma radiation from the ... The Australian government	Scientist Reporter	CUT TO/ close up, looking down, piece of material on ground. Two feet wrapped in protection, enter shot. Camera tilts up slightly to show hands holding geiger counter to ground, meter facing camera. Noise of geiger counter and man's voice.	8
demanded the British government foot at least half the bill for clearing it up.		CUT TO/ Close up, camera near ground, shows lower legs and feet, geiger probe swinging from wire. Feet walk and sensor scans ground.	9
The British maintain that they cleared the site up when they		CUT TO/ shot of stone tablet engraved: TEST SITE TARANAKI A BRITISH ATOMIC WEAPON WAS TEST EXPLODED HERE ON 9 OCT 1957	10
finished the test series in 1957		CUT TO/ long shot of weather recording apparatus	11
but all along the Australians have maintained that the British still has a		CUT TO/ close up geiger meter. Needle swings up and goes off scale.	12
moral responsibility here.		CUT TO/ close up of geiger sensor near ground	13
(2 secs pause) The xxx Aboriginals have historic claims to the land		CUT TO/ mid shot. Aborigine man sitting cross legged on ground in bush, looking out of shot to right, fire in background, dog walks from centre right to bottom and out of shot.	14

Commentary	Speaker	Shot description	No
and they are the true beneficiaries of today's decision. They were cleared off forty years ago to make way for the test series		CUT TO/ mid shot. Two Aboriginal women walk towards camera, several dogs roam, trees in background, camera close to ground.	1!
and they want to go back and they want compensation.		CUT TO/ mid close. Three Aboriginal men sitting on sacks in front of canvas shelter. Looking out of shot to right.	1€
They've got a separate claim against the British for twenty million pounds		CUT TO/ Same man as in shot 14 but closer shot. Surrounded by dogs. Appears to be talking but no voice heard.	17
to make up for the loss of their land over the past forty years		CUT TO/ long shot, trees silhouetted against sunset.	18
The Australian government have been asking the British for compensation for two years now. And it was with some relief that the two ministers from Australia were able to		CUT TO/ mid shot of two white men in dark suits who sit down at table. Camera slightly oblique. Framed map of Australia on wall behind.	19
announce today that they had reached a settlement.		CUT TO/ reverse shot of press corps	20
I think it's been a difficult domestic situation for the British government er I think they have understood for some time that they need to make a contribution but there have been pressures within their government to either pay nothing or a minimal amount.	Minister	CUT TO/ mid close of two men. Camera slightly oblique. One man speaks. Caption identifies as SIMON CREAN, Australian Energy Minister.	21
Lawyers representing the Aboriginal people of south Australia have welcomed the settlement but they say they hope it won't take many more years than the forty the Aboriginal people have already waited for their compensation from the British Government. Sue Lloyd Roberts. BBC News. Central London.	Reporter	CUT TO/Mid close of reporter speaking straight to camera against building identifiable over right shoulder as Australia House. Traffic noise.	22
		CUT TO/ newsreader	

10 The Medieval Concept of the Author

A .J. MINNIS

> In the beginning of this book and of every other, the listeners are
> accustomed to ask who is the efficient cause. And it is very useful to
> know this, for statements of 'authentic' men are the more diligently
> and firmly inscribed in the mind of the hearer.

The English grammarian William Wheteley (*fl.* 1309–16) is addressing his
pupils in the introduction to his course of lectures on the *De disciplina
scolarium*. It is very useful, he assures them, to know the name of the
'efficient cause' or writer of a book, because 'authentic' statements — statements which can be attributed to a named authority — are more worthy of
diligent attention and to be committed to memory. Wheteley explains
that the *De disciplina scolarium* was written by Boethius, the Roman consul
who died in 524. In fact, it was written between 1230 and 1240, probably at
Paris.

This mistaken attribution of a 'modern' work to an 'ancient' and distinguished writer is symptomatic of medieval veneration of the past in general.
Old books were the sources of new learning, as Chaucer remarks:

> . . . out of olde feldes, as men seyth,
> Cometh al this newe corn from yer to yere,
> And out of olde bokes, in good feyth,
> Cometh al this newe science that men lere.

To be old was to be good: the best writers were the more ancient. The
converse often seems to have been true: if a work was good, its medieval
readers were disposed to think that it was old. In order to understand such
attitudes better, it will be necessary in the first place to examine the significance of the common technical term for a distinguished writer, namely,
auctor, and then to proceed with an investigation of how the *auctores* were
studied within the medieval educational system.

The Terms *Auctor* and *Auctoritas*

In a literary context, the term *auctor* denoted someone who was at once a writer and an authority, someone not merely to be read but also to be respected and believed. According to medieval grammarians, the term derived its meaning from four main sources: *auctor* was supposed to be related to the Latin verbs *agere* 'to act or perform', *augere* 'to grow' and *auieo* 'to tie', and to the Greek noun *autentim* 'authority'. An *auctor* 'performed' the act of writing. He brought something into being, caused it to 'grow'. In the more specialised sense related to *auieo*, poets like Virgil and Lucan were *auctores* in that they had 'tied' together their verses with feet and metres. To the ideas of achievement and growth was easily assimilated the idea of authenticity or 'authoritativeness'.

The writings of an *auctor* contained, or possessed, *auctoritas* in the abstract sense of the term, with its strong connotations of veracity and sagacity. In the specific sense, an *auctoritas* was a quotation or an extract from the work of an *auctor*. Writing around 1200, Hugutio of Pisa defined an *auctoritas* as a *sententia digna imitatione*, a profound saying worthy of imitation of implementation. In his *Catholicon* (finished 1286), the Dominican Giovanni de'Balbi of Genoa amplified this with the statement that an *auctoritas* is also worthy of belief: as Aristotle says, an *auctoritas* is a judgment of the wise man in his chosen discipline. De'Balbi used an *auctoritas* of Plato's as an example. Plato says that the heavens are in motion; therefore, we should accept that this is indeed the case, because the man who is proficient and expert in his science must be believed.

The term *auctor* may profitably be regarded as an accolade bestowed upon a popular writer by those later scholars and writers who used extracts from his works as sententious statements or *auctoritates*, gave lectures on his works in the form of textual commentaries, or employed them as literary models. Two criteria for the award of this accolade were tacitly applied: 'intrinsic worth' and 'authenticity'.

To have 'intrinsic worth', a literary work had to conform, in one way or another, with Christian truth; an *auctor* had to say the right things. The Bible was the authoritative book *par excellence*. At the other end of the scale came the fables of the poets, employed in the teaching of grammar. As fictional narrative, fable could be dismissed by its critics as lying; many medieval writers expressed their distrust of such fabrication. According to Conrad of Hirsau (*c.* 1070–*c.* 1150), fables have practically no spiritual significance; they are as nothing when compared with Scripture. Peter Comestor (Chancellor of Notre Dame, Paris, between 1168 and 1178) remarked that the figments of the poets are like the croaking of frogs. The usual defence was that fables, rightly understood, provided philosophical and ethical doctrine: after all,

Priscian had said that fable teaches and delights, and had commended the fables of Aesop. Twelfth-century grammarians rendered acceptable the licentious stories of Ovid by extensive moralisation. Those thinkers influenced by Neoplatonism — notably William of Conches (*c.* 1080–*c.* 1154) and Bernard Silvester (*fl.* 1156) — went much further, in their elaborate mythic interpretations of pagan fables.

To be 'authentic', a saying or a piece of writing had to be the genuine production of a named *auctor*. Works of unknown or uncertain authorship were regarded as 'apocryphal' and believed to possess an *auctoritas* far inferior to that of works which circulated under the names of *auctores*. The standards of authenticity were applied most rigorously in the case of the books of the Bible. Thus, the Dominican Hugh of St Cher (who lectured on the Bible 1230–5) was careful in explaining the terms on which certain apocryphal works are accepted by the Church:

> They are called apocryphal because the author is unknown. But because there is no doubt of their truth they are accepted by the Church, for the teaching of mores rather than for the defence of the faith. However, if neither the author nor the truth were known, they could not be accepted, like the book on the infancy of the Saviour and the assumption of the Blessed Virgin.

It was regarded as a very drastic step to dispute an attribution and deprive a work of its *auctor*. Much more common was the tendency to accept improbable attributions of currently popular works to older and respected writers. Interesting cases in point include the *De disciplina scolarium,* discussed above, and the *Dissuasio Valerii ad Rufinum* produced by Walter Map in the late twelfth century. The quality and popularity of Map's discourse caused some of his contemporaries to doubt that he could have written it. 'My only fault is that I am alive', compained Map; 'I have no intention, however, of correcting this fault by my death.' His title, he explained, contains the names of dead men because this gives pleasure and, more importantly, because if he had not done so the work would have been rejected. Map speculated concerning the fate of the *Dissuasio* after his death:

> I know what will happen after I am gone. When I shall be decaying, then, for the first time, it shall be salted; and every defect in it will be remedied by my decease, and in the most remote future its antiquity will cause the authorship to be credited to me, because, then as now, old copper will be preferred to new gold . . . In every century its own present has been unpopular, and each age from the beginning has preferred the past to itself . . .

In the long term, Map was right (witness the enthusiasm of recent literary critics for his works) but, in the later Middle Ages, the *Dissuasio* was attributed to the first-century Roman historian, Valerius Maximus. The 'authenticity' and *auctoritas* of the work in this attribution were defended in several medieval commentaries.

The thinking we are investigating seems to be circular: the work of an *auctor* was a book worth reading; a book worth reading had to be the work of an *auctor*. No 'modern' writer could decently be called an *auctor* in a period in which men saw themselves as dwarfs standing on the shoulders of giants, i.e. the 'ancients'. In the treatise on the love of books which he composed in the last years of his life, Richard of Bury (Bishop of Durham 1333–45) could claim that, while the novelties of modern writers were always welcome to him, yet he always desired 'with more undoubting avidity' to explore the well-tested labours of the 'ancients'. The precise reason for the ancients' excellence is unclear, according to de Bury: they may have had by nature greater mental powers, or they may have applied themselves more diligently to study. But in his opinion it is obvious that the 'moderns' are barely capable of discussing ancient discoveries, and of acquiring laboriously as pupils those things which the old masters provided. Since the men of bygone days were of a more excellent degree of bodily development than the present age can produce, de Bury continued, it is plausible to suppose that they were distinguished by brighter mental faculties as well, seeing that in their works they are inimitable by posterity. From all this, it would seem that the only good *auctor* was a dead one. Hence the 'fault' which Walter Map was in no hurry to correct.

The Academic Study of *Auctores*

Every discipline, every area of study, had its *auctores*. In grammar, there were Priscian and Donatus together with the ancient poets; in rhetoric, Cicero; in dialectic, Aristotle, Porphyry and Boethius; in arithmetic, Boethius and Martianus Capella; in astronomy, Hyginus and Ptolemy; in medicine, Galen and Constantine the African; in Canon Law, Gratian; in theology, the Bible and, subsequently, Peter Lombard's *Sentences* as well. The study of authoritative texts in the classroom formed the basis of the medieval educational system.

This system had its origins in late antiquity. From the Roman grammarian (*grammaticus*) of the fifth century, the pupil learned the science of speaking with style (*scientia recte loquendi*) and heard the classical poets being explicated (*enarratio poetarum*). The first of these activities comprised explanation of the elements of language, letters, syllables and words; the second comprised explanation of the intellectual content of a text. In his *prelectio* (i.e. lecture or explanatory reading), the grammarian would describe in minute detail the verse-rhythms, difficult or rare words, grammatical and syntactical features, and figures of speech, included in a given passage. He would also elaborate on its historical, legal, geographical, mythological and scientific allusions and details. Pupils were thereby enabled to understand fully each passage of the work.

These teaching methods continued, with occasional modification, into the Middle Ages. John of Salisbury's *Metalogicon* (completed 1159) provides a useful point of reference, since it refers to both past and present educational practice. After paraphrasing the account of *prelectio* which Quintilian had written in the first century, John proceeds to relate how Bernard of Chartres (*c.* 1130), 'the greatest font of literary learning in Gaul in recent times', used to teach grammar. In reading (i.e. lecturing on) the *auctores*, Bernard would point out what was straightforward and in accordance with the rules of composition, and also explain 'grammatical figures, rhetorical embellishment, and sophistical quibbling'. It would seem that Bernard shared some of Quintilian's principles and concerns.

Further insight into the priorities of *prelectio* is provided by a remark of one of Bernard's pupils, William of Conches, once the teacher of John of Salisbury and of the future King Henry II of England. In the prologue to his commentary on the *Timaeus*, William criticised those commentaries and glosses on Plato which attempt to explain the *sententiae* of a work (i.e. its profound and inner meanings) without having first carefully followed and explained 'the letter' of the text. This point of view was shared by Hugh of St Victor (writing *c.* 1127), who advocated the following 'order of exposition' in studying the Bible: one begins with 'the letter', working out the grammatical construction and continuity of a passage; then, one proceeds to expound its *sensus* or most obvious meaning; and, finally, the *sententia* or deeper meaning is sought.

Analysis of both 'the letter' of authoritative texts and of the *sententiae* found therein were, in whatever proportion, essential features of all the teaching conducted within the medieval trivium and quadrivium. (The trivium comprised grammar, rhetoric and dialectic, the inferior group of the seven liberal arts; the quadrivium comprised music, arithmetic, geometry and astronomy, the superior group). In the case of the more specialised disciplines of law, medicine and theology, these procedures were heavily modified to suit the special requirements of the individual subject. But no matter what the subject, the scholar did not compete (he did not even pretend to do so) either with his *auctores* or with the great works which they had left. One's whole ambition was directed to understanding the authoritative texts, 'penetrating their depths, assimilating them and, in the fields of grammar and rhetoric, imitating them'.

11 The Death of the Author

ROLAND BARTHES

In his story *Sarrasine* Balzac, describing a castrato disguised as a woman, writes the following sentence: '*This was woman herself, with her sudden fears, her irrational whims, her instinctive worries, her impetuous boldness, her fussings, and her delicious sensibility.*' Who is speaking thus? Is it the hero of the story bent on remaining ignorant of the castrato hidden beneath the woman? Is it Balzac the individual, furnished by his personal experience with a philosophy of Woman? Is it Balzac the author professing 'literary' ideas on femininity? Is it universal wisdom? Romantic psychology? We shall never know, for the good reason that writing is the destruction of every voice, of every point of origin. Writing is that neutral, composite, oblique space where our subject slips away, the negative where all identity is lost, starting with the very identity of the body writing.

No doubt it has always been that way. As soon as a fact is *narrated* no longer with a view to acting directly on reality but intransitively, that is to say, finally outside of any function other than that of the very practice of the symbol itself, this disconnection occurs, the voice loses its origin, the author enters into his own death, writing begins. The sense of this phenomenon, however, has varied; in ethnographic societies the responsibility for a narrative is never assumed by a person but by a mediator, shaman or relator whose 'performance' — the mastery of the narrative code — may possibly be admired but never his 'genius'. The author is a modern figure, a product of our society insofar as, emerging from the Middle Ages with English empiricism, French rationalism and the personal faith of the Reformation, it discovered the prestige of the individual, of, as it is more nobly put, the 'human person'. It is thus logical that in literature it should be this positivism, the epitome and culmination of capitalist ideology, which has attached the greatest importance to the 'person' of the author. The *author* still reigns in histories of literature, biographies of writers, interviews, magazines, as in the very consciousness of men of letters anxious to unite their person and their work through diaries and memoirs. The image of literature to be found in ordinary culture is tyrannically centred on the author, his person, his life, his tastes, his passions, while criticism still consists for the most part in saying that Baudelaire's work is the failure of Baudelaire the man, Van Gogh's his madness, Tchaikovsky's his vice. The *explanation* of a work is always sought in the man or woman who produced it, as if it were always in the end, through the more or less transparent allegory of the fiction, the voice of a single person, the *author* 'confiding' in us.

Though the sway of the Author remains powerful (the new criticism has often done no more than consolidate it), it goes without saying that certain writers have long since attempted to loosen it. In France, Mallarmé was doubtless the first to see and to foresee in its full extent the necessity to substitute language itself for the person who until then had been supposed to be its owner. For him, for us too, it is language which speaks, not the author; to write is, through a prerequisite impersonality (not at all to be confused with the castrating objectivity of the realist novelist), to reach that point where only language acts, 'performs', and not 'me'. Mallarmé's entire poetics consists in suppressing the author in the interests of writing (which is, as will be seen, to restore the place of the reader). Valéry, encumbered by a psychology of the Ego, considerably diluted Mallarmé's theory but, his taste for classicism leading him to turn to the lessons of rhetoric, he never stopped calling into question and deriding the Author; he stressed the linguistic and, as it were, 'hazardous' nature of his activity, and throughout his prose works he militated in favour of the essentially verbal condition of literature, in the face of which all recourse to the writer's interiority seemed to him pure superstition. Proust himself, despite the apparently psychological character of what are called his *analyses*, was visibly concerned with the task of inexorably blurring, by an extreme subtilization, the relation between the writer and his characters; by making of the narrator not he who has seen and felt nor even he who is writing, but he who *is going to write* (the young man in the novel — but, in fact, how old is he and who is he? — wants to write but cannot; the novel ends when writing at last becomes possible), Proust gave modern writing its epic. By a radical reversal, instead of putting his life into his novel, as is so often maintained, he made of his very life a work for which his own book was the model; so that it is clear to us that Charlus does not imitate Montesquiou but that Montesquiou — in his anecdotal, historical reality — is no more than a secondary fragment, derived from Charlus. Lastly, to go no further than this prehistory of modernity, Surrealism, though unable to accord language a supreme place (language being system and the aim of the movement being, romantically, a direct subversion of codes — itself moreover illusory: a code cannot be destroyed, only 'played off'), contributed to the desacrilization of the image of the Author by ceaselessly recommending the abrupt disappointment of expectations of meaning (the famous surrealist 'jolt'), by entrusting the hand with the task of writing as quickly as possible what the head itself is unaware of (automatic writing), by accepting the principle and the experience of several people writing together. Leaving aside literature itself (such distinctions really becoming invalid), linguistics has recently provided the destruction of the Author with a valuable analytical tool by showing that the whole of the enunciation is an empty process, functioning perfectly without there being any need for it to be filled with the person of the interlocutors. Linguistically, the author is never more than the instance writing, just as *I* is nothing other than the instance saying *I*: language knows a 'subject', not a 'person', and this subject, empty outside of the very enunciation which defines it, suffices to make language 'hold together', suffices, that is to say, to exhaust it.

The removal of the Author (one could talk here with Brecht of a veritable 'distancing', the Author diminishing like a figurine at the far end of the literary stage) is not merely an historical fact or an act of writing; it utterly transforms the modern text (or — which is the same thing — the text is henceforth made and read in such a way that at all its levels the author is absent). The temporality is different. The Author, when believed in, is always conceived of as the past of his own book: book and author stand automatically on a single line divided into a *before* and an *after*. The Author is thought to *nourish* the book, which is to say that he exists before it, thinks, suffers, lives for it, is in the same relation of antecedence to his work as a father to his child. In complete contrast, the modern scriptor is born simultaneously with the text, is in no way equipped with a being preceding or exceeding the writing, is not the subject with the book as predicate; there is no other time than that of the enunciation and every text is eternally written *here and now*. The fact is (or, it follows) that *writing* can no longer designate an operation of recording, notation, representation, 'depiction' (as the Classics would say); rather, it designates exactly what linguists, referring to Oxford philosophy, call a performative, a rare verbal form (exclusively given in the first person and in the present tense) in which the enunciation has no other content (contains no other proposition) than the act by which it is uttered — something like the *I declare* of kings or the *I sing* of very ancient poets. Having buried the Author, the modern scriptor can thus no longer believe, as according to the pathetic view of his predecessors, that this hand is too slow for his thought or passion and that consequently, making a law of necessity, he must emphasize this delay and indefinitely 'polish' his form. For him, on the contrary, the hand, cut off from any voice, borne by a pure gesture of inscription (and not of expression), traces a field without origin — or which, at least, has no other origin than language itself, language which ceaselessly calls into question all origins.

We know now that a text is not a line of words releasing a single 'theological' meaning (the 'message' of the Author-God) but a multi-dimensional space in which a variety of writings, none of them original, blend and clash. The text is a tissue of quotations drawn from the innumerable centres of culture. Similar to Bouvard and Pécuchet, those eternal copyists, at once sublime and comic and whose profound ridiculousness indicates precisely the truth of writing, the writer can only imitate a gesture that is always anterior, never original. His only power is to mix writings, to counter the ones with the others, in such a way as never to rest on any one of them. Did he wish to *express himself*, he ought at least to know that the inner 'thing' he thinks to 'translate' is itself only a ready-formed dictionary, its words only explainable through other words, and so on indefinitely; something experienced in exemplary fashion by the young Thomas de Quincey, he who was so good at Greek that in order to translate absolutely modern ideas and images into that dead language, he had, so Baudelaire tells us (in *Paradis Artificiels*), 'created for himself an unfailing dictionary, vastly more extensive and complex than those resulting from the ordinary patience of purely literary themes'. Succeeding the Author, the scriptor no longer bears within him passions, humours, feelings, impressions, but rather this immense dictionary from which he draws a writing that can know no halt: life never does more than imitate the book, and the book itself is only a tissue of signs, an imitation that is lost, infinitely deferred.

Once the Author is removed, the claim to decipher a text becomes quite futile. To give a text an Author is to impose a limit on that text, to furnish it with a final signified, to close the writing. Such a conception suits criticism very well, the latter then allotting itself the important task of discovering the Author (or its hypostases: society, history, psyché, liberty) beneath the work: when the Author has been found, the text is 'explained' — victory to the critic. Hence there is no surprise in the fact that, historically, the reign of the Author has also been that of the Critic, nor again in the fact that criticism (be it new) is today undermined along with the Author. In the multiplicity of writing, everything is to be *disentangled*, nothing *deciphered*; the structure can be followed, 'run' (like the thread of a stocking) at every point and at every level, but there is nothing beneath: the space of writing is to be ranged over, not pierced; writing ceaselessly posits meaning ceaselessly to evaporate it, carrying out a systematic exemption of meaning. In precisely this way literature (it would be better from now on to say *writing*), by refusing to assign a 'secret', an ultimate meaning, to the text (and to the world as text), liberates what may be called an anti-theological activity, an activity that is truly revolutionary since to refuse to fix meaning is, in the end, to refuse God and his hypostases — reason, science, law.

Let us come back to the Balzac sentence. No one, no 'person', says it: its source, its voice, is not the true place of the writing, which is reading. Another — very precise — example will help to make this clear: recent research (J.-P. Vernant) has demonstrated the constitutively ambiguous nature of Greek tragedy, its texts being woven from words with double meanings that each character understands unilaterally (this perpetual misunderstanding is exactly the 'tragic'); there is, however, someone who understands each word in its duplicity and who, in addition, hears the very deafness of the characters speaking in front of him — this someone being precisely the reader (or here, the listener). Thus is revealed the total existence of writing: a text is made of multiple writings, drawn from many cultures and entering into mutual relations of dialogue, parody, contestation, but there is one place where this multiplicity is focused and that place is the reader, not, as was hitherto said, the author. The reader is the space on which all the quotations that make up a writing are inscribed without any of them being lost; a text's unity lies not in its origin but in its destination. Yet this destination cannot any longer be personal: the reader is without history, biography, psychology; he is simply that *someone* who holds together in a single field all the traces by which the written text is constituted. Which is why it is derisory to condemn the new writing in the name of a humanism hypocritically turned champion of the reader's rights. Classic criticism has never paid any attention to the reader; for it, the writer is the only person in literature. We are now beginning to let ourselves be fooled no longer by the arrogant antiphrastical recriminations of good society in favour of the very thing it sets aside, ignores, smothers, or destroys; we know that to give writing its future, it is necessary to overthrow the myth: the birth of the reader must be at the cost of the death of the Author.

12 The Authoring of Saussure

ROY HARRIS

> . . . quoi que je n'aie pas de plus cher voeu que de ne pas avoir à m'occuper de la langue en général.
>   Cela finira malgré moi par un livre . . .
>
> . . . although I have no dearer wish than not to have to concern myself with language in general.
>   It will come to a book in the end, in spite of my reluctance . . .
>
> — F. de Saussure, letter to A. Meillet, 4.1.1894

History was to prove Saussure right. It produced, *malgré lui* and twenty-two years later, a book: the *Cours de linguistique générale*. Evidently, Saussure had not tried hard enough to prevent that reluctant consummation. His ultimate trump cards (premature decease; fragmentary notes; failure to leave a manuscript) were blandly overtrumped by his pupils and colleagues. It took them barely more than a couple of years to bring out the book that Saussure had managed to avoid writing for the previous twenty.

What Bally and Sechehaye published in 1916 can certainly be read, but it is a book which Saussure never wrote. In one sense, we can no more read the Saussure who was the founder of Saussurean linguistics than we can read the Socrates who was the founder of Socratic philosophy. Our access to Saussure's ideas through reading the *Cours de linguistique générale* is indeed comparable to our access to the ideas of Socrates through reading the Platonic dialogues. Inevitably, all we can read on the page is a second-hand account of what a particular thinker is represented as having said, or as likely to have meant. Saussure and Socrates are classic examples of our cultural reliance on written reports, and even on reports which take the form of imaginative reconstructions. Such reports are, for obvious reasons, wide open to the charge of 'misrepresentation'; but, ironically, the more influential the thinker the less relevant the charge of misrepresentation becomes.

It is a measure of their importance that the possibility of misrepresentation hardly matters in either Saussure's case or that of Socrates. Just as 'Socratic' ideas reached a far wider public through Plato's written reconstruction of them (however misguided) than could ever have been the case

171

otherwise, so more people assimilated 'Saussurean' ideas by reading the *Cours* than ever attended Saussure's lectures or asked him questions about points of linguistic theory. (It may come as something of a shock today to realize that none of Saussure's three courses at Geneva was attended by more than a handful of students.) As readers, we have no option but to read the Saussure who is presented as the author of the *Cours,* unless we renounce all possibility of investigating the source of some of the most basic notions current in contemporary discussions of language. It is not that nothing readable at all survives from the hand of Saussure: but this does not differentiate the Socratic from the Saussurean problem. For there is no doubt that the formative influence was exercised not by Saussure in person but by the text which his editors published after his death.

A quarter of a century after the appearence of the *Cours*, one of its editors wrote:

> Even if Ferdinand de Saussure's *Cours de linguistique générale* were eventually to become entirely outdated, it would be destined to remain alive in the memory of linguistic science because of its powerful and productive influence at a certain point in the evolution of that science. (Sechehaye, 1940: 1)

A quarter of a century had given the editors ample time to realize that as far as most people were concerned 'reading Saussure' was to all intents and purposes reading their version of Saussure's teachings.

The question then is — and has been for many years — how to make sense of reading this Saussure who is the presumptive author of the *Cours*; not whether what we read is a correct or an incorrect account of 'what the real Saussure really meant'. For whatever that may have been is arguably irrecoverable anyway. As mere 'readers', we shall never know what Saussure actually 'said'. (But whether that puts us in a position of disadvantage or, on the contrary, of advantage as compared to his original hearers is debatable: for none of them heard it all.) At the very worst, the Saussure of the *Cours* is a literary — and literal — fabrication of his editors. So might Socrates, conceivably, be a fabrication of Plato's. But as far as modern linguistics is concerned, it would have been necessary, as Voltaire said of God, to invent him had he not existed. In the modern academic world a book demands an author. We cannot blame the editors of the *Cours* for supplying one. They — rightly — sensed that this mode of presentation would be infinitely more authoritative than any publication of the original students' notes.

Less wise than Plato, however, Saussure's editors — on their own initiative — raised the question of authenticity in the reader's mind. Will anyone, they publicly wondered, 'be able to distinguish between Saussure and our interpretation of Saussure?' It is undoubtedly the silliest query executors of Saussure's linguistic testament could possibly have raised; particularly if the executors had already rejected the idea of quoting their source material *verbatim*, and were therefore offering the reader no alternative basis for forming a judgment. Plato was not given to silliness of this order (in part, doubtless, because it never fell to his intellectual lot to endure the nineteenth century).

More unfortunately still, a later generation of Saussureans belatedly took this question of authenticity seriously, and proposed to deal with it by comparing the published text of the *Cours* with the surviving manuscript notes. Textual Pelion was thus piled upon textual Ossa (to the dismay of linguistic historiographers and the delight of university examiners). To say this is not to deny the interest of knowing what Saussure's pupils made of his lectures. It is simply to acknowledge the irony of the fact that this approach to Saussurean linguistics validates at Saussure's expense the methods of philology versus the methods of semiology.

For some scholars, it would seem, it is only a 'philological' approach to the text which has any value at all. At least one eminent commentator on Saussure has been charged outright with lacking the requisite *formation philologique* to undertake a competent exegesis of the *Cours* (Frei, 1950). Evidently 'philological' standards are so high that very few would-be commentators can hope to escape whipping. The shortcomings of my own commentary in that respect will doubtless be judged to be severe, if not positively provocative. Why is the reader not constantly referred to what survives of Saussure's manuscript notes and to his students' notebooks in order to elucidate obscure or contentious points? One reply might be that those who are looking for that kind of philological apparatus already have it available in Engler's monumental critical edition: but that is not the relevant reason. The rejection of a 'philological' approach to the *Cours* in my own commentary is based on conviction that such an approach would be quite misleading. For anyone who is interested in the *Cours* as linguistic theory, the 'philological' questions that can be both asked and answered concerning the text are simply the wrong questions. Quite apart from the fact that it was the Saussure of the *Cours* and not the Saussure of the Geneva lectures who was responsible for the 'Copernican' revolution in linguistic thought, and quite apart from the fallacy that there is just one 'authentic' version of Saussure lurking somewhere behind the textual facade, waiting to be discovered, there are two considerations which combine to call in question whether a 'philological' study of the *Cours* can tell us anything of critical value. One is simply that it begs the question to suppose that the alleged 'sources' confirm or modify certain possible interpretations of the *Cours*: for the 'sources' stand in just as much need of interpretation as the *Cours* itself. The other consideration is that all the crucial theoretical problems are raised in the *Cours* in any case: the 'sources' do not add to that inventory. It is

certainly interesting to have confirmation that Bally and Sechehaye did not
in that crude sense 'miss anything out'; but it would be obviously rash to
conclude that anything not in the 'sources' Bally and Sechehaye simply
invented. In short, apart from failing to reveal omissions, the 'sources' leave
us no wiser on any substantive critical issue. To suppose that subjecting them
to a sufficiently rigorous 'philological' analysis would throw light on any
point of theory is either to confuse theory with biography or else to demand
of philology more than philology is capable of giving.

No attempt either should be made to enter into the labyrinthine and unend-
ing controversy concerning 'influences' on Saussure, important as these issues
may be for historians. Are the key concepts of the *Cours* to be viewed as
deriving specifically from the work of Humboldt, or Paul, or Gabelentz, or
Durkheim, or Whitney . . . ? Or were they, as Bloomfield brusquely claimed
in his review of the book (Bloomfield, 1923), just ideas which had been 'in
the air' for a long time? There is a sense in which detailed answers to such
questions could make a difference to one's reading of Saussure. But there is
also a sense in which they need not matter a jot. Saussure, as it happens, provides an awkward test case for the claims of 'influential' historiography, inas-
much as the Saussurean influence on his successors was manifestly unrelated
to the extent of their curiosity about the influence of Saussure's predecessors
on Saussure. To acknowledge this is not to belittle the researches of historiographers. Nor is it to espouse an idealistic 'context-neutral' approach to
reading the *Cours*. For it is always worth considering what is to be gained by
comparing the ideas of one thinker with those of another working within the
same (or some other) intellectual tradition. Saussure's case is no exception.
It is, indeed, virtually impossible for intelligent readers not to place what
they read within the context of some kind of 'history of ideas', however minimal. To that extent, the concept of historical contextualization is already
implicit in the concept of reading. But the contextualization thus implied is
of a quite different order from the historiographer's.

It is therefore the reader's Saussure, the hypothetically reconstructable
author of the *Cours* who must be the focus of attention and interpretation.
This Saussure is neither complete fact nor complete fiction, neither an
authority on the 'real' Saussure nor an authorial persona. Elusive as he may
be, it is this author who drafted the Magna Carta of modern linguistics. He
is also the author whom Bühler, Hjelmslev, Merleau-Ponty, Lévi-Strauss,
Piaget and Derrida — to mention but a few — read: and their various readings of Saussure became part of the mainstream of twentieth-century
thought.

Perhaps it will be objected that to proceed in this manner is to interpose
'between the image of Saussure and the man Saussure simply the ideological
projection and the epistemological imperfections of two generations of

linguists' (Calvet, 1975: 54). The answer to this objection is that we have no alternative nowadays but to read Saussure through the academic spectacles provided by the subsequent history of Saussurean linguistics. The case is at least less desperate than that of Socrates, whom we read through the distorting lens of two thousand years of Western philosophy.

May it, alternatively, be objected that such an approach to reading Saussure simply conflates author and editors? This is not so. For a reader is still free to distinguish between the two roles whenever there is occasion to do so. The author is the presumptive source of ideas, terminology, arguments and examples: the editors are responsible for their arrangement and the construction of an articulated text. That distinction, contentious though it must inevitably be, is what makes possible the projection of different readings of Saussure, of which his editors have given us just theirs — albeit a consciously 'open' version. Only those readers who cling to the vain hope of uncovering some unique and 'authentic' version of Saussure will be unduly worried by the prospect. His editors clearly were not. Saussure, they tell us, was one of those thinkers for whom thinking is a constant process of intellectual renewal. They 'edited' Saussure in just that spirit; and that is one merit of their version which cannot be denied, however much later critics may carp. Sechehaye subsequently said of Saussure's lectures that Saussure thought aloud in front of his students, in order to make them think for themselves (Sechehaye, 1940: 2). Similarly, to read Saussure is to be invited to re-think Saussure, and it is precisely for this reason that Saussure on linguistic theory is far more worth reading today than many of his more 'advanced' successors.

Saussure had already become compulsory reading for linguists within five years of the publication of the *Cours*, which was widely reviewed (de Mauro, 1972: 366). What linguists read into Saussure is a different question. It was to become almost a commonplace of Saussurean exegesis to point out that even those who were originally most sympathetic and most directly influenced by Saussure (Meillet, for instance; de Mauro, 1972: 368) did not always seem to understand some of his basic ideas. That this should have been so, if it was so, is doubtless an indication of the difficulty which a generation brought up to accept the assumptions of nineteenth-century comparative and historical linguistics experienced in coming to terms with Saussurean structuralism. More eloquent still, perhaps, is what Jespersen says in 1922 in his much acclaimed book *Language, its Nature, Development and Origin*.

He lists the first edition of the *Cours* in his bibliography, but nevertheless begins by announcing: 'The distinctive feature of the science of language as conceived nowadays is its historical character' (Jespersen, 1922: 7). In the four chapters Jespersen gives to the 'History of Linguistic Science', Saussure is mentioned just once, and then simply in an alphabetical list of scholars who 'have dealt with the more general problems of linguistic change or linguistic theory' (Jespersen, 1922: 98). By 1925, however, Jespersen felt obliged to devote a substantial part of the opening chapter of his new book, *Mankind, Nation and Individual from a Linguistic Point of View*, to a criticism of Saussure's distinction between *langue* and *parole* (here misleadingly — but influentially — rendering those terms into English as 'language' and 'speech'). Why that distinction had been passed over in silence three years previously in *Language, its Nature, Development and Origin* Jespersen does not explain. It was not that in 1922 he had not yet read the *Cours*: for he had published a review of it in 1917.

Part of the answer is that Saussure the scholar had already established himself in the minds of his contemporaries in a quite different but less distinguished — and less threatening — role. As Calvet points out (Calvet, 1975: 16), the entry under *Saussure* in the 1923 edition of the *Larousse Universel* refers to his work of 'capital importance' on the primitive system of Indo-European vowels, but makes no mention at all of the *Cours de linguistique générale*. These attested cases of historical myopia go to reinforce the thesis that Saussure falls into that Shakespearian category of those who, retrospectively, 'have greatness thrust upon them'. This leads in turn to an academic reading of Saussure in which the author of the *Cours* was really a happy, orthodox historical comparativist, who suffered intermittently from an unfortunate neurosis about terminological distinctions. Or, to borrow Calvet's metaphor, Saussure appears as an intellectual Columbus who by accident discovered America while exploring in search of the Indies.

Another eloquent piece of evidence about academic readings of Saussure comes from Leonard Bloomfield's book *Language*, published a decade after Jespersen's. Here too Saussure is given a single passing mention (Bloomfield, 1935: 19) in an introductory chapter on the history of linguistics. At first sight, it might seem that, like Jespersen in 1922, Bloomfield had somehow failed to register the fact that the *Cours* was major landmark in the development of the subject. This is not the case, however. Bloomfield too had published a previous review of the *Cours* (Bloomfield, 1923). This review makes interesting reading. In it, Bloomfield begins by acknowledging Saussure's standing as the scholar who first faced the problems involved in constructing a comprehensive theory of language. Bloomfield says of Saussure, 'in lecturing on "general linguistics" he stood very nearly alone, for strange as it may seem, the nineteenth century, which studied intensively the history of one family of languages, took little or no interest in general aspects of human speech.' Here, in effect, Bloomfield acknowledges Saussure as the founder of modern general linguistics, even though Bloomfield's earlier book *An Introduction to the Study of Language* had come out in 1914, thus preceding the original publication of the *Cours* by two years. Saussure, says Bloomfield, 'has here first mapped out the world in which historical

Indo-European grammar (the great achievement of the past century) is merely a single province: he has given us the theoretical basis for a science of human speech.' But by the time he wrote *Language*, Bloomfield had changed his first estimate of Saussure's *Cours* and its significance.

The reason for the disparity between Bloomfield's eulogy of Saussure in 1923 and his virtual dismissal of Saussure ten years later is not difficult to explain. The Bloomfield of the 1923 review is Bloomfield in his pre-behaviourist period; and in his pre-behaviourist period Bloomfield was a follower of the psychologist Wundt. So the 1923 review gives us a reading of the *Cours* as viewed by an American Wundtian who was also a Germanic philologist of the traditional stamp (and a student of Amerindian languages as well). But ten years later Bloomfield had rejected Wundt in favour of Watson. His reading of Saussure had altered accordingly. Saussure was now read not as the adventurous founder of modern linguistics, but as a perpetuator of the endemic psychologism of late-nineteenth-century approaches to language. That later Bloomfieldian reading was to dictate the relationship between American and European versions of structuralism for the next quarter of a century.

A complementary but interestingly different Anglo-Saxon reading of Saussure is manifest in the objections to the *Cours* raised by Ogden & Richards (1923), Gardiner (1932) and Firth (1950). Nevertheless, although different individual positions might be taken whether in Europe or America, few theorists were prepared to deny that the distinctions drawn by Saussure provided the basis on which a modern science of language might be established. In this respect, Saussure eventually appeared to be less innovative and less controversial than had formerly been supposed. Thus whereas Firth in 1950 (Firth, 1950: 179) could still classify professional linguists into four groups ('Saussureans, anti-Saussureans, post-Saussureans, or non-Saussureans'), by 1957, the centenary year of Saussure's birth, a fellow professional linguist could make the bland pronouncement: 'We are all Saussureans now' (Spence, 1957: 15).

As the case-history of Bloomfield demonstrates, the question of 'reading Saussure' merges inextricably with that of reading readings of Saussure. For when Bloomfield wrote *Language* nothing of the readable Saussure had changed since 1916 (with the exception of trivial emendations to the 1922 edition). Furthermore, it would be a mistake to infer from the way in which Bloomfield's *Language* deliberately ignores Saussure that Saussurean ideas left no trace in American academic linguistics of the interwar period. Bloomfield himself admitted to Jakobson that reading the *Cours* was one of the events which had most influenced him (de Mauro, 1972: 371). Editing a collection of papers spanning the period 1925–1956, Joos (1957: 18) wrote: 'At least half of these authors had read the *Cours*. The others got it second-hand: in an atmosphere so saturated with those ideas, it has been impossible to escape that. The difference is hard to detect, and it is generally unsafe to accuse a contemporary linguist of not having read the *Cours* . . .' In other words, by the late 1950s the experience of reading Saussure seemed to have been so thoroughly absorbed as to make a distinction between Saussureans and non-Saussureans meaningless.

However, as if to give the lie to the dictum that 'we are all Saussureans now', there appeared in the very same year of 1957 the first manifesto of a new school of transatlantic linguistics which apparently owed little if anything to Saussure, however directly or indirectly assimilated. This was A. N. Chomsky's *Syntactic Structures*. The new theory proposed to treat a language as 'a set (finite or infinite) of sentences, each finite in length and constructed out of a finite set of elements' (Chomsky, 1957: 13) — a definition which might well have made the author of the *Cours* turn in his authorial grave. The essential novelty of transformational-generative grammar, as proposed in *Syntactic Structures*, was the eminently unSaussurean notion of considering languages as mathematical systems, on a par with the formal systems of mathematical logic. In retrospect, that approach may well now appear to have been naive or misguided; but in 1957 — to some at least — it looked full of promise. So rapidly did the new school win adherents that it doubtless seemed to many by the late 1950s that the advent of transformational grammar meant that Saussurean ideas had at last exhausted their usefulness, and a radically different era of linguistic theorizing had dawned.

From its inception, transformational-generative linguistics was based on a distinctly second-hand — if not third-hand — idea. Already in the nineteenth century, Boole had mathematicized logic. Subsequently Frege re-mathematicized it, by generalizing function-theory instead of algebra. The formal linguistics of the twentieth century was destined to follow — surprise, surprise — an exactly parallel course. Saussure's thinking about language owed nothing to this 'mathematical' tradition whatsoever, and was in spirit opposed rather than congenial to any unification of logical and linguistic formalism.

All the more remarkable is the fact that in less than ten years from the publication of *Syntactic Structures* a significantly altered and much more Saussurean theory of language was being proclaimed under the same 'transformational-generative' banner. This new version of transformational-generative linguistics drew a fundamental distinction between linguistic 'competence' and linguistic 'performance': furthermore the distinction was acknowledged as echoing Saussure's classic dichotomy between *langue* and *parole* (Chomsky, 1964: 62; Chomsky, 1965:4), and the 'generative grammar internalized by someone who has acquired a language' identified as the Saussurean *langue* (Chomsky, 1964: 52). It can hardly be dismissed as mere coincidence that the first English translation of the *Cours* was published in the U.S.A. in 1959, and that in the 1957 manifesto of transformationalism Saussure's name had not even appeared in a footnote. In other words, it took less than a decade (a mere hiccough in the history of linguistics) before we were 'all Saussureans again'. Needless to say, the recently discovered author of the *Cours* had to be castigated for failure to teach transformationalism *avant la lettre* (Chomsky, 1964: 59–60; Chomsky, 1965: 4); but, nevertheless, a reading of Saussure had evidently left its mark on the formulation of a doctrine which was to become as important in the linguistics of the 60s and 70s as Saussurean structuralism itself had been in the linguistics of the 20s and 30s.

References

Bloomfield, L. (1923) Review of Ferdinand de Saussure's 'Cours de linguistique général'. *Modern Language Journal* Vol. 8.
— (1935) *Language*. London.
Calvet, L. (1975) *Pour et contre Saussure*. Paris.
Chomsky, A. N. (1957) *Syntactic Structures*. The Hague.
— (1964) *Structure of Language*. Englewood Cliffs.
— (1965) *Aspects of the Theory of Syntax*. Cambridge, Mass.
Firth, J. R. (1950) Personality and language in society. *The Sociological Review* Vol. 42.
Frei, H. (1950) Saussure contre Saussure. *Cahiers Ferdinand de Saussure* Vol. 9.
Gardiner, A. H. (1932) *The Theory of Speech and Language*. Oxford.
Jespersen, O. (1922) *Language: Its Nature, Development and Origin*. London.
Joos, M. (ed.) (1957) *Readings in Linguistics I. The Development of Descriptive Linguistics in America* 1925–56. Chicago.
Mauro de T. (1972) *Edition critique du 'Cours de linguistique générale' de F. de Saussure*. Paris.
Ogden, C. K. and Richards, I. A. (1923) *The Meaning of Meaning*. London.
Sechehaye, A. (1940) Les trois linguistiques saussuriennes. *Vox Romanica* Vol. 5.
Spence, N. C. W. (1957) A hardy perennial: The problem of langue and parole. *Archivum Linguisticum* Vol. 9.

13 The Influence of Popular Fiction: An Oppositional Text

GEMMA MOSS

The concerns that English teachers bring to their reception of pupils' writing are both for the form of that writing — the rules which underpin its production — and for the relationship of that writing to its author — what it tells us about who they are. I could put this second point in another way. Our concern for the relationship between text and author is governed by our concern for the production of good people, something which is at least as rule-bound as the production of their work. We have rules about what it means to be a good person, alive to the sensitive business of living; rules about what it means to be a good feminist, ready to take up the challenges of patriarchy. Our personal concern for children is played out against a background of texts. We look for children to produce texts of the sort we promote as offering the best versions of themselves. Identity, reading, writing are all somehow intimately connected, tangled up in the versions of English teaching we most commonly employ.

I am not sure that we have got the connections right. What is the relationship between writing and the self? In what sense might we consider the author to be present in their own text (if at all)? What is the relationship between other texts, other readings, and children's own writing? The Leavisite, Media Studies and anti-sexist, anti-racist arguments propose that texts exert a powerful influence on writers both in the production of their own texts and in the way they live out their lives, and will inevitably do so without the application of critical skills which encourage distance from the text. Is this model right? Are we right to worry about girls so much and in particular to insist on the need for their full presence in the texts they read or write? Should we be more concerned about boys, and if so how could we show that concern without casting them as victims of the system in much the same way that we cast girls?

One way of beginning to answer these questions is to take a close look at some actual pieces of children's writing. This is what I propose to do now. All of the pieces I examined were written for me by members of my fourth-year CSE/O level group at various points during the year. They were homeworks, but neither the titles nor the content were either chosen or guided by me, nor did they stem from any work we were doing in class — they were free choice! I begin with a piece of work which derives much of its sense of shape and structure from popular fiction. It was written for homework by Angelique at the very beginning of the year that I taught her. In the following year, when I was no longer her English teacher, I interviewed her at length about her writing on three separate occasions and I will be quoting from those interviews later on. Angelique is Black, her school predominantly white.

In the reading of Angelique's text that follows my aim has been not only to mark the traces of familiar formulas as they appear in her work, but to examine how she uses these traces to shape her own meaning. It seems to me that the interest of the piece stems from the way in which Angelique puts her text together — a process of construction which relies not only on a knowledge of other texts, and their partial reproduction here, but also on her own experience and social knowledge. Within Angelique's writing these do not remain discrete categories but blur and melt into each other; in the process her own text establishes its own coherence. My reading seeks to re-create the coming into meaning of Anglique's text.

The piece is called 'Again!'

AGAIN!

'Why me though?', that's all I keep asking, why me? It all began when my mum had allowed me to go out of Bristol with a few friends, it wasn't usual but I ended up telling my mum what good friends I had and what they wouldn't do and what they would do (within reason of course!).

Anyway we took the train to London, Paul, Nick, Clare and me. It was hilarious on the train down. Nick and Clare had an arguement and Clare started throwing things at him. Paul and I walked out and Paul tried to get us a private apartment to get away from Nick and Clare but the man (him being a porter) said he didn't trust us, and wondered if we knew something of birth control. We just walked off into another carriage and sat down. Paul put his arm round me. I felt embarassed because an old woman kept staring. I shrugged him off, and kissed him when the lady had turned round.

'Wonder what Nick and Clare are up to?' said Paul looking closely.

'Probably tearing each others eyes out' I said. We both laughed.

At that Clare walked in. 'I wanna go home' she flopped on the seat next to the old woman. The old woman instantly walked out.

'Snobby bitch' remarked Clare.

'Oh Clare don't spoil the trip. We'll enjoy ourselves, we'll all go to the Fair' I said.

'Don't you two ever argue?' Clare said angrily.

'Well . . . course we do' I smiled.

'When?' Paul asked me.

'Well . . . loads of times' I said looking at him 'Why?'

'Nope, we've never argued' Paul said scratching his head, he pretended to be thinking.

'Yes we have Paul' I pinched him and gave him a 'Shut up' stare.

'Tell me when, then I'll shut up' Paul kissed me creeping around me slowly.

'Paul Richards and Angela Campbell give over' Clare butted in. We nearly got into a real fuss Paul and I did! Anyway, the rest of the journey is unimportant so I'll skip the rest.

We got off at Paddington.

Paul and I walked off into a café in London. It wasn't bad we had a sandwich and a coke we started talking about the arguement we had.

'Paul we have had arguments before.'

'I know but I just wanted her not feel . . . well . . . never mind!' He never finished his sentence and I was hurt and upset when I asked him to finish he told me not to nag.

'What was going on' I thought to myself.

Nick appeared on the scene stuffing his face with a jam doughnut Clare just sat beside him sipping an orangeade.

'Bloody stupid cow you deliberately spilled that on me' Nick turned to Clare. Clare had spilt her drink on Nicks trousers.

'You sod, calling me a cow'

'Well you are one, who do you think you are?' Nick took a serviette and wiped his trousers.

'Look shut up you two' I said 'people are looking'

'Let them bloody look' Paul took my hand and lead me out of the café.

We sat outside on the wall and kissed.

'I hope we don't ever fight like they do' I said holding his hand.

'Thought you said we didn't fight.'

'Well not recently' I argued.

'Yeah I know' Paul looked down.

I had been out with Paul before for two months but he left me and went out with Clare, yeah my friend, but we weren't friends then so it didn't matter much to me. I know I couldn't stand it happening again. Clare soon came out crying.

'Nick slapped me and he has finished with me' Paul instantly let go off my hand. He stroked Clare's cheek with his hand 'Did he hurt you?' Paul asked.

'Course he bleedin' did' Clare sniffed.

'Bastard' Paul said.

'Paul?' I saw the way he looked at her the way he touched her.

'Paul? It's not over again is it?'

'I still love you Ange, I don't want to hurt you again.'

'No Paul No, you can't love her again?' But it was too late. He held Clares hand and walked over to the café.

Clare let go of his hand and shook her head. She turned her back on Paul and kissed Nick lovingly. Paul walked slowly back. He saw me crying and he held my hand, I let go.

'I'm sorry Ange I didn't mean anything' Paul tried to kiss me.

'No, No I won't let your last kiss remain a memory like the first one you'll only hurt me again I couldn't bear it I loved you Paul' I laughed 'probably still do . . . but never Paul ever'.

Funny that evening, on the way home Paul and I sat apart, whilst Nick and Clare kissed.

★

'Why me though?' that's all I keep asking, why me?

The story opens with words spoken by the lead character, the narrator. It reminds me of the beginning of a photo-love story, with a close-up of the central character, establishing her mood through what she says. Angelique's story works on the same principles: the words spoken, a small action performed, focus my attention on the different characters. I can almost frame each separate picture:

At that Clare walked in. 'I wanna go home' she flopped on the seat next to the old woman.

The first phrase would become the text in the corner of the picture, what Clare says would appear in bubbles and the picture would show Clare sitting on the seat.

The old woman instantly walked out.

'Snobby bitch' remarked Clare.

The next picture would show Clare scowling as the woman leaves the carriage, the bubbles enclosing her remarks.

About the only passages which couldn't be packaged in this way are those which set the context of the story: the negotiations with Mum over whether the narrator can go up to London, and later on the information that Paul had once ditched the narrator for Clare. Each episode is self-contained, yet gains its full meaning by its relationship to the episodes which have gone before and follow after.

The narrator is obviously young — Angelique's own age. This is apparent in her relationship with her mum:

> my mum had allowed me to go out of Bristol with a few friends, it
> wasn't usual but I ended up telling my mum what good friends I had
> and what they wouldn't do and what they would do (within reason of
> course!).

This places the narrator as an adolescent, someone whose behaviour is of parental concern, who may be misled by friends into behaving irresponsibly; '(within reason of course!)' comments on the nature of the guarantees the narrator has given her mother and suggests both her independence and her acquiescence in her mother's concern.

I am continually reminded of the age of this group of friends throughout the story. Clare starts throwing things at Nick during an argument on the train journey down. This episode is preceded by the comment: 'It was hilarious on the train down.' The fight between Nick and Clare is not serious, therefore, just larking about. The friends are on their way to the Fair: '"We'll enjoy ourselves, we'll all go to the Fair" I said.' When they arrive in London they go to a café and have sandwiches, Coke, a doughnut and orangeade. These concerns and interests belong to childhood. Childhood, adolescence, both create different contexts in which to read the characters' actions.

Being young also means being at the receiving end of adult disapproval:

> the man (him being a porter) said he didn't trust us, and wondered if
> we knew something of birth control . . . an old woman kept staring

This sense of 'them and us' is part of a whole tradition of children's literature from *Just William* to *Grange Hill*. By tradition it can be a focus for stories. It is also part of Angelique's own experience, the stories she tells about herself. In her first interview with me she said:

> I wear my Dad's hats, and I wear shirts from my Dad's . . . My Mum thinks I'm weird, and she thinks there's something wrong with me, she thinks I'm a lesbian, or something . . . I think she's worried about me, you know. She thinks just because I wear my Dad's shirts or [laughs] something like that, there must be something wrong with me . . . I combed my hair like, um, once I combed my hair. Do you know Grace Jones?

Gemma: Yeah . . . oh yeah! [laughs]

Angelique: Oh, I'll never forget, I wouldn't never the risk that again . . . ever . . . just to avoid argument, I wouldn't ever do it again.

There are two points I want to make about this extract, both of which have a bearing on Angelique's text. First, her comments arose as part of a discussion about sexism and the way it stops girls doing what they want to do. For Angelique the conflict with her parents is about what she may do as a girl. Her mother disapproves of her wearing her dad's shirts because it seems to signify an 'abnormal' sexuality. Wearing shirts may be natural for a boy; it is not natural for a girl. So what Angelique has to do to gain approval depends on an adult view of gender-appropriate behaviour. Youth is subdivided into girls and boys. The process of conflict and its resolution between adults and young girls is part of the latter's construction as female within our (patriarchal) society.

This notion that being young and female presents specific problems not shared by boys is there in Angelique's own story. At the beginning the narrator's mother worries about what the narrator will do if she goes out for a day with her friends. As she is a girl, this means worrying about sex rather than violence. The incident with the porter highlights this. The porter doesn't trust Paul and the narrator on their own. He imagines the presence of a girl and a boy means that they will indulge in sexual behaviour inappropriate to the young (rather than that they will wreck the carriage). When Paul and the narrator sit down together,

> Paul put his arm round me. I felt embarassed because an old woman kept staring. I shrugged him off, and kissed him when the lady had turned round.

It is the narrator as a girl, not Paul, the boy, who feels nervous about revealing the nature of their relationship in public, who can kiss only when the old lady is not looking. For her to be seen to behave sexually is to run the risk of adult disapproval, to be labelled promiscuous, common, cheap. It is girls', not boys' sexuality which signifies in this way.

This leads me to my second point: the extent to which it is possible to challenge the adult order. The extract I have quoted from Angelique's interview shows her contesting the adult's view of appropriate (female) behaviour but also, if need be, compromising — on her Grace Jones hairstyle, in this instance. But giving in doesn't mean utter submission. In her second interview I asked her about the differences in the writing she produces in school and the writing she does for herself at home. She talked about the difficulties of writing in patois in school:

> I remember doing a thing on what I liked for English, for Mr H — and, it was writing about stories and what I've achieved. I wrote this story, and he said to me 'Well how will people like *me* be able to read that story' . . . you know [smiles] and that really got to me because the only way a person who wants to read patois, you must *know* a certain amount of it because how on earth can I go round starting to pick out the bits of patois and starting to try and abbreviate it cos it *is not*, it's not a foreign language it's just a slang . . . I felt really, really, mad about it . . . 'how would a person like me be able to understand that!' . . . I thought, well, there is one way a person like you could understand it, but I won't bother to write it down.

Holding back, not challenging the views of others, can be a way of escaping those views when you lack the power to challenge them directly.

Mixed in with the judgement by adults of young people's behaviour is the question of gender. Appropriate young female behaviour is different from young male behaviour. Angelique's text shows that she is aware of this. Within her story, how does the narrator, a girl, react to this sort of pressure on her behaviour? She concedes to the adult view and does nothing whilst the old lady is looking at her; as soon as she looks away, she kisses Paul. For the narrator, a girl, behaving as she wants to means finding a space in which do so, a space cleared of others' readings of her actions.

I began my analysis of this story by commenting on the similarities between the organisation of photo-love stories and Angelique's text in terms of the handling of dialogue and action. Photo-love stories take as their theme girl–boy relationships explored as romance. In Angelique's story the four friends are quickly established as two couples: 'Nick and Clare had an arguement . . . Paul and I walked out.' Once their names have been linked in this way I begin to read the story in the context of romance. I expect the friends' focus of interest to be particularised, to be centred on their partner, their loyalties not to be to the group as a whole but to their special friend. My expectations are fulfilled as the group splits up: 'Paul tried to get us a private apartment to get away from Nick and Clare . . .', Nick and Clare's argument is private, between them as a couple. Precluded from joining in, Paul and Angela go elsewhere.

> 'Wonder what Nick and Clare are up to?' said Paul looking closely.
> 'Probably tearing each others eyes out' I said. We both laughed.

Paul and Angela are sitting peacefully with each other. They can guess that Nick and Clare will still be arguing. Paul and Angela become the steady, loving couple; Nick and Clare the bickerers who can't stop rowing. Points of comparison are established. But the arrival of Clare on her own breaks up the structuring of the group of friends as two couples, for Angela's attention passes to Clare. She is fed up — '"I wanna go home"' — and Angela's response re-establishes the group identity: '"Oh Clare don't spoil the trip. We'll enjoy ourselves, we'll all go to the Fair".' Even if Clare is fed up with Nick, the day out need not be wasted; the friends can still have fun. Clare pushes the participants in the conversation back into their position as partners in a couple: '"Don't you two ever argue?" Clare said angrily.' Her question stresses the difference between Nick and Clare, Paul and Angela: the former arguing, moody, unhappy; the latter content, calm.

There are two ways of viewing this contrast. Not arguing can mean security, trust, a perfect match, the perfect couple, by whose measure the other couple appear dissatisfied, ill matched, likely to break up. Or the calmness of those who don't row can tip into placidity, contrasted with the strength of feeling, the anguish of true love. Angelique plays with both images and resolves them in her final sentence: 'Funny that evening, on the way home Paul and I sat apart whilst Nick and Clare kissed.' The perfect couple, the couple who seemed likely to succeed — that is, end the story with a secure relationship — have broken up. The question the romance story asks about its key characters, the boys and girls who encounter each other within it, is: how will their relationship work out? To work out well the relationship must end intact, its stability secured, but for the moment this remains a question hovering above the text, guiding my reading. At this point in the story other considerations are also at play.

I want to return to the exchange between Clare, Angela and Paul and examine the different ways in which the dialogue of these three characters positions them. Angela has talked about the friends as a group of young people; Clare has placed them as two couples. Angela's response to Clare's moody discontent with her own relationship is to help Clare out. In order to try to stop her feeling gloomy about the rows between her and Nick, she suggests that her own relationship with Paul is just the same:

'Don't you two ever argue?' Clare said angrily.

'Well . . . course we do' I smiled.

Angela refuses to accept the polarity on which Clare insists. She offers friendship and a sense of solidarity. What she does is determined by how Clare feels; her own allegiance to Paul takes second place.

Paul's response is different:

'Nope, we've never argued' Paul said scratching his head, he pretended to be thinking.

He is still playing the couples game, reminding Angela of their status as a couple and scoring off Clare by showing her that his relationship with Angela is better than hers with Nick. For Angela, accepting his response will mean exluding Clare. She is caught between contradictory obligations — to her friend, to her boyfriend:

> 'Yes we have Paul' I pinched him and gave him a 'Shut up' stare.
>
> 'Tell me when, then I'll shut up' Paul kissed me creeping around me slowly.

Being in a couple means negotiating for what she wants, in a tight space, a space defined by others.

Angelique, the story-teller, is quite clear that in her romances what the boys want and what the girls want is often different, and part of the function of her stories is to settle that conflict. In her third interview with me she said:

> I think in my stories I really want the boy to be understanding. You always get these blokes that go off and two-time you and all this sort of thing . . . every girl wouldn't want their boyfriends to do that . . . the people I know they're always telling me that their boyfriend did this, and my boyfriend's hitting me about . . . When I'm writing my stories I want everybody to know that if I have a boyfriend my boyfriend ain't going to hit me about. If anything I'm going to hit him about.

Being in a couple means struggling over power.

In Angelique's story the struggle between Paul and Angela begins when Paul refuses to understand what Angela is doing (protecting Clare). His lack of understanding and reluctance to talk about it leave her hurt:

> He never finished his sentence and I was hurt and upset when I asked him to finish he told me not to nag.
>
> 'What was going on' I thought to myself.

She is on her own. The story continually fluctuates over where she is: safely inside a couple, her partnership assured by a touch, a kiss:

> 'Let them bloody look' Paul took my hand and lead me out of the café. We sat outside on the wall and kissed;

made to feel uneasy by that relationship:

> I felt embarassed . . .
>
> I was hurt and upset . . .

part of a group of young people with allegiances to the group rather than a pair: '"We'll all go to the Fair".' Angelique's story uses the formation of the group of friends into two couples as a starting point to do more than ask the question: 'Which couple will succeed?' By focusing also on the conflicting demands of the boyfriend and friend, by juxtaposing the different aspects of the group of friends, she can raise questions about what being in a couple means.

So far, in thinking about the presentation of girl–boy relationships in Angelique's text, I have examined the way in which the group of friends has been subdivided into two couples, and shown that this configuration brings with it the expectation that the story will centre around the securing or undermining of these pairs of relationships: an expectation which Angelique's final sentence, with its sense of symmetry, acknowledges. I have gone on to show how elements in her story undercut this tight focus and leave a space for other issues to be raised. What about romance? How does this figure in her text? The romance works by foregrounding emotions. Does the heroine love the hero, will he love her? Will the heroine be happy, her feelings shared by her lover, whose kiss promises a future together — or will she end the story bereft of her loved one, lonely, incomplete, sad? Either way, the romance can be filled with turbulent emotions, emotions which threaten to swamp the actions which generate them. Every gesture can become a sign of deep feeling.

Angelique's text is curiously empty of romance at the beginning. Paul puts his arm round the narrator, or kisses her, but her attention is elsewhere — on the old lady staring, or on Clare and her feelings. The one point the text offers at which they could become more absorbed in each other is quickly passed over:

'Wonder what Nick and Clare are up to' said Paul looking closely.

The phrase 'looking closely' spoken by a boy to a girl suggests a moment of intimacy, a move towards a romantic encounter. But Angela's response:

'Probably tearing each others eyes out' I said. We both laughed.

refuses this overture and re-positions the exchange as a moment of child-like glee. Angela's relationship with Paul seems domestic. There is little sense of passion. She simply wants them to be comfortable and at ease with each other:

'I hope we don't ever fight like they do' I said holding his hand.

Things begin to change as the misunderstanding between Angela and Paul deepens. Suddenly inserted into the text is a brief reference to Angela's past history of involvement with Paul and Clare:

I had been out with Paul before for two months but he left me and went out with Clare, yeah my friend, but we weren't friends then so it didn't matter much to me. I know I couldn't stand it happening again.

Another way of reading what is going on emerges here. Paul has already finished his relationship with Angela once. Do their present conflicting interests presage another split, Angela to be left on her own, alone, unhappy? The reference to Clare sets up other echoes by reference to other texts. The girl whose best friend betrays her, seizing the boy, causing heartache: a story in which the establishment of a couple takes precedence over friendship, girls compete for the boy and destroy trust in each other. But it is an echo which the narrator summons up to dismiss: 'We weren't friends then so it didn't matter much to me.' Her own action earlier in protecting Clare stands. Nevertheless, the intensity of emotion with which Angela contemplates being on her own — 'I know I couldn't stand it happening again' — prepares the way for romance to enter the text. Romance reorientates my understanding of what the characters do. It offers me a new way of reading their actions as gestures become signs of deep feeling.

What is strange about this is that as romance enters, the coherence of the text itself begins to shake. Suddenly all sorts of question marks begin to hang over what is said. I find myself echoing Angela's 'What is going on?' Part of the answer lies in the way romance is introduced. It seems to sprawl in undigested chunks across the page. Precisely because there has been no preparation for this sort of outburst, its conventionalised nature stands out in high relief. Denaturalised, rendered painfully visible, it spins away from the narrative confines of the text that has gone before, refusing to be tied down by it, to stay in its place.

I want to examine this part of the text closely from the point where Clare comes out of the café:

Clare soon came out crying.

'Nick slapped me and he has finished with me'

The row in the café has moved from the childish resonance of just larking about to a lovers' quarrel. Clare is no longer sulky, she is upset, yet the words she uses to describe how her relationship with Nick has ended still carry the child's view with them.

Paul's response concludes the switching of gear, true entry into romance:

Paul instantly let go off my hand. He stroked Clare's cheek with his hand.

He caresses her, a gesture of intimacy and affection. It is also a gesture of exclusion: Angela stands outside this exchange with no role to play. Like

Angela in her response to Clare on the train, Paul gives priority to Clare, the outsider; but because of the language used to describe his movement the gesture is positioned by romance, not friendship, and so speaks of his own self-interest, his claim on Clare, his desire to relinquish Angela in her favour.

> 'Did he hurt you?' Paul asked.
>
> 'Course he bleedin' did' Clare sniffed.
>
> 'Bastard' Paul said.

Again there is a contrast in tone. Clare obstinately refuses to shift into romance. Her answer reminds me of her youth. Paul's tone is that of the avenging male about to do battle with his rival for the girl's favour. He asks about Nick, not about Clare:

> 'Paul?' I saw the way he looked at her the way he touched her.
>
> 'Paul? It's not over again is it?'

Angela confirms my interpretation of Paul's actions within the framework of romance. Her words could have come straight out of a popular song. I don't have to be told how Paul is looking at and touching Clare. His show of affection triggers off the appropriate response in Angela: pain and grief, two moves in a sequence which leads to the disintegration of a relationship. Yet the next exchange is puzzling:

> 'I still love you Ange, I don't want to hurt you again.'
>
> 'No Paul No, you can't love her again?'

Paul counters the narrator's view of his actions but his remarks are swept aside: the narrator is the disappointed lover in full voice and immediately after Paul's declaration of loyalty to her the text confirms her view of him: 'But it was too late. He held Clare's hand and walked over to the café.' This could provide a convenient stopping place for the text: girl loses boy to the other girl, a tradition in which the other girl stands accused of betrayal and the heroine must accept defeat with tears. Angelique refuses this ending:

> Clare let go of his hand and shook her head. She turned her back on Paul and kissed Nick lovingly.

Angela's friend refuses Paul's offer and seals her rejection of him by kissing Nick.

> Paul walked slowly back. He saw me crying and he held my hand, I let go.

What is Paul up to? Trying his luck where he can, as Angela and Clare imagine, or helping out a friend? This time it is Angela who removes her hand, distancing herself from him:

> 'I'm sorry Ange I didn't mean anything' Paul tried to kiss me.

His excuse will not do. The language of romance has found him out, and pinned him down as the fickle lover whose words cannot be trusted:

> 'No, No I won't let your last kiss remain a memory like the first one you'll only hurt me again I couldn't bear it I loved you Paul' I laughed 'probably still do . . . but never Paul ever.'

Paul's return to Angela makes sense if this is still a story about childhood sweethearts, young people out for the day to enjoy themselves as a group, when no one's relationship is serious. Why not then talk of love to Angela and hold another girl's hand, comforting her? The language of romance has displaced the action, moving it away from the sphere of carefree youth to the world of maturity, passion, heartache, jealousy. In this arena lovers who betray each other's trust cannot return. Paul's route back to Angela is barred by her outburst. It draws heavily on the genre of romance. The fact that its meaning is hard to follow, that its relationship to the events that have taken place is awkward rather than clear, that its own message and tone are contradictory, doesn't matter. What it does is take the position of disappointed lover and turn it into one of strength. Angela, who has been deserted by Paul, now pushes him away. She makes the choice, she will not have him. In Angelique's hands the romance and all its attendant clichés turn the text upside down, confound our expectations. She ends the story with her heroine sad, but in control; alone, but determined to be so.

To summarise, Angelique's story interweaves several different, often contradictory threads: youth, romance, couples, friends, each of which evoke their own stories, lying beyond the text. They refer outwards, whether to other stories told in books — a literary tradition — or to the stories she tells about herself: her own experience shaped with others', formed through language. Reading her particular story I catch the references; and the characters, their actions, twist and turn as I place them within different contexts. The text seems to me not so much settled and secure as making up its mind, playing one thread off against another, shifting its ground. What emerges is a sense of the confined space within which the heroine, as a girl, has to operate: a space crisscrossed by contradictory demands made on her as a friend, girlfriend, lover. This sense of claustrophobia is not shared by the other characters in the story. Clare says what she likes and refuses to be swayed by others into losing sight of her own feelings. She takes risks — '"You sod, calling me a cow"' — but does so primarily by remaining childlike, obstinately moody. Paul pays no attention except to what he wants — '"Let them bloody look"' — but his single-minded purpose is selfish; he cannot be trusted to do anything except follow his own whims. Where does that leave those who care for him?

The juxtaposition of these varying approaches leaves Angelique's text uncertain. It is not the monolithic reproduction of a given order, a unitary whole, but fragmentary. It raises questions about what it might mean to leave childhood behind, to grow into womanhood and enter into relationships with men. On whose terms could this, should this, take place? What is at stake?

Angelique wrote several romances for me during the year I taught her. [. . .] Although different in tone and setting, all her romances shared certain features. First, in all of them the girl ends up rejecting the boy — there are no happily-ever-afters; nor does the girl watch the boy walk out on her: she pushes him. Second, the boys themselves are not the focus for an unconditional surrender to the emotions on the part of the narrator — a common feature of the romance. There is always something about them that renders them ultimately untrustworthy and provides the motive for the girl to disentangle herself. Third, it is easy to read all these stories as if the narrator were white. Part of this is inevitably the effect of my reading rather than the text itself. For me (a white woman in a white culture) to read them otherwise, something in the setting or the language would have to mark the presence of Blackness. Unmarked, constructed within a form (romance) which I am familiar with, which brings with it images of whiteness, my expectations generate a cast of white characters. Yet this was not a feature of Angelique's writing as a whole. Increasingly during the year she brought in pieces of writing she was doing for herself at home, where the characters were explicitly Black and much of the language was patois. Why the difference in the romances she wrote for school? How far was she aware of the difference in her own writing? What do these differences suggest?

Angelique talked to me at length about her writing in the three interviews I did with her in the fifth year and it is to these interviews that I now want to turn. What quickly becomes clear from the transcripts is that here is someone who has thought hard about what being Black and female means, how it affects her own life. Answering my questions meant reminding herself of debates she had already had, as well as reflecting on them afresh:

> When it comes to the discussion on women, I always find myself getting annoyed because, I talk with my mother about this sort of thing and she seems to think a woman's place is in the home . . . having to cook, clean and that sort of thing.

She introduced the question of race before I did. Explaining why her favourite programmes on television were 'No Problem' and 'Front Line', she said:

> I think it's just because it's lots of Black people acting. You hardly see any Black actors . . . on the tele.

Gemma: Well, I was going to ask you about that, because when you were talking about the books . . . quite a lot of the books that you're talking about have got Black heroines . . . and I wondered if that was important for you, in terms of your choice of book.

Angelique: I think the reason I choose so many books by Black authors is because of the school I'm in. There's hardly, I have never seen anyone in this school pick up a book, no one has ever done Black history in this school, so I look it out for myself . . . If I was probably in a . . . in a Black school, where there was a high majority of Black, I probably wouldn't take much notice of it . . . — but — I think — once I'm in this school — and once no one ain't going to teach me it — then I'll look for it myself.

She is confident in what she has to say, and articulate. I asked her whether being Black or being female was more important to her, and she was quite clear on her answer: 'I would say one's more important than the other and that is because of being Black.'

How does this picture of Angelique as someone aware of the problems of racism and sexism square with her writing, and what does it have to say about the status of her romances? Angelique accepts that her romances are peopled with white characters and that to say this is to say something significant: 'when you write about a white person, a Black person, it's a completely different thing.' Pinning that difference down, explaining it to me in words, was difficult and I didn't always help to make the process easier. I raised the question in my first interview and we pursued it in the second and the third sessions. I'll try to bring together what Angelique said.

The sort of writing she does is dependent on the context within which it is produced. The first pieces of work she showed me which centred on Black characters were written at home primarily for herself, although this distinction blurred during the year that I taught her, and Black characters began to emerge in her school work. One of her reasons for not introducing explicitly Black characters in her school work is the reception she expects:

I just know that if I start writing patois on a piece of paper, one of the teachers will come up to me and say 'What does this mean, what does that mean?' [. . .] I suppose it's normal 'cos they don't understand it, but I can't write patois in English because it's not patois.

In the teacher's eyes patois becomes incorrect use of English, but to make it correct, conform to the standard, would mean losing the flavour of the language, the very reason why she's included it.

Writing for herself at home means writing without constraints:

When I write in my own stories I can just write what I want, you know, write patois, the Jamaican things . . . and I can write anything I want even if it's not about Jamaica I can write something. Let the pen just run loose, you know, and really get across what I'm feeling on the book. In school you have to cut that down to a certain amount.

Even when race is on the agenda at school, talking about it means being careful, remembering her audience, not getting too annoyed: 'We talk about it in school, we talk about it in English, but, if I get too carried away, I have to control myself slightly.'

Writing for herself means being able to let go and re-create the Black world she left behind when her family moved out from the inner city to the white suburbs:

> When I left St Werburghs, I was really heartbroken because living on the street I lived on you could hear a West Indian mother opening the door and telling her son to get off the street because there's a car coming. You could smell the West Indian food cooking, the noise, you could hear a boy down the road playing his stereo unit from inside the house and that sort of thing. All those I really missed. I tell you I really missed them . . . and listening to a bunch of Jamaicans talk . . . specially the men when they get going. It's beautiful. When I moved up to Kingswood all that went. At first I didn't worry about it, nothing like that, but I started watching tele programmes like 'No Problem' and things like that and I really realised how much I missed it and I read the *Gleaner*, and that sort of thing and so I thought, well, I don't have it up here, I don't have that sort of thing at Kingswood, so I can *make* it happen so I started the stories and it brought it alive.

Her sources for this sort of writing are her own knowledge of the Black community and the stories they tell about themselves, and she is conscious that these ways of telling are specific to that community. Explaining a particular scene in one of her Black stories called 'Ebony and Ivory' where the mother can't bring herself to talk openly to her daughter, Angelique said:

> I think when it comes to talking love, romance, sex . . . between an old-fashioned Jamaican parent, it's very difficult because they've been taught, when they were younger, that that's a no-no word, sex.

She went on to illustrate this point by recounting an anecdote about her mother and grandmother. It is this sense of cultural difference which explains why her romances centre around white characters: 'I feel, I *do* feel, that Black people and white people act differently when it comes to romances.' Her knowledge of how people behave in romances does not tally with her knowledge of the Black community:

> They find it hard to express, Jamaicans anyway they find, most of them find it really hard to show loving, love and emotion. Its sort of like . . . you know . . . Jamaicans are supposed to be

strong, tough, the guys anyway . . . you know . . . they told you . . .

Gemma: I was wondering if that's what you mean when you say love, whether really what you're talking about is in a sense romantic love, yeah!

Angelique: Yeah! Roman, romance, yeah!

Gemma: It's like . . .

Angelique: They're like that, they do, I mean . . .

Gemma: . . . being gentle.

Angelique: Yeah and gentle and kind. That sort of thing's not . . . it's not . . . the sort of thing . . .

Gemma: . . . the sort of thing . . .

Angelique: that they sort of like *do*, you know . . .

This sense of a difference in style is then picked up on and expanded by her in a story she told about her aunt who, whilst shouting at her son that he certainly couldn't have a bracelet she was wearing, was taking the bracelet off and giving it to him: 'That's our way of saying I, oh, I want to give it to you my love, . . . my son.'

The register of romance finds different expression in the Black community, whilst Angelique's acquaintance with the former has been made through reading books which deal exclusively with white characters. This affects her writing: 'I've never once read a Black romance . . . so I tend to write the stories as I have read in books.' To position herself in a romance story, she also has to position herself as white: 'Usually when I'm writing a romance, a story, it's usually just me, but playing a white character, d'you know what I mean?'

The books on which she models such writing are exclusively white and have little bearing on Black culture. To write a romance, therefore, she 'plays' a white part. She followed up that comment by drawing a distinction between writing about Black and white characters:

If I'm going to write something that's got to do with Black people then I'm really going to prepare it first, I mean I *think* about when I'm going to write something to do with a Black person yet when I'm writing something to do with a white person I just write it.

At this point in the interview I was confused. In a previous session she had talked about writing for herself at home as straightforward, easy compared to the constraints of writing in school: 'I thought I'm going to make it, so I wrote it out, do it, be how I feel.' Now she was talking about the ease of writing with a white voice, playing a white role.

Gemma: What I'm wondering is, when you say, when you're writing as a white person you just write, that would leave me, doesn't that mean you're writing more as you?

Angelique: Well, yeah, I suppose it does really but, I can't explain it really. I suppose when I'm writing as a white person . . . it's more enough, I really just, it's all the books I've read. I've never read in my whole life really a Black romance. There's hardly any ones that I know actually. And so the ones I have read I tend to just write, sort of like copy in other words what they've written into my own type of words. I just write. With a Black romance there are certain things that you've got to get right.

The genre proposes white characters. To take the genre on board is to accept its setting. Alter the setting and she would have to alter the characterisation, the romance's exploration of events, its conventions. Yet it is these conventions she wants to explore — not, I would argue, at the expense of exploring her identity as Black, but alongside it. The simple reason for this is that the romance is the most obvious space in which to examine girl–boy relationships. This is one of the main reasons why feminists dislike it. Support for this view comes from the way in which Angelique talks about her own romance writing. She has thought carefully about what she is doing and is involved in what she is writing. She consistently talks about the narrator-heroines in the first person:

> the girl, I end up saying, 'cos it's like me really the way I think I would act . . . I end up saying 'Well you shouldn't have come running back to me should you' really sarcastic but knowing in my heart that probably I would really want this guy back.

But being involved doesn't just mean taking on board everything the convention has to offer. She is critical of the form, both in what it has to say about girls —

> I cannot, I hate reading a story where the girl's all 'Ahh', the Cinderella type of thing. It really annoys me because it's so stupid. That is the reason why we have so many stereotypes about women

— and the image it creates of boys:

> with the man with the most black hair and blue eyes, the irresistible blue eyes, the one with the blue eyes is supposed to be heartless and cold and the woman with the brown eyes is nice and warm, that sort of thing, it's really rubbish.

Instead, she works within the conventions to establish her own meanings: 'When I'm writing a story to me the girl has always got to be a strong character.'

The problems girls encounter with boys in her stories are not to do with whether they have a boyfriend or not but on whose terms the relationship will be conducted, and here she places control in the hands of the girl:

> If [the boys] start . . . not being the way I want them to be in my stories, in my romance like they're begging me to come back to them, that sort of thing [smiles] I say '*No!* I'm not going' and all this sort of thing and walk off.

It is the boys who have to put up with being powerless, cajole the girl into staying within the relationship, and ultimately they lose. She punctures the smooth and attractive pose in which they're presented in the magazines:

> I done a description of Steve's room, page three all over the place, money thrown down where he's come home from work, his YTS scheme [. . .] his room looks a complete state . . . that sort of thing, when I read a magazine all you see is . . . hmmm . . . well dressed, suit, nice tie, you know the sort of things that they write about, really rubbish [laughs].

To this extent she has adapted the romance genre to her own purposes. However, as I've already shown, this doesn't leave her free to do anything she wants. There are constraints, amongst them the question of how to end her stories. Romance offers two possibilities for closure: happy — the girl gets the boy of her dreams; or sad — she is left on her own. Either way the resolution is beyond the girl's control. It just happens, and it is final. Angelique's preoccupations, in particular with the wresting of control from the boy, fit uneasily within this format:

> I don't think there really is an ending in any of my stories.

She comes to a temporary resting place: temporary because the solution is fragile, open to continuing negotiation.

> the last story I wrote, that Steve one, um, they ended up breaking up and him coming back to her and saying 'Oh will you please' and she's saying 'No, it's not worth it because you're only going to do the same thing to me again!'
>
> That's the sort of thing it is and then I pick it up again, if I feel like writing another story, sometimes we go out with each other again, sometimes we just don't bother . . . it's not worth it.

It is difficult to reconcile her conflicting desires: wanting the boy and yet not wanting to be dominated by him, used by him.

> I end up saying 'Well you shouldn't have come running back to me should you' really sarcastic, but knowing in my heart that probably I would really want this guy back.

The endings in her own stories are uneasy. They do not conform to the stark distinction drawn in romance (happy/sad) — the point they have reached is more subtle. But to think about them in terms other than those proposed by romance is hard.

> It was just the sort of ending where she was going to go off and find another boyfriend and at the time, *now* when you think about all this business about women being stereotyped and all this, *now* I think of it as a woman going off and having her own independence without a male tying her down, but then, I didn't think of it that way.

Gemma: Did it seem to you when you wrote it as a happy or a sad ending then?

Angelique: Sad ending, I think, well not sad ending but just that she wouldn't have Steve.

I have been attempting to map out in my account of Angelique and her writing a far more complex interaction between the writer and her text than the customary arguments about popular culture and popular fiction allow for. Angelique's writing cannot be understood in terms of entirely passive consumers hopelessly trapped and subdued by an all-powerful popular fiction, relentlessly undermining their perception of the real world. Angelique's romance writing is about modification, adaptation, transformation of the genre within which she is working. Her text exploits the contradictory ways of reading offered by her sources to open up new spaces and to pose her own questions about identity, emotion, power. If it is not the seamless text, the unitary whole which the argument about popular fiction assumes, the same holds true if her writing is viewed by the standards of good literature. I want to argue that it is precisely here, in its fragmentation, that its strength lies.

All this implies freedom for the writer. There are also constraints. Angelique's interview points to what is excluded in her writing for school, the difficulties of writing about herself as Black within that institution. The agenda of the romance is for her a partial one. But in saying this one further point must be borne in mind. She is very aware of her identity as a Black girl. Even without the pressures of the institution within which she writes, where would she look for a genre which addresses itself to both these issues? Her politics must take her into two separate camps. Whilst this may not be ideal, it is an inevitable result of writing within the culture in which she is placed and from which she must draw.

14 Encoding/Decoding[1]

STUART HALL

Traditionally, mass-communications research has conceptualized the process of communication in terms of a circulation circuit or loop. This model has been criticized for its linearity — sender/message/receiver — for its concentration on the level of message exchange and for the absence of a structured conception of the different moments as a complex structure of relations. But it is also possible (and useful) to think of this process in terms of a structure produced and sustained through the articulation of linked but distinctive moments — production, circulation, distribution/consumption, reproduction. This would be to think of the process as a 'complex structure in dominance', sustained through the articulation of connected practices, each of which, however, retains its distinctiveness and has its own specific modality, its own forms and conditions of existence. This second approach, homologous to that which forms the skeleton of commodity production offered in Marx's *Grundrisse* and in *Capital*, has the added advantage of bringing out more sharply how a continuous circuit — production–distribution–production — can be sustained through a 'passage of forms'. It also highlights the specificity of the forms in which the product of the process 'appears' in each moment, and thus what distinguishes discursive 'production' from other types of production in our society and in modern media systems.

The 'object' of these practices is meanings and messages in the form of sign-vehicles of a specific kind organized, like any form of communication or language, through the operation of codes within the syntagmatic chain of a discourse. The apparatuses, relations and practices of production thus issue, at a certain moment (the moment of 'production/circulation') in the form of symbolic vehicles constituted within the rules of 'language'. It is in this discursive form that the circulation of the 'product' takes place. The process thus requires, at the production end, its material instruments — its 'means' — as well as its own sets of social (production) relations — the organization and combination of practices within media apparatuses. But it is in the *discursive* form that the circulation of the product takes place, as well as its distribution to different audiences. Once accomplished, the discourse must then be translated — transformed, again — into social practices if the circuit

200

is to be both completed and effective. If no 'meaning' is taken, there can be no 'consumption'. If the meaning is not articulated in practice, it has no effect. The value of this approach is that while each of the moments, in articulation, is necessary to the circuit as a whole, no one moment can fully guarantee the next moment with which it is articulated. Since each has its specific modality and conditions of existence, each can constitute its own break or interruption of the 'passage of forms' on whose continuity the flow of effective production (that is, 'reproduction') depends.

Thus while in no way wanting to limit research to 'following only those leads which emerge from content analysis' (Halloran, 1973), we must recognize that the discursive form of the message has a privileged position in the communicative exchange (from the viewpoint of circulation), and that the moments of 'encoding' and 'decoding', though only 'relatively autonomous' in relation to the communicative process as a whole, are *determinate* moments. A 'raw' historical event cannot, *in that form*, be transmitted by, say, a television newscast. Events can only be signified within the aural-visual forms of the televisual discourse. In the moment when a historical event passes under the sign of discourse, it is subject to all the complex formal 'rules' by which language signifies. To put it paradoxically, the event must become a 'story' before it can become a *communicative event*. In that moment the formal sub-rules of discourse are 'in dominance', without, of course, subordinating out of existence the historical event so signified, the social relations in which the rules are set to work or the social and political consequences of the event having been signified in this way. The 'message form' is the necessary 'form of appearance' of the event in its passage from source to receiver. Thus the transposition into and out of the 'message form' (or the mode of symbolic exchange) is not a random 'moment', which we can take up or ignore at our convenience. The 'message form' is a determinate moment; though, at another level, it comprises the surface movements of the communications system only and requires, at another stage, to be integrated into the social relations of the communication process as a whole, of which it forms only a part.

From this general perspective, we may crudely characterize the television communicative process as follows. The institutional structures of broadcasting, with their practices and networks of production, their organized relations and technical infrastructures, are required to produce a programme. Using the analogy of *Capital*, this is the 'labour process' in the discursive mode. Production, here, constructs the message. In one sense, then, the circuit begins here. Of course, the production process is not without its 'discursive' aspect: it, too, is framed throughout by meanings and ideas: knowledge-in-use concerning the routines of production, historically defined technical skills, professional ideologies, institutional knowledge, definitions and assumptions, assumptions about the audience and so on frame the constitution of the programme through this production structure. Further, though the production structures of television originate the television discourse, they do not constitute a closed system. They draw topics, treatments, agendas, events, personnel, images of the audience, 'definitions of the situation' from other sources and other discursive formations within the wider socio-cultural and political structure of which they are a differentiated part. Philip Elliott has expressed this point succinctly, within a more traditional framework, in his discussion of the way in which the audience is both the 'source' and the 'receiver' of the television message. Thus — to borrow Marx's terms — circulation and reception are, indeed, 'moments' of the production process in television and are reincorporated, via a number of skewed and structured 'feedbacks', into the production process itself. The consumption or reception of the television message is thus also itself a 'moment' of the production process in its larger sense, though the latter is 'predominant' because it is the 'point of departure for the realization' of the message. Production and reception of the television message are not, therefore, identical, but they are related: they are differentiated moments within the totality formed by the social relations of the communicative process as a whole.

At a certain point, however, the broadcasting structures must yield encoded messages in the form of a meaningful discourse. The institution-societal relations of production must pass under the discursive rules of language for its product to be 'realized'. This initiates a further differentiated moment, in which the formal rules of discourse and language are in dominance. Before this message can have an 'effect' (however defined), satisfy a 'need' or be put to a 'use', it must first be appropriated as a meaningful discourse and be meaningfully decoded. It is this set of decoded meanings which 'have an effect', influence, entertain, instruct or persuade, with very complex perceptual, cognitive, emotional, ideological or behavioural consequences. In a 'determinate' moment the structure employs a code and yields a 'message': at another determinate moment the 'message', via its decodings, issues into the structure of social practices. We are now fully aware that this re-entry into the practices of audience reception and 'use' cannot be understood in simple behavioural terms. The typical processes identified in positivistic research on isolated elements — effects, uses, 'gratifications' — are themselves framed by structures of understanding, as well as being produced by social and economic relations, which shape their 'realization' at the reception end of the chain and which permit the meanings signified in the discourse to be transposed into practice or consciousness (to acquire social use value or political effectivity).

Clearly, what we have labelled in the diagram 'meaning structures 1' and 'meaning structures 2' may not be the same. They do not constitute an 'immediate identity'. The codes of encoding and decoding may not be perfectly symmetrical. The degrees of symmetry — that is, the degrees of 'under-

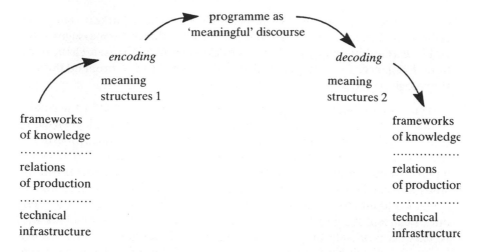

standing' and 'misunderstanding' in the communicative exchange — depend on the degrees of symmetry/asymmetry (relations of equivalence) established between the positions of the 'personifications', encoder-producer and decoder-receiver. But this in turn depends on the degrees of identity/non-identity between the codes which perfectly or imperfectly transmit, interrupt or systematically distort what has been transmitted. The lack of fit between the codes has a great deal to do with the structural differences of relation and position between broadcasters and audiences, but it also has something to do with the asymmetry between the codes of 'source' and 'receiver' at the moment of transformation into and out of the discursive form. What are called 'distortions' or 'misunderstandings' arise precisely from the *lack of equivalence* between the two sides in the communicative exchange. Once again, this defines the 'relative autonomy', but 'determinateness', of the entry and exit of the message in its discursive moments.

The application of this rudimentary paradigm has already begun to transform our understanding of the older term, television 'content'. We are just beginning to see how it might also transform our understanding of audience reception, 'reading' and response as well. Beginnings and endings have been announced in communications research before, so we must be cautious. But there seems some ground for thinking that a new and exciting phase in so-called audience research, of a quite new kind, may be opening up. At either end of the communicative chain the use of the semiotic paradigm promises to dispel the lingering behaviourism which has dogged mass-media research for so long, especially in its approach to content. Though we know the television programme is not a behavioural input, like a tap on the knee cap, it seems to have been almost impossible for traditional researchers to conceptualize the communicative process without lapsing into one or other variant of low-flying behaviourism. We know, as Gerbner has remarked, that representations of violence on the TV screen 'are not violence but messages about violence' (Gerbner *et al.*, 1970): but we have continued to research the question of violence, for example, as if we were unable to comprehend this epistemological distinction.

The televisual sign is a complex one. It is itself constituted by the combination of two types of discourse, visual and aural. Moreover, it is an iconic sign, in Pierce's terminology, because 'it possesses some of the properties of the thing represented' (Pierce, 1931). This is a point which has led to a great deal of confusion and has provided the site of intense controversy in the study of visual language. Since the visual discourse translates a three-dimensional world into two-dimensional planes, it cannot, of course, *be* the referent or concept it signifies. The dog in the film can bark but it cannot bite! Reality exists outside language, but it is constantly mediated by and through language: and what we can know and say has to be produced in and through discourse. Discursive 'knowledge' is the product not of the transparent representation of the 'real' in language but of the articulation of language on real relations and conditions. Thus there is no intelligible discourse without the operation of a code. Iconic signs are therefore coded signs too — even if the codes here work differently from those of other signs. There is no degree zero in language. Naturalism and 'realism' — the apparent fidelity of the representation to the thing or concept represented — is the result, the effect, of a certain specific articulation of language on the 'real'. It is the result of a discursive practice.

Certain codes may, of course, be so widely distributed in a specific language community or culture, and be learned at so early an age, that they appear not to be constructed — the effect of an articulation between sign and referent — but to be 'naturally' given. Simple visual signs appear to have achieved a 'near-universality' in this sense: though evidence remains that even apparently 'natural' visual codes are culture-specific. However, this does not mean that no codes have intervened; rather, that the codes have been profoundly *naturalized*. The operation of naturalized codes reveals not the transparency and 'naturalness' of language but the depth, the habituation and the near-universality of the codes in use. They produce apparently 'natural' recognitions. This has the (ideological) effect of concealing the practices of coding which are present. But we must not be fooled by appearances. Actually, what naturalized codes demonstrate is the degree of habituation produced when there is a fundamental alignment and reciprocity — an achieved equivalence — between the encoding and decoding sides of an exchange of meanings. The functioning of the codes on the decoding side will frequently assume the status of naturalized perceptions. This leads us to think that the visual sign for 'cow' actually *is* (rather than *represents*) the animal, cow. But if we think of the visual representation of a cow in a manual on animal husbandry — and, even more, of the linguistic sign 'cow' — we can see that both, in different degrees, are *arbitrary* with respect to the concept of the animal they represent. The articulation of an arbitrary sign — whether visual or verbal — with the concept of a referent is the product not of nature but of convention, and the conventionalism of discourses requires the intervention, the support, of codes. Thus Eco has argued that iconic signs 'look like objects in the real world because they reproduce the conditions (that is, the codes) of perception in the viewer' (Eco, n.d.). These 'conditions of perception' are, however, the result of a highly coded, even if virtually unconscious, set of operations — decodings. This is as true of the photographic or televisual image as it is of any other sign. Iconic signs are, however, particularly vulnerable to being 'read' as natural because visual codes of perception are very widely distributed and because this type of sign is less arbitrary than a linguistic sign: the linguistic sign, 'cow' possess *none* of the properties of the thing represented, whereas the visual sign appears to possess *some* of those properties.

This may help us to clarify a confusion in current linguistic theory and to define precisely how some key terms are being used in this article. Linguistic theory frequently employs the distinction 'denotation' and 'connotation'. The term 'denotation' is widely equated with the literal meaning of a sign: because this literal meaning is almost universally recognized, especially when visual discourse is being employed, 'denotation' has often been confused with a literal transcription of 'reality' in language — and thus with a 'natural sign', one produced without the intervention of a code. 'Connotation', on the other hand, is employed simply to refer to less fixed and therefore more conventionalized and changeable, associative meanings, which clearly vary from instance to instance and therefore must depend on the intervention of codes.

We do *not* use the distinction — denotation/connotation — in this way. From our point of view, the distinction is an *analytic* one only. It is useful, in analysis, to be able to apply a rough rule of thumb which distinguishes those aspects of a sign which appear to be taken, in any language community at any point in time, as its 'literal' meaning (denotation) from the more associative meanings for the sign which it is possible to generate (connotation). But analytic distinctions must not be confused with distinctions in the real world. There will be very few instances in which signs organised in a discourse signify *only* their 'literal' (that is, near-universally consensualized) meaning. In actual discourse most signs will combine both the denotative and the connotative *aspects* (as redefined above). It may, then, be asked why we retain the distinction at all. It is largely a matter of analytic value. It is because signs appear to acquire their full ideological value — appear to be open to articulation with wider ideological discourses and meanings — at the level of their 'associative' meanings (that is, at the connotative level) — for here 'meanings' are *not* apparently fixed in natural perception (that is, they are not fully naturalized), and their fluidity of meaning and association can be more fully exploited and transformed. So it is at the connotative *level* of the sign that situational ideologies alter and transform signification. At this level we can see more clearly the active intervention of ideologies in and on discourse: here, the sign is open to new accentuations and, in Volosinov's terms, enters fully into the struggle over meanings — the class struggle in language. This does not mean that the denotative or 'literal' meaning is outside ideology. Indeed, we could say that its ideological value is strongly *fixed* — because it has become so fully universal and 'natural'. The terms 'denotation' and 'connotation', then, are merely useful analytic tools for distinguishing, in particular contexts, between not the presence/absence of ideology in language but the different levels at which ideologies and discourses intersect.

The level of connotation of the visual sign, of its contextual reference and positioning in different discursive fields of meaning and association, is the point where *already coded* signs intersect with the deep semantic codes of a culture and take on additional, more active ideological dimensions. We might take an example from advertising discourse. Here, too, there is no 'purely denotative', and certainly no 'natural', representation. Every visual sign in advertising connotes a quality, situation, value or inference, which is present as an implication or implied meaning, depending on the connotational positioning. In Barthes's example, the sweater always signifies a 'warm garment' (denotation) and thus the activity/value of 'keeping warm'. but it is also possible, at its more connotative levels, to signify 'the coming of winter' or 'a cold day'. And, in the specialized sub-codes of fashion, sweater may also connote a fashionable style of *haute couture* or, alternatively, an informal style of dress. But set against the right visual background and positioned by the romantic sub-code, it may connote 'long autumn walk in the woods' (Barthes, 1971). Codes of this order clearly contract relations for the sign with the wider universe of ideologies in a society. These codes are the means by which power and ideology are made to signify in particular discourses. They refer signs to the 'maps of meaning' into which any culture is classified; and those 'maps of social reality' have the whole range of social meanings, practices, and usages, power and interest 'written in' to them. The connotative levels of signifiers, Barthes remarked, 'have a close communication with culture, knowledge, history and it is through them, so to speak, that the environmental world invades the linguistic and semantic system. They are, if you like, the fragments of ideology' (Barthes, 1967).

The so-called denotative *level* of the televisual sign is fixed by certain, very complex (but limited or 'closed') codes. But its connotative *level*, though also bounded, is more open, subject to more active *transformations*, which exploit its polysemic values. Any such already constituted sign is potentially transformable into more than one connotative configuration. Polysemy must not, however, be confused with pluralism. Connotative codes are *not* equal among themselves. Any society/culture tends, with varying degrees of closure, to impose its classifications of the social and cultural and political world. These constitute a *dominant cultural order*, though it is neither univocal nor uncontested. This question of the 'structure of discourses in dominance' is a crucial point. The different areas of social life appear to be mapped out into discursive domains, hierarchically organized into *dominant or preferred meanings*. New, problematic or troubling events, which breach our expectancies and run counter to our 'common-sense constructs', to our 'taken-for-granted' knowledge of social structures, must be assigned to their discursive domains before they can be said to 'make sense'. The most common way of 'mapping' them is to assign the new to some domain or other of the existing 'maps of problematic social reality'. We say *dominant*, not 'determined', because it is always possible to order, classify, assign and decode an event within more than one 'mapping'. But we say 'dominant' because there exists a pattern of 'preferred readings'; and these both have the institutional/political/ideological order imprinted in them and have themselves become institutionalized. The domains of 'preferred meanings' have the whole social order embedded in them as a set of meanings, practices and beliefs: the everyday knowledge of social structures, of 'how things work for all practical purposes in this culture', the rank order of power and interest and the structure of legitimations, limits and sanctions. Thus to clarify a 'misunderstanding' at the connotative level, we must refer, *through* the codes, to the orders of social life, of economic and political power and of ideology. Further, since these mappings are 'structured in dominance' but not closed, the communicative process consists not in the unproblematic assignment of every visual item to its given position within a set of prearranged codes, but of *performative rules* — rules of competence and use, of logics-in-use — which seek actively to *enforce* or *pre-fer* one semantic domain over another and rule items into and out of their appropriate meaning-sets. Formal semiology has too often neglected this practice of *interpretative work*, though this constitutes, in fact, the real relations of broadcast practices in television.

In speaking of *dominant meanings*, then, we are not talking about a one-sided process which governs how all events will be signified. It consists of the 'work' required to enforce, win plausibility for and command as legitimate a *decoding* of the event within the limit of dominant definitions in which it has been connotatively signified. Terni has remarked:

> By the word *reading* we mean not only the capacity to identify and decode a certain number of signs, but also the subjective capacity to put them into a creative relation between themselves and with other signs: a capacity which is, by itself, the condition for a complete awareness of one's total environment. (Terni, 1973)

Our quarrel here is with the notion of 'subjective capacity', as if the referent of a televisional discourse were an objective fact but the interpretative level were an individualized and private matter. Quite the opposite seems to be the case. The televisual practice takes 'objective' (that is, systemic) responsibility precisely for the relations which disparate signs contract with one another in any discursive instance, and thus continually rearranges, delimits and prescribes into what 'awareness of one's total environment' these items are arranged.

This brings us to the question of misunderstandings. Television producers who find their message 'failing to get across' are frequently concerned to straighten out the kinks in the communication chain, thus facilitating the 'effectiveness' of their communication. Much research which claims the objectivity of 'policy-oriented analysis' reproduces this administrative goal by attempting to discover how much of a message the audience recalls and to improve the extent of understanding. No doubt misunderstandings of a literal kind do exist. The viewer does not know the terms employed, cannot follow the complex logic of argument or exposition, is unfamiliar with the language, finds the concepts too alien or difficult or is foxed by the expository narrative. But more often broadcasters are concerned that the audience has failed to take the meanings as they — the broadcasters — intended. What they really mean to say is that viewers are not operating within the 'dominant' or 'preferred' code. Their ideal is 'perfectly transparent communication'. Instead, what they have to confront is 'systematically distorted communication'.

In recent years discrepancies of this kind have usually been explained by reference to 'selective perception'. This is the door via which a residual pluralism evades the compulsions of a highly structured, asymmetrical and non-equivalent process. Of course, there will always be private, individual, variant readings. But 'selective perception' is almost never as selective, random or privatized as the concept suggests. The patterns exhibit, across individual variants, significant clusterings. Any new approach to audience studies will therefore have to begin with a critique of 'selective perception' theory.

It was argued earlier that since there is no necessary correspondence between encoding and decoding, the former can attempt to 'pre-fer' but cannot prescribe or guarantee the latter, which has its own conditions of existence. Unless they are wildly aberrant, encoding will have the effect of constructing some of the limits and parameters within which decodings will operate. If there were no limits, audiences could simply read whatever they liked into any message. No doubt some total misunderstandings of this kind do exist. But the vast range must contain *some* degree of reciprocity between encoding and decoding moments, otherwise we could not speak of an effective communicative exchange at all. Nevertheless, this 'correspondence' is not given but constructed. It is not 'natural' but the product of an articulation between two distinct moments. And the former cannot determine or guarantee, in a simple sense, which decoding codes will be employed. Otherwise communication would be a perfectly equivalent circuit, and every message would be an instance of 'perfectly transparent communication'. We must think, then, of the variant articulations in which encoding/decoding can be combined. To elaborate on this, we offer a hypothetical analysis of some possible decoding positions, in order to reinforce the point of 'no necessary correspondence'.

We identify *three* hypothetical positions from which decodings of a televisual discourse may be constructed. These need to be empirically tested and refined. But the argument that decodings do not follow inevitably from encodings, that they are not identical, reinforces the argument of 'no necessary correspondence'. It also helps to deconstruct the common-sense meaning of 'misunderstanding' in terms of a theory of 'systematically distorted communication'.

The first hypothetical position is that of the *dominant-hegemonic position*. When the viewer takes the connoted meaning from, say, a television newscast or current affairs programme full and straight, and decodes the message in terms of the reference code in which it has been encoded, we might say that the viewer is *operating inside the dominant code*. This is the ideal-typical case of 'perfectly transparent communication' — or as close as we are likely to come to it 'for all practical purposes'. Within this we can distinguish the positions produced by the *professional code*. This is the position (produced by what we perhaps ought to identify as the operation of a 'meta-code') which the professional broadcasters assume when encoding a message which has *already* been signified in a hegemonic manner. The professional code is 'relatively independent' of the dominant code, in that it applies criteria and transformational operations of its own, especially those of a technico-practical nature. The professional code, however, operates *within* the 'hegemony' of the dominant code. Indeed, it serves to reproduce the dominant definitions precisely by bracketing their hegemonic quality and operating instead with displaced professional codings which foreground such apparently neutral-technical questions as visual quality, news and presentational values, televisual quality, 'professionalism' and so on. The hegemonic interpretations of, say, the politics of Northern Ireland, or the Chilean *coup* or the Industrial Relations Bill are principally generated by political and military elites: the particular choice of presentational occasions and formats, the selection of personnel, the choice of images, the staging of debates are selected and combined through the operation of the professional code. How the broadcasting professionals are able *both* to operate with 'relatively autonomous' codes of their own *and* to act in such a way as to reproduce (not without contradiction) the hegemonic signification of events is a complex matter which cannot be further spelled out here. It must suffice to say that the professionals are linked with the defining elites not only by the institutional position of broadcasting itself as an 'ideological apparatus' (see Althusser, 1971), but also by the structure of *access* (that is, the systematic 'over-accessing' of selective elite personnel and their 'definition of the situation' in television). It may even be said that the professional codes serve to reproduce hegemonic definitions specifically by *not overtly* biasing their operations in a dominant direction: ideological reproduction therefore takes place here inadvertently, unconsciously, 'behind men's backs'. Of course, conflicts, contradictions and even misunderstandings regularly arise between the dominant and the professional significations and their signifying agencies.

The second position we would identify is that of the *negotiated code* or position. Majority audiences probably understand quite adequately what has been dominantly defined and professionally signified. The dominant definitions, however, are hegemonic precisely because they represent definitions of situations and events which are 'in dominance' (*global*). Dominant definitions connect events, implicitly or explicitly, to grand totalizations, to the great syntagmatic views-of-the-world: they take 'large views' of issues: they relate events to the 'national interest' or to the level of geo-politics, even if they make these connections in truncated, inverted or mystified ways. The definition of a hegemonic viewpoint is (a) that it defines within its terms the mental horizon, the universe, of possible meanings, of a whole sector of relations in a society or culture; and (b) that it carries with it the stamp of legitimacy — it appears coterminous with what is 'natural', 'inevitable', 'taken for granted' about the social order. Decoding within the *negotiated version* contains a mixture of adaptive and oppositional elements: it acknowledges the legitimacy of the hegemonic definitions to make the grand significations (abstract), while, at a more restricted, situational (situated) level, it makes it own ground rules — it operates with exceptions to the rule. It accords the privileged position to the dominant definitions of events while reserving the right to make a more negotiated application to 'local conditions', to its own more *corporate* positions. This negotiated version of the dominant ideology is thus shot through with contradictions, though these are only on certain occasions brought to full visibility. Negotiated codes operate through what we might call particular or situated logics: and these logics are sustained by their differential and unequal relation to the discourses and logics of power. The simplest example of a negotiated code is that which governs the response of a worker to the notion of an Industrial Relations Bill limiting the right to strike or to arguments for a wages freeze. At the level of the 'national interest' economic debate the decoder may adopt the hegemonic definition, agreeing that 'we must all pay ourselves less in order to combat inflation'. This, however, may have little or no relation to his/her willingness to go on strike for better pay and conditions or to oppose the Industrial Relations Bill at the level of shop-floor or union organization. We suspect that the great majority of so-called 'misunderstandings' arise from the contradictions and disjunctures between hegemonic-dominant encodings and negotiated-corporate decodings. It is just these mismatches in the levels which most provoke defining elites and professionals to identify a 'failure in communications'.

Finally, it is possible for a viewer perfectly to understand both the literal and the connotative inflection given by a discourse but to decode the message in a *globally* contrary way. He/she detotalizes the message in the preferred code in order to retotalize the message within some alternative framework of reference. This is the case of the viewer who listens to a debate on the need to limit wages but 'reads' every mention of the 'national interest' as 'class interest'. He/she is operating with what we must call an *oppositional code*. One of the most significant political moments (they also coincide with crisis points within the broadcasting organizations themselves, for obvious reasons) is the point when events which are normally signified and decoded in a negotiated way begin to be given an oppositional reading. Here the 'politics of signification' — the struggle in discourse — is joined.

Notes

1. This article is an edited extract from 'Encoding and Decoding in Television Discourse', CCCS Stencilled Paper No. 7.

References

Eco, U. (n.d.) Articulations of the cinematic code. *Cinemantics* No. 1.
Gerbner *et al.* (1970) *Violence in TV Drama: A Study of Trends and Symbolic Functions.* Philadelphia: University of Pennsylviania.
Halloran, J. D. (1973) Understanding Television. Paper for the Council of Europe Colloquy on 'Understanding Television'. University of Leicester.
Pierce, C. (1931) Speculative Grammar. In *Collected Papers*. Cambridge, MA: Harvard University Press.

15 Double Talk in News Broadcasts: A Cross-Cultural Comparison of Pictures and Texts in Television News

ULRIKE H. MEINHOF

Media research has a long and productive history in this country. Research has usually focused on one of three aspects: the producers or the production process, the responders/readers or viewers and their conditions of reception, and the texts, the actual media product. In terms of academic disciplines, media research involves sociologists, linguists, semioticians, to name but a few. But there is increasingly an interest in bringing together these three foci in a unified, dynamic, interactive model.

In the introduction to this paper I want to briefly analyze developments in discourse analysis especially in relation to the changing role which the readers/viewers are given in responding to texts. This will mean moving from purely text-internal readings, where readers are theorized as decoders of fixed meanings to more dynamic models, where meanings are negotiated by actively participating readers. In the main part of the paper I want to explore such a dynamic model of discourse comprehension in relation to one particular genre of discourse, television news broadcast, with examples from England and West Germany. In the conclusion I will sketch some of the pedagogic implications which arise from such an analysis of the comprehension process.

Changing Roles of Texts and Readers

In the first section I want to explore how text and news analysis have changed by moving from a notion of closed texts to one of open texts; and

212

how readers have changed from being text-based subjects to complex actively participating viewers.

Text-based/closed text models

Common to what I want to call 'closed text models'[1] is their placing the meaning of the communication in the text itself. The text encodes meanings which readers decode. In a more ideological formulation: the text has the power to impose its reading upon viewers.

From the many different text-based models in text analysis I want to briefly mention three very influential ideological approaches, which are central to the debate within media studies and semiotics.

- *Content analysis* (cf. Glasgow University Media Group: 1976, 1980): Ideology is seen as encoded in the content of the text. Analysis concentrates on topics and themes, the representation of opinions, who is given a voice, who is excluded.

- *Early sociosemiotic analysis* (cf. Fowler, Kress, Hodge & Trew, 1979): Ideology is seen as encoded in the form of the text. Analysis concentrates on linguistic forms and transformations, such as the study of transitivity structures; active/passive transformations; modality and so on.

- *Screen theory* (cf. McCabe, 1986; Heath, 1977): Comprises a critique of realism which, it is argued, dissolves the contradictions which viewers ought to feel. (For an excellent summary see Fiske, 1987: Chap. 3)

In these models, as in one of my own papers on press representations of subversive women (Meinhof, 1986), readers/viewers are either not specifically addressed or, as in Screen theory, seen as 'text-based' subjects; that is, as reading subjects constructed by the text.

Reader-based models

Reader-based models, in contrast to the above, tend to operate with a more open version of what the text means. Here the difference between a postulated 'inscribed' reader and the real reader becomes crucial. There is no difference from the point of view of analysis between an 'inscribed reader' (Volosinov, 1973) and textual strategies, which encode a preferred reading. These strategies are open to different forms of textual analysis. Real readers, in contrast, are living people; social beings with different backgrounds, different contexts in which they read or view the texts. The allowance for a discrepancy between inscribed readers and real readers shifts the analysis away from fixed meanings in closed texts which the readers extract or decode to a multiplicity of actual responses '. . . Text-as-meaning is produced at the moment of reading, not at the moment of writing . . . (this) takes away from that text the status of being the originator of that meaning' (Fiske, 1987: 305).

How are such more open text models realized in news analysis?

- *Ethnography of viewing*: Studies observe and analyze viewers' actual responses (Morley, 1980, 1986; Palmer, 1986; Lewis, 1985), and in some instances show discrepancies between encoding and decoding processes.

- *Postulating a discrepancy* between 'preferred readings' (dominant ideology), the 'inscribed readers or addressees', and actual readers (social beings). This makes allowances for deviant and/or subversive readings (cf. Barthes, 1975; Hall *et al.*, 1980).

Reading the News

The larger context of this paper is how one might theorize and study the interrelation between textual strategies, or inscribed readers, and actual readers. The opening up of a text by incorporating viewer response requires a different theorizing of the relationship between all components in a communicative situation: viewers/readers — text — contextual features of text productions including the authors — contextual features of text reception: it requires a very active, dynamic model where texts become multi-accentuated or 'polysemic' (cf. Volosinov, 1973; Bahktin, 1981).

Opening of text at level of production

News texts are the result of different processes of production, which are not usually transparent to the viewer. To give a few of the most obvious examples: there are basically three types of news formats: the studio announcements and readings by the newscaster, the film on the scene with the reporter present, and the news film taken on the scene of the event with a voice-over. From the viewer's point of view, there is a clear difference in style and presentation between the studio film, on the one hand, and the filming on the scene with or without a reporter present. But from the point of production techniques and exercise of control over the news broadcast, there is a highly significant difference between film produced on location by the news teams themselves where they exercise control over filming and text; and film which is bought in from one of the international news agencies, which is later on texted in the studio (cf. Burger, 1984 for a more detailed analysis). This difference is largely obscured to the viewer, but is, of course, important for the relationship between pictures and text, allowing for a whole range of interconnections between the various agents involved in the creation of the news item.

Opening the text at the level of reception

In responding to news texts we respond to different interrelations between different modes of representations: visual (pictorial, written), and oral.

Comprehension is influenced by inferences which readers make between modes to arrive at an interpretation of what is going on. We are not usually aware of the sources of our information, and whether it is in response to the pictures or the text.[2] Inferences depend on culture-specific knowledge, much of it highly conventionalized and activated by home viewers in a largely automatic and intuitive way. Viewers possess and apply different types of knowledge in responding, beginning with an understanding of what constitutes the genre of TV news in their culture. Whether we are watching a news broadcast, a party political broadcast, an advert, or something like Crimewatch, depends on generic knowledge which we build up from experience. (In Panama, for example, the news used to be accompanied by music which built up in drama depending on the item.)

To understand the sophisticated inferences which viewers make in order to comprehend any news item, we must find ways of describing the interplay between viewers and the news broadcast. Since each news item on TV is doubly encoded, i.e. through a visual and an oral channel, close attention has to be given to the relationship between these in any one news item. At this point in news analysis we are far from sure whether viewers respond to the visual and the oral channel in an equally balanced way, whether certain channels dominate, or how individual preferences and differences in the context of viewing might affect any such balance. It would, for example, be feasible to hypothesize that the referential function, or, in Hallidayan terms (Halliday, 1978) the *ideational* function of a news item is more fully realized in the verbal part of the news text, whereas the interpersonal function might dominate in the visual. This would provide us with a temptingly neat division:

- *news text:* field-dominated — emphasizes information about the event

- *news film:* tenor-dominated — appeals to attitudes and feelings about the event.

However, although one can find plenty of examples from the news which could back up such an analysis, this does not allow for the dynamic interplay between channels with which viewers in my experience arrive at single representations of a news item. There is considerable scope for empirical work.

Defining the object of study

So how can we approach the interplay between the different channels which viewers respond to simultaneously as they watch an item on TV news? From a sociosemiotic perspective we can begin by isolating the following three action components in a news item and see how they are realized in the pictures and in the text of the news item:

- *the actors:* originators, causes of actions, or events;
- *the activities or events;*
- *the affected, the effect, or outcome.*

By studying how text and picture relate to these components independently, we can first of all clarify the sophisticated inferences which viewers must make if they are to form a single representation of a news item. These relations may help to reveal preferred readings, i.e. textual strategies which invite the viewer to form a particular ideological response and possible contradictions between them. We may also be able to show the spaces for dispreferred readings, spaces for the viewers to disrupt.

Relating pictures and text

In my study of German and English news films I identified three types of interrelations between text and picture, which I want to describe under the headings of overlap, displacement, and dichotomy.

- *Overlap:* The film footage and the text share the same action component. Examples: Text and film both refer to the Prime Minister or to the victims of a disaster. The relationship between text and picture may be direct or metonymic, as in a flag or map representing a country. Overlap is typical for studio announcements, for the opening of the news story. Different conventions, such as the showing of pictures, graphs, or headlines next to the newsreader act as advance notifiers for viewers. But overlap also occurs in films. Pictures show the actors (for example in 1998 the East German citizens crossing the border of Hungary), the text describes who they are; why they are leaving for the West, etc.

- *Displacement:* Film footage and text represent different action components of the same event. Example: The text reports the causes, the film shows the effects of an event. There are obvious cases such as disasters, where the filming must, by definition, follow the event itself. The text will announce that an earthquake has happened, the pictures will show the effect of the disaster.

  More interestingly for an ideological analysis are those, where displacement is not the inevitable result of having to film after the event has taken place. News reports about strikes are very interesting in this respect. In the English news report about the summer 1988 strike by the Spanish air traffic controllers, the text talked about the strikers and the strike (actors and activities), the pictures showed the suffering masses at Gatwick airport (the effect). In terms of balance between cause and effect, there was an over-representation of the effect, and an under-representation of actors, their grievances, their reasons for striking. Not all strike items are represented with a technique of displacement. Contrast in the same year the reporting of the striking Polish steel workers, which produced an overlap between text and pictures. When strike and striking workers were referred to in the text, the film camera stayed right in the middle of the striking workers, leading up to interviews with them, and questions about their reasons for striking. In these representations, the effect of the strike on, for example, the Polish economy was under-represented.

• *Dichotomy:* Film footage and text represent action components of different events. Example: the text reports an event/the film shows unrelated images filmed on the location of the event. Dichotomy is very typical for news film bought in from a news agency, and later texted in the studio.

In news reports of the withdrawal of Soviet troops from Afghanistan in January 1989, the text on the German satellite news programme *Blick* (Sat 1) described the situation in Kabul as under the threat of collapse adding comments about an acute food shortage there. The pictures, however, showed an unrelated street scene from Kabul.

Similarly, in a report of the Nicaraguan president Ortega visiting the FRG, the Sat 1 news film showed a state visit at the highest diplomatic level. The text talked about a begging tour, discussed Ortega's combat uniform as a sign of the desperate struggle for his survival. The follow-up explanation of why Nicaragua has such economic problems, which mentioned Reagan's support for the Contras as a key factor, was under-laid by films of Nicaraguan street scenes, where women were buying vegetables and similar such scenes, and not, for example, by pictures of Contras in armed combat or training.

The viewers' response

How do viewers respond to such doubly-encoded presentations, where the action component of the text and the action component of the picture are divergent? Viewers must make inferences across the channels to combine the different action components to a single representation of the news item. By articulating these and raising them to the level of consciousness, we can see the influence which text and picture exercise on each other to invite a preferred reading of the particular time, and, at the same time, the gaps and contradictions which stop news texts from achieving a clear, monolithic message.

To return to the example of Afghanistan. One of my students had chosen this item about the Soviet troop withdrawal from Afghanistan from the German satellite programme Sat 1 (31/1/89) for a seminar the next day. On a computer program which I am developing for the purposes of news comprehension and analysis, Interactive News[3] I had prepared a transcription of the text on one half of the screen, and my own description of the film footage on the other.

Below is a translation of part of that transcript:

Afghanistan: the rapid withdrawal 31/1/89

Text	Picture
(1) The Soviet troops in Afghanistan will presumably be leaving the country by the end of this week. This was announced by Western diplomats in I. According to the Geneva agreement, the Soviets have to withdraw their troops by the 15th of February.	Studio report.
(2) Blue skies and sunshine in Kabul. After heavy snowfalls, the airport was reopened today. Immediately, the Soviet transport planes resumed their flights. They took the troops back to the SU, and returned to Kabul carrying food supplies.	Film: Airplane ascending into blue-sky. Close-up of airplane.
(3) The Afghan capital is about to collapse. The troops of the resistance fighters have closed in on the city even more tightly.	Street scene of Kabul. Men & children in front of small shops. A water carrier.
Kabul can only be given food supplies via the air.	Man with a water canister on the back of his bike.

As you can see from the transcription, the film in the sequence 'Afghanistan 3' showed a street scene in Kabul, a picture of a water carrier, followed by a picture of a man on a bike with a water-canister on his back. Since the text spoke of food shortage, I thought that the image of the man with his water-canister added to the general sense of a deep crisis in Kabul. In the seminar the next day, the students reported that they had seen the same footage on the BBC news the previous evening, and that the canister on the bike contained petrol and not water. Of course, as we could easily check, the content of this canister was not mentioned in either news programme. But because of the spoken context in which the image of the man on the bike appeared, we made different inferences about its content. The German news spoke of a food shortage in Kabul, the English news of a petrol shortage. Of course, it is not particularly significant which it was, petrol or water, and we will never know. In any case, an anthropologist told me later, that (a) the people of Kabul always move water about in canisters, even when there isn't a crisis, and (b) that it is quite possible that petrol would be transported in these water canisters at a time of shortage (Brian Street, personal communication). But what does matter, is that the source of the information, whether it was petrol or water that needed to be transported, and one's sense of the gravity of the crisis, was partly a result of our/the viewers' inferences *across* visual and oral channels.

Is it then not a contradiction to deny that this particular text carries its meaning? Clearly a preferred reading of this news item has to be Kabul in crisis. But there is a difference between an analysis which positions the meaning of the canister in the news text itself, as a signal of either water or petrol shortage, with the viewer as the passive recipient of that news message, and a more open analysis which emphasizes the various possible responses which viewers can have because of different inferences across channels. A 'dispreferred' reading would, for example, take the street scene of Kabul as no more than any ordinary street scene in Afghanistan, and possibly resist the interpretation of an extreme crisis, or at least question it on the basis of the visual information. How flexible the images themselves are can be appreciated if one compares more recent pictures of the same kind of street scene in Kabul which are now taken as indications of a Kabul which is resisting the rebels.

Thus similar footage on the BBC and German Sat 1 — a street scene in Kabul — can represent different accounts of the situation there: first a difference in urgency, from Kabul is under threat, to Kabul is about to fall; then a turn-around in interpretation: Kabul is successfully resisting the rebels.

Similarly, news about government reaction to the student demonstrations in China in Spring 1989 re-interpreted the same kind of visual information within the space of a few days: pictures of tanks continuing to roll into the city centre of Beijing was interpreted on a Tuesday on German Satellite news as a sign of an impending civil war. On Thursday, two days later, the almost identical footage was made to represent the end of the democracy movement, and the firm control of Deng Xiaoping over the army.

So what are the sources for the various readings and responses? I do not wish to deny textual strategies which can be seen to encourage preferred readings. The question one could ask is: do we see the pictures we are told to see, as in the Afghanistan example? Or, in contrast, do the pictures tell the real story by giving us the feeling of immediacy, influencing our attitudes, and adding those to a seemingly neutral text (as in the example of the striking air traffic controllers, where the viewer's attention was directed to the unfortunate air travellers stranded at Gatwick airport)?

I want to argue that it is neither of these, but a dynamic between these multiple representations and the viewers. Because the news item is not 'just there' but has to be activated by the viewers, a whole range of different responses is feasible. It is not possible to close off the text in either of the above mentioned directions. The possibilities for different and/or dispreferred responses arise from differences amongst the viewers themselves, and therefore depend on a multitude of factors, such as their discrepant knowledges and abilities, their willingness to make inferences across channels, and their level of involvement with the item. There are also differences in responses amongst viewers because of differences in what they are doing at the time, i.e. differences because of context of viewing. Viewers have many options (see also Hodge & Kress, 1988: 51) and many mixed ways of responding to and receiving texts. This includes the power to refuse and disrupt, have a conversation, make fun, comment, disagree, not to pay attention, and switch off.

A sociosemiotic study of text and pictures as separate action components allows us to analyse the preferred readings, such as those mentioned in the case of the two strikes. Overlap between text and pictures in the case of the Polish steel workers showed a clear empathy with the position of the striking workers, displacement in the case of the Spanish air-traffic controllers removed the empathy from the strikers and onto the affected. But we cannot restrict our analysis to text-internal features — the relationship between viewers and texts have also to be taken into account. This includes the contextual features of news productions and the authoring of these productions, as well as the contextual features of news reception. Thus, by incorporating the relationship between all the participants in a communicative situation, we are not identifying the preferred reading with the multiple meanings which texts have for viewers. The text becomes a 'meaning potential', to borrow Halliday's expression (Halliday, 1978), whose meaning is realized in a variety of (potentially conflictual) readings.

Summary of the news analysis

Openness at the level of production implies that there is not a singular monolithic text, but that meaning is affected by different interactions between the various producing agents of a news feature. The methodology for analysis is an investigation of this interaction and a refusal of realism as a criterion for why features are filmed and texted in the way they are. The text can thus never be closed, because there are too many constraints and contradictions in the construction of the text and the interplay between text and pictures. Although it is possible to read off a preferred reading by analysing textual strategies which favour a particular reception, the meaning cannot be singular.

Openness at the level of reception implies that there is not a single receptive audience manipulated by single monolithic texts, but socially situated people with their different knowledges. Therefore no text is more than a meaning potential; a preferred reading is only one of many possible other readings, and no audience is just a receptacle for a given set of messages. Instead, due to the factors just described, there are multiple realizations of the meaning of a text, which in turn depend on the viewers' motivation and ability to rapidly and intuitively draw inferences across visual and oral channels. Viewers must actively create their own texts by responding to a sophisticated interplay of visual and oral stimuli, they must be willing and able to activate their previous knowledge and engage with the broadcast. This kind of response can be consciously refused by viewers, it can be not given unintentionally because of the context of viewing or a lack of knowledge; preferred readings can be consciously subverted or unintentionally not received. (For a discussion of why a large number of viewers do not recall news items see Lewis, 1987.)

Teaching With and About the News

What pedagogic questions does this analysis of the comprehension process raise for using television news either in mother tongue or in foreign language teaching?

Within one's own cultural context, an analysis like the one I just presented, should help to clarify the interplay between news production, channels of news texts, the news, and the viewers with their different presuppositions and habits, and create a metalanguage for analysing the news. This will improve the comprehensibility of a broadcast and allow a more efficient viewing; but at the same time by making the textual strategies more transparent, it will strengthen the viewers' resistance to possible preferred readings and thus empower them to reject and/or subvert these readings.

To viewers outside the cultural circle and in a foreign language, much more attention must be given to the knowledge types involved in comprehending such culture-bound texts as news broadcast. TV news conventions presuppose a vast amount of cultural knowledge in their readers, as anyone knows who has seen news abroad, or tried to use news films for foreign language teaching. TV news is specifically geared to a home audience. Viewers must know the conventions; they must be able to distinguish between what is an advert, what is news, what is a party political broadcast. They must know the length, the patterning of items. News schemata, such as disaster events, strikes, elections, etc. structure our comprehension and our expectations. Apart from structural and schematic knowledge, viewers must bring to the news knowledge about the content, i.e. culture-specific world knowledge. This is more than just recognizing the people shown on the screen, but implies a whole perspective of how we interpret the rest of the world. Together, these knowledge types enable us to anticipate the news texts themselves, to tune in to what is likely to come. By understanding the comprehension strategies which native speakers intuitively employ on the basis of their cultural presuppositions, and their world knowledge, including their ability to form single representations from simultaneously received pictures and texts, we can help to understand the sources for misunderstanding which arise for viewers outside the intended circle of addressees.

Helping the foreign learner to develop comprehension strategies includes a conscious building up of metalinguistic and contextual knowledge. As I have explained elsewhere, this is not only an effective way of teaching about a culture, it is also a highly efficient comprehension strategy for difficult texts in print or on TV (cf. Meinhof, 1987, 1990).

Helping viewers to come to terms with a difficult type of discourse such as the news does not imply that the burden is entirely on the viewers. As Lewis has cogently argued, the producers of TV news would be well advised to note the kinds of meanings which viewers do construct, and the discrepancies between the encoding and decoding processes (Lewis, 1985). More participation by the viewers can be encouraged not only by giving viewers insights into metalinguistic processes, but also by asking producers to take note of concrete comprehension problems which viewers do experience for some of the reasons I set out in this paper.

Notes

1. With the terms 'open' and 'closed' I am borrowing the terminology of Eco (1981). My own usage differs from Eco's in that I am restricting the terms to different ways of interpreting meanings in texts. Eco, on the other hand, characterizes particular narratives as open or closed, depending on the range of interpretative proposals which the text validates (Eco, 1981: 33). Crudely put, his aim is to interpret the texts, mine is to analyse the methods used for the interpretation and the analysis of texts.
2. See also Lewis (1985) reporting on the disparate responses of viewers to the question of who is the 'author' of an opinion in news reporting.
3. Interactive News is a new support facility which I am developing on the basis of Hypercard on an Apple Macintosh SE and a linear video-cassette-recorder. Aimed at first and second language learners at schools and universities, IN integrates the teaching of a language with the teaching of cultural topics and of a metalanguage for analysing texts. It combines the facilities of a cognitive support tool for comprehending off-air TV news programmes with a system for annotating these programmes and for building up a resource bank of linguistic and cultural data. For a detailed description see Meinhof (1990). The project is supported by a research grant from the British Association of Applied Linguistics (BAAL) and the educational division of Apple Macintosh, UK.

References

Bahktin, M. (1981) *The Dialogic Imagination*. Austin: Texas University Press.
Barthes, R. (1975) *S/Z*. London: Cape.

Burger, H. (1984) *Die Sprache der Massenmedien*. Berlin: de Gruyter.
Drummond, P. and Paterson, R. (1985) *Television in Transition*. London: BFI.
Eco, U. (1981) *The Role of the Reader*. London: Hutchinson.
Fiske, J. (1987) *Television Culture*. London: Methuen.
Fowler, R. *et al.* (eds) (1979) *Language and Control*. London: Routledge.
Glasgow University Media Group (1976) *Bad News*. London: Routledge.
— (1980) *More Bad News*. London: Routledge.
Hall, S. *et al.* (eds) (1980) *Culture, Media, Language*. London: Hutchinson.
Halliday, M. A. K. (1978) *Language as Social Semiotic*. London: Arnold.
Heath, S. and Skirrow, G. (1977) Television: A world in action. *Screen* 18, 2.
Hodge, R. and Kress, G. (1988) *Social Semiotic*. Cambridge: Polity Press.
Lewis, J. (1985) Decoding television news. In P. Drummond and R. Paterson.
McCabe, J. (1986) (ed.) *High Culture/Low Culture*. Manchester: Manchester University Press.
Meinhof, U. H. (1986) Revolting women: Subversion and its media representation. In S. Reynolds (ed.) *Women, State and Revolution*. Brighton: Wheatsheaf.
— (1987) Predicting texts. In T. Bloor and J. Norrish (eds) *Written Language (British Papers in Applied Linguistics 2)*. BAAL/CILT.
— (1990) Television news, the computer, and foreign language teaching. In S. Anivan (ed.) *Language Methodology for the Nineties. RELC Anthology*, 24. Singapore University Press.
Morley, D. (1980) *The 'Nationwide' Audience*. London: BFI.
— (1986) *Family Television: Cultural Power and Domestic Leisure*. London: Comedian.
Palmer (1986) *The Lively Audience: A Study of Children Around the TV Set*. Sydney: Allen & Unwin.
Volosinov, V. (1973) *Marxism and the Philosophy of Language*. New York: Seminar Press.

16 The Lively Audience

PATRICIA PALMER

The word 'passive', when applied to children's television viewing has never been meant as a compliment, either to children or to the television they watch. It is also a misleading description of the way children watch TV. The impetus for the present study of children and television came from a growing recognition by researchers that children's relationship with TV was more complex and interesting than earlier studies seemed to indicate. At the beginning, three questions were asked to define the purpose of the research and give direction to its progress.

(1) How do children define and discuss television content?

(2) What do children do when they watch television?

(3) What part does television play in relationships with friends and family, in games and activities?

Palmer (1986) presents a full analysis and discussion of the different features of children's television viewing. These are summarised below to give a concise picture of the nature of television viewing for children, based on this research project.

Definition

Children define 'television' in terms of those regularly appearing programs which they enjoy most. Viewing for children is associated with fun, excitement and finding out about the world. Television also gives structure to the day. It is something to look forward to and, for children with little to do, it fills in spare time. Programs which children don't like are usually ignored, though children use strong language to criticise them when asked. Advertisements do not feature in children's talk about television.

Children's favourite programs depend on their physical and social maturity, as defined by their age and sex. Girls and boys, divided further into 8–9-year-olds and 11–12-year-olds, described qualitites of favourite shows which were consistent with those of their own groups and different in some respects from those of other groups. Children's TV experience is therefore not the same. What they seek and what they enjoy from television is very different even within the age range used for this study.

Adaptation

Television is an important part of most children's lives. They have even created a special environment for themselves around the TV where they can watch in relaxed comfort and feel involved in what is happening on the screen. For some children, pets are a part of this TV space. The placement of the television is important in providing a social and physical environment for children's viewing. Most children still watch TV in a public and shared space in the family home. Access to the television also conveys to children a sense of their own significance within the family.

Observations of children show them to be manipulators of the set. They enjoy switching it on and playing with it. They are confident and able in adjusting the set to find their programs, but they rarely switch it off.

Children have adapted themselves to the presence of television in many ways. However, television is also made to fit in with other interests. Children describe television in relation to other family routines. A wide range of activities are also carried out in the vicinity of TV, to the extent that sometimes TV provides a 'background' to family life.

Interaction

While they watch TV, children are not usually still and silent for long. Their television behaviour varies according to the program content, their company while viewing, the usual routines of the family and their own particular viewing style.

From observations, eleven different kinds of 'interaction' have been described for children. These forms of interaction varied in the extent to which children were attentive to the screen. At their least attentive, children 'monitored' programs by sight or sound while they spent most of their time on some other activity. Some behaviours were clearly 'interactive' because children expressed events from TV programs in their own words or actions. Other forms of interaction were inferred from children's body posture and physical orientation to the set.

The range of interactions was for some children very wide. Their behaviour during a short spell of viewing would include periods of intent viewing punctuated by expressive behaviour such as performance of TV jingles or discussion of information with whoever viewed with them. Other children had a characteristic pattern of interaction which involved intent viewing of their favourite programs and distraction during commercials.

No single pattern of interactions could be said to be 'typical' of children's television viewing.

Review

With friends, children do most of their talk and acting out from TV. It is also likely that friends will agree about the programs they enjoy most. Talk about television with friends is part of a daily routine. It is common for children to discuss favourite shows at school the morning after they are broadcast, and to arrange which movies they will watch in the evening. TV talk also provides an important basis of shared experience for children. Because of its social function of maintaining group cohesiveness, friends are rarely critical of each other's favourite programs in their conversations.

Talk sometimes leads to the acting out of parts of programs to share the 'best bits' or to fill in the story for friends who miss the show. One group of girls in the study regularly acted out sections from their favourite shows. To do this, they memorised speeches as they watched the night before. Some children play games based on TV shows. This seems to be more common for younger children who adapt objects and play spaces to represent characters and scenes from their TV shows. In all of the games and most of the talk, the aim is to 'replay' the TV show as faithfully to the original as possible. The mistakes children make in their performance provide further amusement. Sometimes children use their acting out to comment on TV programs or do a send-up of them.

Selection

Children as young as eight years old know the programs they like best on TV and make deliberate choices, even when what is available is a very narrow selection. Their favourite programs usually come from those shown in the early evening timeslot. However, one-third of the children in this study also included programs made for children in their choice of favourites.

Children are familiar with the programs made specially for them but many find them disappointing. A welcome improvement would be shows which related more strongly to their other interests and their actual tastes in television programs. They would like to see more children like themselves on TV.

New directions for children's TV would include programming for them in prime time and structuring programs to take account of children's ways of interacting with the medium. Continuous feedback about children's interests and needs, not just their patterns of consumption, should be incorporated into the production process.

A Different Understanding of the Child Audience

Considering the research evidence, in the past fragmented and now systematic, that children interact with TV programs and do other tasks while they watch TV, how is it that the notion of the 'passive child viewer' was applied to all children for all of their TV viewing? According to one view, the passive child was just assumed as part of a way of thinking which was based on behaviouristic psychology, prevalent during the 1950s and 1960s (Heller, 1982).

The astounding popularity of television with children when it was first introduced and the way it displaced, for a time, many other unstructured activities also had an impact on adult ways of thinking about TV for children. The amount of television children watch is still quoted in a way which presupposes adult amazement and disapproval. We speak of 'heavy' or 'light' viewers as if there is indeed a measurable 'amount' of the thing called TV viewing which has entered into the child's system and stays there like a dead weight. In this way, television viewing is considered in isolation from all other forms of human communication and given a singular place in children's lives which they do not give it themselves.

Most importantly, what is meant by 'passive' has rarely been defined or held up for scrutiny. There are few researchers who have argued that the television medium induces particular mental states and also set out to prove it. One of the most widely quoted examples, the research of Emery & Emery (1975), has recently been the subject of extensive testing and review by researchers of the Australian Broadcasting Tribunal. In this revision, they directly tested the Emery & Emery proposition that television viewing, regardless of content, produced an alteration in brain activity characterised by an increase in alpha and lower frequency activity and a decrease in beta activity. These changes in the EEG (electroencephalogram) would mean that the brain was less able to process and recall information gained during television viewing.

The test of Emery & Emery's results involved the laboratory study of EEG responses of 24 13-year-olds under four viewing conditions: written text projected by slide onto a screen, written text shown on a TV monitor, a television interview and a television documentary.

The experiment results were not in accordance with the original findings. The researchers state: 'the mechanism of electrophysiological effects implicated by Emery & Emery (1975) does not accord with strict theoretical analysis and has failed to gain empirical support' (Australian Broadcasting Tribunal, 1983: 28). Instead, changes in the brain functioning were found which related to the content of the TV presentations, the most striking of these being when written text was shown on TV. The 'effects' found in this study related to variations in the content shown on TV and not to the difference between media (slide projector and video screen).

Ironically, the argument about children's television viewing put forward by Emery & Emery and based on their now-questionable results, was that its effect on their brains would make children 'hyperactive' rather than passive (Emery & Emery, 1975: 105). Their view is still consistent with the 'passive' concept because it gives to television as a medium the ability to control children rather than seeing children as exercising their own influence over the television environment.

Studies such as the Emerys' are unusual in specifying television's presumed effects on the brain. 'Passive' has most often been applied in a more general fashion to describe children's quiet, absorbed attention as they watch TV. Their supposed physical inactivity has been taken to indicate an accompanying mental inactivity, a kind of non-responsive acceptance of TV messages in toto.

If this notion had been looked at carefully by the researchers who studied television's 'effects' on children's behaviour, the inconsistencies within their own way of thinking would have become obvious. For children to reproduce in their own activities the 'effects' of their TV viewing, they must at least remember and select what has been seen, apply it to their own situation and reconstruct the behaviour in their own setting. Television's so-called 'effects' could not be demonstrated without the child's active participation in viewing and in recreating scenes from TV.

The notion of the passive child viewer has essentially been a value judgment based on the cursory observation that children are not like adults when it comes to television viewing. They are not critical, reflective or self-aware in the way adults think is important. What has gone unrecognised is the way children do deal with their TV experience. They are sometimes irreverent, even rude in their comments on TV programs. And although they do not talk about programs much to adults, talk and play from TV is an important activity with friends.

It is unfortunate that the awareness of genuine differences between adults and children in the experience of TV viewing has led to a negative value being placed on the whole of TV viewing for children, or even on the TV itself. When these differences begin to be explored an understanding of the child–TV relationship emerges which holds some promise for the ways television could be developed for its child audience.

The 'Active' Child Viewer

In two main areas of research, a different view of the child's relationship with television is being put forward. The first is concerned with children's cognitive development and how this relates to children's processing of television messages. The second is more narrowly focused on children's attention to TV.

To those working in the area of children's cognitive development, television viewing is not understood to be a kind of conditioned response but part of a continuous process of adaptation, in which the child's experience of the medium, as well as his or her social understanding in general, is brought into play (Wartella *et al.*, 1979). The central place of the child as a purposeful actor in this set-up is brought out in a recent article, which looks specifically at the question of how to regard the child viewer. Here the authors set forward a model of television viewing as 'active' and 'interactive'. They state: 'as the child views, her interpretation of the message influences how she will interpret subsequent messages'. Because the meaning and structure in television messages is complex the child must become engaged in a 'dynamic communication of diverse messages'. The demands made on children by their television viewing are conveyed in the description of the child viewer as someone who must 'bootstrap her way into a more complete understanding of . . . television's messages' (Rice & Wartella, 1981: 372).

The work of Salomon and others supports this conception of children's active processing of television messages by the results they obtained when they experimentally manipulated children's expectations of how much 'mental effort' to invest in television viewing. Children who were told to watch a TV story 'for fun' were much less able to draw inferences from it afterwards than children who were asked to watch it 'to see how much you can learn from it' (Salomon & Leigh, 1984: 131). Children therefore made their own expectations come true. The attitude they took towards a TV program affected the depth with which they processed the information.

The second research area which is challenging conventional assumptions about the nature of children's television viewing is based on the study of children's attention to television. Anderson and his colleagues describe the outcome of one study of 5-year-olds watching 'Sesame Street', half of the children with toys present and the other half with no toys: 'We were led to the conclusion that the 5-year-olds in the toys group were attending quite strategically, distributing their attention between toy play and viewing so that they looked at what for them were the most informative parts of the program . . . we developed a new respect for children and also a hypothesis of comprehension-guided television viewing' (Anderson & Lorch, 1983: 14–15). The authors quote more recent studies which support the premise that visual attention is guided by the child's comprehension of television content.

Such a premise is opposite to those which formed the basis of previous attention research, where specific features of television images were thought to control children's attention to the screen. The authors' tentative theory is that attention to television is actively guided by the viewer's efforts to understand the television program. The child viewer does not 'passively incorporate any and all content in a uniform manner', but 'applies his or her own experience and understanding to that content' (Anderson & Lorch, 1983: 29–30).

These researchers are emphasising the process of selection in children's television viewing and the close relationship between what they attend to on television and the children's developing understanding of their environment. Anderson and his colleagues are careful not to insist, at this stage, that all of children's viewing in all situations can be described as 'active'. Instead they set out some of the important issues about children's attention to television which have yet to be researched for their theory to have a firm basis. One of these issues is the influence of the television viewing environment itself on children's attention to television. However, their findings are compelling because they are consistent with the understanding of the child viewer being put forward by Wartella, Salomon and others working within the cognitive developmental framework.

The Lively Audience

The results from the present research project complement those in the areas of cognitive development and attention, and give support to the notion of the active child viewer. Being used on a Symbolic Interactionist perspective, the emphasis in this study is on the construction of meaning within social groups and the way these meanings are enacted in social life. With such a theoretical basis, the research reported here has 'filled out' some of the areas of knowledge about children's relationship with TV which were previously hardly known.

These areas include knowledge of how children set about viewing, and their behaviour as they watch TV in the normal social and physical context of the home. The process of defining and sharing television experience in friendship networks outside the family is also sketched, and seems a promising way to explore television as children understand it.

The word 'lively' has been chosen to describe children as an audience because it was found that in their own talking and playing about the set, and in their viewing behaviour, children were not passive respondents. Rather, they were engaged in the human task of giving their own lives structure and meaning, using whatever was at hand to do so, within the bounds of their physical and social development. 'Lively' refers to children's conscious choice of favourite programs and to their activities in front of the TV set. Both of these demonstrate a relationship with television based on the ability to make decisions about the salience of programs and the competing appeal of other activities.

Children are not always physically active in front of the TV. While some children will be most vocal and active during their best-loved programs, many choose these times to give their absorbed and intense concentration to the TV screen. However, their viewing is 'lively' in the sense of being directed in a consistent and purposeful way. For some children, the word 'lively' is too tame. The pace and energy of their physical and verbal activity around the TV comes as a shock to those expecting a placid viewer.

'Lively' also describes how children bring TV stories and events to life again in their talk, activity and games. However undeserving a TV program may appear to be, the sheer enjoyment and enthusiasm in children's account of it, if it is a favourite, says much about the curiosity and interest they bring to their television viewing.

'Lively' rather than 'active' has been chosen as a description of the child audience for a number of reasons. First, the word 'active' has been used in the context of studies about children's possessing of television information. The present project does not deal with children's mental states but instead sets out to describe their social behaviour, by their own report and by observation. 'Lively' clearly refers to children's behaviour, rather than being a statement about the kind of mental activity in which they are engaged.

Another reason for eschewing the use of 'active' to describe children as a television audience is its different meaning as developed by another group of researchers adopting the 'Uses and Gratifications' perspective. While there may be points of overlap between this perspective and that of Symbolic Interactionism, there is little to be gained from confusing the language and assumptions of these two different approaches. Although it is not directly stated in the Uses and Gratifications perspective, there seems to be an association between the idea of being an active audience and the idea of being mentally focused on television viewing.

One study within this tradition employs a definition of the 'active audience' which even runs counter to the understanding of the 'lively audience' in the present study. In their research Levy & Windahl (1984) assumed a close association between attention and 'active viewing' so that viewers who perform other activities while they watch TV are regarded as being less 'active' viewers.

The 'lively' audience of this study has more in common with the children described by Anderson & Lorch (1983) as attending 'strategically' to television as they played. Children's behaviour in front of the TV in the present study exhibited recurrent patterns which were related to program content as well as social context, and which appeared to be initiated and directed by the child rather than the TV.

Pessimism or Promise?

A reassessment of children's relationship with television and a rejection of the notion of children as passive viewers has far-reaching consequences. In particular, it challenges those with vested interests and prejudices to reconsider the significance of television in children's lives. There are two areas where such a reassessment has major implications. The first is, most obviously, the provision of television for children and the second, the relationship of television to children's education.

Television production

The need for programs made specially for children has been recognised by concerned individuals in Australia, and supported by such groups as the Australian Council for Children's Film and Television and the Australian Children's Television Foundation. Regulations exist which require commercial television stations to broadcast only 'C' programs between 4 and 5 on weekday afternoons. 'C' programs are those which have been designed for children aged six to thirteen and which contribute to the social, emotional or intellectual development of children. The Children's Program Committee of the Australian Broadcasting Tribunal, the regulatory body, have the responsibility of awarding 'C' classifications before they are broadcast to those programs which fulfil the established criteria. The regulations and the system of preclassification are both expressions of a basic concern for the needs of children and a belief that television programs can make a positive contribution to their development.

However, the individuals and groups who press for special programming and the broadcast regulations and practices reflecting their concern are not totally established and secure. There is an ambivalence towards providing for children on television that undermines any action in this area, relying as it does on broad community support. The ambivalence comes from uncertainty about the nature of children's relationship with television.

If television itself is harmful for children, then perhaps even the best programs may do damage? Surely 'good' parents should not even admit to allowing their children access to such a dubious form of recreation, let alone be vocal in their demands for more and better programs? The view of children as a passive audience lies at the heart of uncertainties about television in relation to children.

Marie Winn, an American journalist, has been the most vocal proponent of the view that it is the television medium itself and therefore for children the mere act of viewing it, that does harm. Winn only admits to one state of viewing for children which she describes as follows: 'they watch the screen and passively soak in images, words and sounds hour after hour, as if in a dream' (Winn, 1985: 194) and 'the younger viewer is so completely absorbed in the television experience that manipulating the sensations is harder to accomplish than manipulation of real-life material. The mind takes in the television images as they arrive and stores them intact' (Winn, 1985: 135). Moreover, she regards this process as dehumanising because the child's 'passive participation leaves him unchanged in a human sense' (Winn, 1985: 77). These assertions about the nature of children's TV viewing are matched with strong criticism of parents who allow their children access to television. Indeed the central argument of her book, *The Plug-In Drug* is not that children are addicted to TV, but that negligent, selfish parents have become dependent on it for child control.

The most glaring inadequacy of this point of view is the failure to take TV programs into account at all. 'Television' is consistently referred to as a machine. There is no sense in which it is also understood to be a form of human communication. Winn exhorts parents to triumph over 'the mechanical rival', to get rid of the TV set, and fill 'the vacuum created by the absence of television' with 'people-centred rather than machine-centred activities' (Winn, 1985: 166, 221). Her real opinion is that TV should be abolished, and those who seek to improve programming for children should be treated with disdain: 'to work for better programs . . . is not unlike dealing with alcoholism by striving to replace cheap whisky with Chivas Regal' (Winn, 1985: xi).

While there is some collective wisdom about living with TV in statements quoted throughout her book, it nevertheless paints a false picture, because it is based on an assumption about children's TV viewing which is incorrect and misleading. All children do not always watch TV passively. The types of attention they give TV and their accompanying mental states are not unique to the television experience, but resemble other, everyday forms of interaction and communication. Their viewing behaviour also varies according to the programs they watch, and even in response to particular features within programs.

Most importantly, television is not a machine which grabs at children's minds, but a form of technology which acts as a medium of communication for the TV programs and other short messages transmitted onto its small screen. Television programs are the work of human hands, minds and imaginations. They are products of human communication, though they do not take place through the medium of direct interpersonal contact.

Children understand this. They define television in terms of its programs, and the feelings they associate with viewing their best-loved shows. By contrast, the monolithic and threatening picture of television which has become so much a part of the thinking of adults does not arise from adults' own experience of television viewing, but from their difficulties 'in integrating this new medium into their behaviour' (Corset, 1983: 188).

When adults turn their attention from condemnation of television as a medium, and focus it on television programs, there is much to criticise and change, if television is to work in children's interests. Children at present watch and enjoy many programs which are very limited in the world they reveal to children and the demands they make for participation. Such a situation speaks for children's ingenuity and determination to create interest and excitement in their lives. However, poor programs are also the consequence of holding low expectations of the television medium for its child audience. By relegating it to 'mere entertainment' for children and an inferior form of entertainment at that, adults in Australia have left it to commercial television companies for the most part to define the quality and potential of television for children.

When children are regarded as active viewers in the way they think, pay attention or 'manage' their TV environment, a new importance is given to the content of TV programs, especially with the availability of new television technologies such as video and interactive cable systems. Anderson and Lorch for example are two researchers who are optimistic about the future of television for children; their optimism is based on their findings which demonstrate that children attend strategically to television programs. They maintain that 'the new video technologies should be well received insofar as these technologies offer greater choice of content and direct interaction' (Anderson & Lorch, 1983: 29–30).

Another group of researchers which has sought to understand children's own definitions of television and the place it has in their lives has come to a similar, positive conclusion about the possibilities of television for children. Corset (1983) describes a group of French studies which used a range of novel methods to enter into children's ways of thinking about television. These methods included drawings of children watching TV, playing 'TV' with a video camera, role-plays and extensive talk about a science fiction character.

In these studies, differences in children's television preferences are described as well as the close association of television with other aspects of family life. They confirm the importance of where the television is placed in the home and the emotional climate which attends its use by family members. On the basis of research findings, Corset is enthusiastic about the potential of television as a source of shared experience and knowledge about the world:

> If we consider children's way of life and their needs . . . it would appear that television, rather than being a new problem to be solved, is a real chance to be seized . . . To explain something by referring to television is to proceed from a subject which is familiar to children and which they find interesting because it concerns their behaviour directly . . . The possibilities it offers are thus manifold and the range of questions to be treated covers a large share of what the child needs to know in order to understand the world. (Pierre *et al.* cited in Corset, 1983: 207–8)

The findings of the present study that children interact with television in many different ways, some of them involving an application and extension of what they see on TV, point to a similar potential for creative development. The members of the 'lively' audience described here have many capabilities which are not reflected in the programs being made, even those which are supposedly made especially for them. In particular, children's enjoyment of active participation during some programs, and their use of TV with friends, if taken seriously, could lead to a very different style of TV program or series.

Television and education

Inklings of the pervasiveness and significance of television in children's thinking have appeared in research about TV games (James, 1982) and in this project. Children's use of both the structure and content of narratives from TV in their talk and games demonstrates their eagerness to imitate and adapt TV scenarios to their own experience. There can be no doubt that television is now the main medium for story-telling in our society. The 'stories' in the form of drama programs, cartoons or even news, documentaries and advertisements give children a wider sense of the world than is possible within their own neighbourhood. There seems every reason to believe that, through the stories it tells, television is one of the main sources of information about social life for children.

This is certainly the view of one researcher who goes so far as to compare television messages with school curricula: 'while one of the major missions of commercial television is to entertain, the effect of that entertainment is to provide social learning messages that reach children just as those associated with the planned curriculum of an educational institution do' (Berry, 1980: 78). Television, he argues, functions as an 'unplanned curriculum' in which professional writers, producers and directors do the planning and creative work akin to that of teachers in schools. It is the dramatisation of social roles and events together with their consequences that provide learning experiences for children. He concludes that 'because of the unplanned yet powerful influence of television portrayals, adults have a responsibility to prepare children to be wise consumers of television'.

Some of the French studies reviewed above were conducted as part of a new approach to teaching about television in French schools. The aim of the program was to 'improve and enrich children's experience and encourage them to develop an active response in front of the screen in order to make them more alert and selective' (Cohn, 1981: 30). The program, 'Jeunes Téléspectateurs Actifs', which began at the end of 1979, was based on the view that 'television is above all, a language that must be learned — a language whose influence is felt by all but which is taught by no one' (Cohn, 1981: 29).

In this program, carried out in local groups, the approach to television was a positive one. Television was considered as a 'new and original element in the French education system'. This is probably one of the first examples of educational planning to be based on a clearly articulated view that children are an active TV audience. Children were encouraged not just to understand and criticise what they saw on TV but to develop further those abilities which had been established as characteristic of children's viewing.

Television is an integral part of the daily routines, thinking and behaviour of most children. It also informs their view of the world and of themselves. Schooling is inadequate which does not encourage students to reflect on the information and values they have heard on TV or which does not provide them with skills to understand and interpret its messages. It fails to acknowledge the changed world of human communication in which children must find their own place.

There are some educators who would take issue with such a conclusion and would seek to exclude television from being any part of school study. Postman is the most recent writer to call for a change in school curricula which would counteract the harmful effects of television. It is interesting to note that his argument is based on assumptions about the medium, and about children's lack of engagement with it, which are called into serious question by the research detailed throughout this book. Postman asserts:

> There is a sense in which pictures and other graphic images may be said
> to be 'cognitively regressive'. Television . . . has the potential to put
> our minds to sleep . . . People watch television. They do not read it.
> Nor do they much listen to it . . . Television offers a fairly primitive but
> irresistible alternative to the linear and sequential logic of the printed
> word and tends to make the rigors of a literate education irrelevant . . .
> Watching television not only requires no skills but develops no skills
> . . . it does not make complex demands on either mind or behaviour.
> (Postman, 1983: 73, 78–80)

Postman's statements reveal the prejudices of a person from an earlier
communications tradition against visual media and images because they
do not communicate with the 'printed word'. Postman's mind seems shut
against the possibility that mental processing of television messages may be
every bit as demanding as reading the printed word and that teaching these
skills at school might be an important preparation for adulthood.

What Postman does acknowledge is that television programs are a kind of
curriculum. However, in his opinion school curricula should be designed
which deliberately counter the form and content of television programs.
Winn puts this view most eloquently: 'With school remaining the last bastion
of the printed word and the last chance of ensuring its survival, any movement of the education establishment away from this single, all-important
goal must be seen as unprofitable and even dangerous' (Winn, 1985: 95).

In Australia the relationship of television to education does not yet seem
an important issue, except in the development of courses of study in mass
media. Teachers and school administrators seem to be fairly successful at
keeping the subject of television outside formal class time. It is ironic that
children nevertheless spend much of their time at school in discussions about
television, though this takes place in children's free time and in their own
playground space.

This almost tangible division between school and television represents a
lost opportunity for adults to work alongside children as they develop an
understanding of themselves and their world. Certain groups within our
community, for example migrants and girls, are ignored or treated badly
in most television programs, and this view of the world should not go
unchallenged, to repeat itself in the lives of those children viewing.

Schools may well provide one of the few places where children are forced
to withdraw for a time from a constant flux of electronically produced
sounds and images. It would be making more constructive use of this down-
time in media exposure to help children reflect upon the messages they see
and hear outside school and reconstruct them according to their own understanding and experience.

Children are a precious resource and television a powerful one. Beyond those institutions concerned more narrowly with schooling, there is the need to develop a clear idea of what we aspire to in the lives of our young people. Both education and television will be important in shaping their future.

Edward Palmer, a researcher who works for the Children's Television Workshop, one arena where education and entertainment television join forces, argues strongly for the need to 'define a comprehensive policy in children's television to support national objectives' (Palmer, 1983: 6). In Australia, we have not yet seen the importance of forming such a policy. The research presented here will I hope encourage those working with children, with television and in education, to look beyond existing practices and create new kinds of television for an audience of children we have only lately begun to understand and to respect.

References

Anderson, D. R. and Lorch, E. P. (1983) Looking at television: Action or reaction. In J. Bryant and D. R. Anderson *Children's Understanding of Television*. New York: Academic Press.

Australian Broadcasting Tribunal (1983) *Electroencephalographic Responses of Children to Television*. Melbourne: ABT.

Berry, G. L. (1980) Children, television and social class roles: The medium as unplanned educational curriculum. In L. Palmer and A. Dorr (eds) *Children and the Faces of Television: Teaching, Violence, Selling*. New York: Academic Press.

Cohn, E. (1981) France wants active young televiewers. *Television and Children* 4, 29–32.

Corset, P. (1983) Television in the lives of French children: A review of recent research. In M. Meyer (ed.) *Children and the Formal Features of Television*. Munich: Saur, K. G.

Emery, F. and Emery, M. (1975) *A Choice of Futures — To Enlighten or Inform*. Canberra: Centre for Continuing Education, Australian National University.

Heller, M. A. (1982) The contribution of critical scholarship to television research. In B. J. Dervin and M. J. Voigt (eds) *Progress in Communication Science* Vol. 3. Norwood, NJ: Ablex.

James, N. C. and McCain, T. A. (1982) Television games preschool children play: Patterns, themes and uses. *Journal of Broadcasting* 26, 783–98.

Levy, M. R. and Windahl, S. (1984) Audience activity and gratifications. *Communication Research* 11, 51–78.

Palmer, P. (1983) *Favourite TV Programmes: What Children Say and the Games they Play* (Progress Report 2). Sydney: Department of Government, University of Sydney.

— (1986) *Television in the Lives of Young Teenage Girls*. Sydney: New South Wales Ministry of Education.

Postman, N. (1983) *The Disappearance of Childhood*. London: W. H. Allen.

Rice, M. and Wartella, E. (1981) Television as a medium of communication: Implications for how to regard the child viewers. *Journal of Broadcasting* 25, 365–72.

Salomon, G. and Leigh, T. (1984) Predispositions about learning from print and television. *Journal of Communication* 34, 119–35.

Wartella, E., Lemish, A. and Alexander, D. (1979) The mass media environment of children. *American Behavioral Scientist* 23, 33–52.

Winn, M. (1985) *The Plug-In Drug* (revised edn). New York: Penguin.

17 Television Pleasures

JOHN FISKE

Whatever the controversy about television's role in our culture, there is no doubt that people enjoy it, and that watching it is a major source of pleasure in our lives. This word 'pleasure' occurs widely in recent critical writings and appears to be crucial to our understanding of popularity. But, like many widely used terms, it is remarkably difficult to pin down and define. It is also multidiscursive, that is, it means differently in different discourses.

Thus, the psychoanalytic use of the term tends to relate it with desire and places it as the main motivator of human action. Feminist work deriving from Lacan suggests that while masculine and feminine pleasures may be experienced differently in patriarchy, in general the origin of pleasure and unpleasure is located in the early psychic process common to all human infants, and its essential structure is laid down before social influences such as gender, class, race education, or religion come into the picture. In psychoanalytic terms, the pleasure principle comes close to being a human universal.

Barthes (1975b), however, use the word '*plaisir*' to refer to a pleasure which is essentially cultural in origin, and the more ecstatic '*jouissance*' to refer to a physical pleasure, located, like sexual orgasm, in the senses of the body rather than in the workings of the subconscious. '*Jouissance*' has similarities with Freud's 'affect' in which the intensity of the experience is its important dimension.

Then there is a third discursive use, which is broadly social in emphasis. It seeks the meaning of pleasure in its relationship to the social structure and to the social practices of the subjects who experience it. While the first two uses look for essentially abstract and singular meanings, this third one tends towards more concrete and plural ones.

These three categories, the psychoanalytic, the physical, and the social, constantly leak into each other, and the pleasure or pleasures experienced at any one time are likely to include elements of all. The categories are, like all categories, explanatory strategies, they exist for a heuristic purpose, not in their own right. But while it is important to insist on the differences between

239

them, it is equally important to point out that all of them depend, to a greater or lesser extent, on the relationship between pleasure and power. Broadly, the psychoanalytic view of pleasure sees it as the product of accommodation to the dominant ideology. According to Mulvey (1975), pleasure is the reward offered to the conforming spectator by patriarchal cinema: it is the prime hegemonic agent.

In both its other discourses, however, pleasure can be associated with resistance and subversion. For Barthes as for many of the postmodernists, pleasure can be the opposite of ideology, not, as for Mulvey, its reward.

Psychoanalysis and Pleasure

Mulvey (1975) in her influential article 'Visual Pleasure and Narrative Cinema' turned for her theoretical base to Freud's theory of voyeurism — the pleasure and power of looking. She argues that the spectator of mainstream Hollywood cinema is positioned like the peeping Tom: the screen is like the window of the lighted room through which the invisible, unacknowledged voyeur looks. His (for voyeurism is a masculine pleasure) ability to see the secret, the private lives of others, gives the voyeur a power over them. This voyeuristic pleasure is produced by the masculine look at the female body, so the typical progress of Hollywood narrative is male action that advances the plot alternating with interruptions during which the female body is gazed at or possessed by the male protagonist. The male protagonist becomes the embodiment of the masculine spectator and the masculine 'look' of the camera upon the pro-filmic event. The visual pleasure of looking at and possessing the female is a reward for successful male action in the preceding segment of narrative. This produces a masculine reading subject, even though the cinema audience may be composed of both males and females. In patriarchy, women can be constructed as masculine subjects and can consequently experience masculine pleasures. They, like men, can subject the female body to a masculine gaze.

Alongside the power of voyeurism goes the cinematic practice of the fetishization of the female. A fetish, according to Freud, is the overvaluation of a threat. The movie camera 'worships' the female form to excess, as a way of defusing the castration threat and Oedipal guilt that the woman bears. This produces the cinematic fragmentation of the female body, as the camera worships, in close-up, the eyes, lips, thighs, hair, and almost any part of the female body.

For Mulvey, the pleasures produced by the satisfaction of the voyeuristic desire are perfectly aligned with the requirements of patriarchy and she comes close to constructing an unbreakable relationship among patriarchy, pleasure, and the natural differences between male and female. She appears to ground patriarchy in human nature and to explain the pleasure of cinema by treating patriarchal power as indistinguishable from the nature of human sexuality. As a feminist, she is thus led to a call for a destruction of pleasure as we currently experience it, and for its replacement by a new pleasure, the pleasure of defamiliarizing what is taken for granted and in producing a new way of seeing.

But mainstream pleasure results from finding the structures of infant sexuality reproduced in the structures of mainstream cinema, which leads the spectator to accommodate himself or herself to the dominant ideology, by adopting the textually produced subject position with all its subjection to the demands of patriarchy and of human sexuality. Pleasure is thus reactionary, for both the dominant ideology and Freudian explanations of sexuality work to naturalize the patriarchal status quo. Mulvey does, however, admit of the possibility of a radical pleasure, but does not elaborate in any detail how this may be produced.

Mulvey's argument may hold up well for cinema, but it translates less convincingly to television. The huge, bright cinema screen and the anonymous darkness of the auditorium reproduce much more precisely the situation of the peeping Tom than does the far less imperative television screen situated in the family living room in the middle of ordinary family life. Television is more interactive than voyeuristic. Its realism, which certainly has a voyeuristic dimension, is constantly fractured both by the segmentation of the television text and by its mode of reception. Its viewers, unlike cinema spectators, are not granted the same voyeuristic power over, and pleasure in, the image, just as they are less subjected to the positioning of the realist narrative.

While there are problems with applying Mulvey's theory of pleasure to television, it still has some explanatory power. The fragmentation of the female body into a fetish object is commonplace in commercials, particularly those for cosmetic products. The mobilization of masculine desire in the female viewer and the construction for her of a masculine reading position from which she can make sense of her own body through masculine eyes is an obvious economic strategy of the industry.

Similarly, there are numerous representations of the female body as an object of the masculine gaze and a producer of the voyeuristic power/pleasure. The models that decorate the prizes in game shows, or that provide much of the 'scenery' in shows like *Miami Vice* or *Mike Hammer,* are clear evidence of this voyeuristic pleasure at work. So, too, is television's tendency to confine women on the screen to the age of maximum sexuality and to physical types that conform to the patriarchal sense of attractiveness and normalcy for the women. Fat women, for instance, appear only rarely, as do pregnant women. In Australia, 1985, a female announcer/reporter was barred from appearing on screen when she was visibly pregnant. She invoked the law on sexual discrimination, won her case, and was allowed to introduce an opera. But the voyeuristic pleasure of the male requires an 'available' woman, so that she can be possessed by the look: a pregnant woman, however sexually attractive, is not available for possession in the same way.

But this view of pleasure can only account for *some* of television's appeal. In particular, it allows for no possibility of resistance to the dominant ideology and no possibility of viewer-generated meanings, or at least, that there is no pleasure to be gained from these possibilities.

Pleasure and Social Control

Barthes's (1975b) twofold notion of pleasure provides one way of addressing these difficulties. He uses the words *plaisir* and *jouissance* to distinguish between two different types of pleasure produced in the reading of a text. He stresses that pleasure, of either type, is not to be found in the text itself, but in its conjuncture with the reader; the theory is concerned not with what the text *is* but with what it *does*. He frequently uses the metaphor of the economy of the text, a metaphor that likens the generation and circulation of meanings and pleasures to the generation and circulation of wealth. The words or images in the text are exchanged for pleasure, the commodity that the reader buys is not a sense of the world, but pleasure in the processes of representing and figuring that world.

Freud, though not quoted directly by Barthes, is lurking just below the surface of his theory, firstly in Barthes's assumption that human beings always seek pleasure and avoid unpleasure, and secondly in his belief that pleasure in our society always produces two policemen — a political one and a psychoanalytic one. Pleasure is, in western societies, typically classed as an indulgence, the expression of selfishness, idleness, vanity and thus productive of guilt. The Church's constant attempt to curb the 'pleasures' of the flesh was eagerly taken up by capitalism and transformed into the Protestant work ethic with its acceptance of only that pleasure which had been 'earned' and which was used responsibly (i.e. to prepare the worker for more work). Bennett (1983a) has traced the ways in which the nineteenth-century middle classes attempted to control and channel the leisure of the emerging working class into ideologically acceptable forms.

The long tradition of attacks on television (preceded by attacks on comics and other popular forms) is part of this movement. The attacks use the discourses of morality, legality, or aesthetics in order to displace their actual origin in class-based social power. Television is immoral, the arguments typically run, because it shows extramarital sex, or it undermines law and order in its glorification of violence and crime, and it degrades people's ability to discriminate through its crudities, its crassness, and its appeal to the lowest common denominator. Similar arguments were used to ban the popular fairs and festivals in the nineteenth century (see Waites, Bennett & Martin, 1982) and stem from the same unvoiced fear that the pleasures of the subordinate classes are necessarily disruptive because they lie outside the control of the bourgeoisie. But class power is obviously open to contestation, so pleasure cannot be suppressed openly in the name of class: rather attempts to control it have to be seen to work through more universally accepted and thus less challengeable discourses such as those of morality, the law, or aesthetics.

Casting the popular as the degraded, the illegal, or the immoral justifies the policing action of the bourgeoisie in their constant attempts to devalue or curb it. It also legitimates Barthes's psychoanalytic policeman and the guilt through which he works. The histories of capitalism and of Christianity show how their fear of pleasure as disruptive, as hostile to their social power, produces the desire to subject it to moral, economic, and political control.

For Barthes pleasure is opposed to ideological control, though *plaisir* less so than *jouissance*. *Plaisir* is a mundane pleasure that is essentially confirming, particularly of one's sense of identity. It is a product of culture and the sense of identity produced by that culture. While Mulvey's (1975) masculine pleasure of mainstream cinema may be similar to *plaisir*, Barthes allows, in the way that Mulvey does not, for an oppositional pleasure. The pleasure experienced by more liberal or even radical viewers of *Hill Street Blues* or *Cagney and Lacey* is a form of *plaisir* to be found in confirming their social identity as one that opposes or at least interrogates dominant social values. Barthes gives comparatively little attention to *plaisir*, yet it is this more mundane, everyday sort of pleasure that is probably more typical of television. The conditions under which television is normally watched are not conducive to that intensity of experience which is necessary for *jouissance*. But *plaisir*, with its stronger political and social dimension, may be at least as progressive and interrogative a form of pleasure as *jouissance* whose roots seem to lie primarily in ideological evasion. *Plaisir*, too, is plural: the variety of social identities it confirms requires us to think of a diversity of *plaisirs*, whereas there is only one *jouissance*. And diversity is, itself, both an agency and an effect of resistance.

Jouissance is translated into English as bliss, ecstasy, or orgasm, and Barthes constantly uses sexual metaphors to explain it. It is a pleasure of the body, experienced through heightened sensualities that relate it to human nature, rather than culture. It is produced by the physical signifiers of the text — the 'grain' that some singing voices have, but others, technically as perfect, lack. It is located in the body of the text and is responded to by the body of the reader — Barthes (1975b) uses words like flesh, throat, patina, voluptuousness, to describe it. It is, he says, an articulation of the body, not of meaning or of language:

> the language lined with flesh, a text where we can hear the grain of the throat, the patina of consonants, the voluptuousness of vowels, a whole carnal stereophony: the articulation of the body, of the tongue, not that of meaning, of language. A certain art of singing can give an idea of this local writing; but since melody is dead, we may find it more easily today at the cinema. In fact, it suffices that the cinema capture the sound of speech *close up* (this is, in fact, the generalized definition of the 'grain' of writing) and make us hear in their materiality, their sensuality, the breath, the gutturals, the fleshiness of the lips, a whole presence of the human muzzle (that the voice, that writing, be as fresh, supple, lubricated, delicately granular and vibrant as an animal's muzzle) to succeed in shifting the signified a great distance and in throwing, so to speak, the anonymous body of the actor into my ear: it granulates, it crackles, it caresses, it grates, it cuts, it comes: that is bliss (*jouissance*). (pp. 66–7)

Jouissance escapes the control of culture and of meaning by 'distancing the signified' and thus foregrounding the signifier, particularly the way it is materialized (the grain, the breath of the voice, the fleshiness of the lips). It is found in the material body of the sign, in the sensuality of the body of the reader. In this way it is always erotic and its peak is properly described as orgasm.

Jouissance occurs at the moment of the breakdown of culture. 'Neither culture nor its destruction is erotic: it is the seam between them, the fault, the flow, which becomes so' (Barthes 1975b: 7). Sexual orgasm is the moment when the body escapes culture, or, at least, makes that escape appear possible. The body and its sensualities oppose subjectivity, they provide a pleasure that is not to be found in the subject and its construction in culture by ideology.

The close-ups in soap opera may produce *jouissance*. The intense materiality of emotion in the magnified quiver of the mouth's corner, the narrowing of the eyes, the breathy wetness of the voice may produce tears in the viewer quite independent of, or even counter to, the narrative of what is said, of what is felt, and the way they work in the subjectivity. The loss is experienced in the body as the loss of subjectivity. (Ecstasy or orgasm can, of course, produce tears as an appropriate physical response.) 'A good cry' which Brown (1987a) identifies as one of the pleasures of soap opera is not only the *plaisir* of expressing emotions and an identity which social life frequently represses, but often the *jouissance* of reading with the body, of establishing a presence that is outside culture, outside ideology, because it is not concerned with meaning (either of self or of the world) but with presence and intensity.

While the distinction between *plaisir* and *jouissance* is often difficult to make in practice, the importance of Barthes's theory lies in its shift of attention to readers in their differences away from the central, universal notions of pleasure deriving from a mix of psychoanalysis and ideology. Pleasure is decentralized and is part of the reading that creates a text out of a work central to it, then, is the sense that the reader has some control over the production of meaning.

Lovell (1983) offers an account of pleasure that has superficial similarities to Mulvey's because it is gender-specific, and to Barthes's, because it admits of resisting pleasures, but differs from both in its historical specificity which inserts it into patriarchal capitalism. She suggests that the clear division established by nineteenth-century capitalism between the public-political world of the man and the private-domestic world of the woman has resulted in the feminization of pleasure in the way it has been confined to private and personal life, while the world of 'the serious' has been left to the masculine. But her earlier work (Lovell, 1980) has shown how popular pleasures can be resistive, so we may argue that the privatization of pleasure allows for its articulation in the body and the senses, and its feminization allows it to be articulated with the culture of the repressed. Schwichtenburg (1986) insists that 'it is important . . . to render pleasure out of bounds', for this sort of pleasure lies in the refusal of the social control inscribed in the 'bounds'. While there is clearly a pleasure in exerting social power, the popular pleasures of the subordinate are necessarily found in resisting, evading, or offending this power. Popular pleasures are those that empower the subordinate, and they thus offer political resistance, even if only momentarily and even if only in a limited terrain.

Pleasure, Play and Control

Barthes (1977) suggests that the pleasure of creating a text out of a work involves playing with the text, and he exploits the full polysemy of 'play' in his ideas. Firstly, he says, the text has 'play' in it, like a door whose hinges are loose. This 'play' is exploited by the reader who 'plays' the text as a musician plays a score: s/he interprets it, activates it, gives it a living presence. In doing this, the reader plays a text as one plays a game: s/he voluntarily accepts the rules of the text in order to participate in the practice that those rules make possible and pleasurable; the practice is, of course, the production of meanings and identities. In a text, as in a game, the rules are there to construct a space within which freedom and control of self are possible. Games and texts construct ordered worlds within which the players/readers can experience the pleasures of both freedom and control: in particular, for our purposes, playing the text involves the freedom of making and control-ling meanings.

Freud draws our attention to the infant's 'fort-da' game in which the child continually throws away a loved object only to demand its return. His explanation is that the game is enacting the disappearance and reappearance of the mother, and that in playing it the child is not only symbolizing his or her anxieties about the mother's return, but is also beginning to use symbols to control the meanings of his or her environment, and in so doing is explor-ing the relationship between the real and its representation.

Palmer (1986) provides many examples of children playing with tele-vision. At the simplest level, children enjoyed the control that the set gave them over the signifiers themselves — they played with the channel switches or tuning buttons to distort the image or make it disappear and reappear in a sort of electronic fort-da game. She comments on one, not untypical, pair: 'Part of the delight of Amy and her brother seemed to come from playing out their mastery over the little box' (p. 58).

This empowering play with the mechanism of reproduction extended to playing with the representations themselves. Sometimes this took the form of fairly straightfoward re-enactment, as when girls in the schoolyard replayed scenes from the previous night's episode of *Prisoner*, but some-times these re-enactments were satirical — they were critical reformulations of representations of which the children disapproved. The fact that children explored their television shows from inside their experience of watching them instead of adopting the adult critical method of treating them as objects for analysis in no way invalidates the critical process in which they were engaged. Indeed, children's play may be more productive than adult criti-cism, for it can involve a remaking of the program to suit their social experi-ence that is more creative than the dismissive negativity typical of so many adults. This 're-making' is a source of pleasure and power:

> Make-believe play and pretending is commonly associated with good feelings, with 'interest and joy'. Researchers have suggested that this is because play is a kind of 'power transformation by which the child . . . reconstitutes a miniature world which follows his or her rules' (Singer & Singer, 1980: 1).   (Palmer, 1986: 113)

Similarly, Seal argues that children's games frequently explore the boun-dary between the symbolic and the real. The arguments between the child who plays according to the rules — 'You're dead' — and the one who brings 'reality' into it — 'No I'm not — see I'm still breathing' — are arguments about who has the power to construct a representation of reality that is binding upon others.

This is fundamentally similar to the play of women viewers of soap opera that both Ang (1985) and Hobson (1982) report. The pleasure of these viewers in playing with the relationship between the representation and the real questions the power of the program to control the representational illusion and is a way of exercising control over their own viewing practices. Their active choice of whom to 'identify' with (e.g. Sue Ellen or Pamela in *Dallas*) and their choice to identify or not in the process that I have called 'implication-extrication' are both examples of exerting control through play.

The play may not in itself be resistive or subversive, but the control or empowerment that it entails produces a self-esteem in the subordinate that at least makes resistance or subversion possible. Radway (1984) has found that some women readers of romance novels reported that they chose to read the novels in the face of husbandly disapproval and found meanings in them that supported feminine values and criticized masculine ones. This choice and this validation of a subordinated value system gave them the self-confidence to assert themselves more strongly and to resist the patriarchal power of the male in the family.

Similarly, a study of young girl fans of Madonna (Fiske, 1987) showed that a major source of their pleasure was Madonna's control over her own image (or meaning) and the sense that this control could be devolved to them. They consistently saw Madonna as a woman who used the discourse of patriarchal sexuality to assert her control over that discourse and therefore over her own sexuality. Her sexuality was not represented in music video as a source of pleasure for men, but for herself and her girl fans. She used signs and images from a masculine discourse in order to assert her independence from men, from male approval, and therefore from that discourse. This was a particularly important source of pleasure for young girls because, as Williamson (1986) points out:

> she retains all the bravado and exhibitionism that most girls start off with until the onset of 'womanhood' knocks it out of them . . . She does in public what most girls do in private, like a little girl in an adult world with no one to say 'No'. This gives an enormous sense of released energy, which is itself positive . . . And Madonna is never a victim, never passive, [her] persona is one of conscious ebullient confidence in her sexual image, utterly unembarrassed: this is the exact opposite of the sense of shame that poisons young girls' enjoyment of their own bodies from the moment they open a teenage magazine. (p. 47)

Madonna's music videos explore this boundary between the rules that conventionally govern the representation of sexuality in patriarchy and the

sociosexual experience of young girls and their subcultural needs. They
rapidly adopted the Madonna 'look' which tore the signs of conventional
female fashion (lacy gloves, ribbons, religious jewelry, peroxided hair, etc.)
out of their original context and thus freed them from their original meanings. The meanings of the Madonna look, as of the Madonna videos, cannot
be precisely specified. But that is precisely the point, the pleasure that they
give is not the pleasure of *what* they say, but of their assertion of the right and
the power of a severely subordinated subculture to make their own statements, their own meanings. Madonna's invitation to her girl fans to play
with the conventions of patriarchy shows them that they are not necessarily
subject to those conventions but can exercise some control over their
relationship to patriarchy and thus over the sense of their identity.

Madonna's emphasis on style, on 'the Madonna look,' is a denial of
meaning and of the ideology and power that it would bear. It is an assertion
of the surface — the crucifix is a shape not a meaning — of the signifier, and
of the ease with which the powerless can play with images/commodities to
gain the power and pleasure of making their own personalized image-
identity.

Rules have inscribed within them both the power they convey and its
origin. Gilligan (1982) makes the point that men in patriarchy think and
work through rules, because rules allow them to dominate: the women playing with the system of representation in soap opera are like children playing
in that both subordinated 'classes' are using play to question the rules that
maintain their subordination. Rules, then, work in a similar way to ideology
to maintain the power base in its current location. Like ideology, they
emanate from a sociocentral source and attempt to construct social identities
in relation to this sociocentrality.

But pleasure is not produced or experienced centrally: pleasure is decen-
tered or centrifugal. So the school students' readings of *Prisoner* were
pleasurable because they were centered in their interests, were in their control, and because they resisted the centered, centripetal power that constantly worked to subject them. Many of the programs that are most popular
with children are productive of this centrifugal pleasure that questions the
rules and the central control of the system.

Barthes's shift from his earlier work where he saw ideology as central to
the understanding of texts in culture (e.g. *Mythologies*) to his foregounding
of pleasure (e.g. *The Pleasure of the Text*) is a shift from the centripetal to the
centrifugal. The centrifugal model of pleasure allows for a diversity of
pleasures 'around the circumference' and suggests a line of force in active
opposition to the centripetal force that attempts to center control at a point
of ideological and social unity. So Barthes moves away from seeking to
explain a text by referring to its singular ideology towards the plurality of

pleasures it can offer in its moments of reading. Pleasure may be *provoked* by the text, but it can only be *experienced* by the reader in the reading. It can thus differ from reader to reader, and even from reading to reading. Barthes suggests that any one reader reading any one text at different times may experience different pleasures, or none, at each reading. While this notion locates pleasure in the reader rather than the text and emphasizes difference rather than homogeneity, it does imply a randomness which is little help in explaining the process.

I would prefer to suggest that the variety of pleasures is a function of the variety of socially situated viewers. For those in easy accommodation with the dominant ideology, this pleasure will be conforming and reactionary, but it will still be experienced as self-generated: the subject will feel that he or she is voluntarily adopting a social position that happens to conform to the dominant ideology and is finding genuine pleasure in it. This, of course, is pleasure acting as the motor of hegemony.

But for those whose accommodation to the system is less complete, an essential component of pleasure must be an evasion, or at least a negotiation, of dominant ideological practice, the ability to shake oneself free from its constraints. This then opens up spaces for subcultures or groups to find their own pleasures in relationship to the ideology they are evading. Pleasure, in this subcultural role, helps to preserve and legitimate the heterogeneity of society and is thus properly seen as oppositonal to the homogenizing force of ideology and can be summed up as the pleasure/power to be different. Television, like the society it serves, contains both tendencies in active contradiction.

Pleasure and Rule Breaking

One of the pleasures of play is its ability to explore the relationships between rules and freedom. Rules are the means by which social control is exercised, and result in a social order that works to control the disruptive, anarchic forces of nature. Play enacts the opposition between freedom and control, between nature and culture.

Huizinga (1949) concludes that play, or the spirit of play, is essential to all cultural forms, including those of law, war, diplomacy, business, marriage, education, and the arts. The essence of play is that it is voluntary and therefore free, and that it creates order. The order that it creates is in the control of the players or, at least, is one voluntarily accepted by them, but the orderliness is never total, for it has built into it chanciness, the impossibility of knowing what will happen. The main structuring principle of play is the tension between social order and the 'freedom' of anarchy or chance.

In sport this tension is as controlled as much as possible, technically by the referee and socially by the surrounding moral system of 'responsibility' that centers sport into the dominant ideology. So 'responsible' television coverage and commentary underpins the authority of the referee and the ideology of 'fair play' which means playing both within the rules and the larger 'spirit' of the game. But 'popular' taste demands that television zoom in on the moments of rule-breaking, the fouls and fights, the professional 'plays' that operate on or beyond the boundaries of the rules.

In *Rock 'n' Wrestling*, for example, the impotence of the referee is a major part of the pleasure. The constant rule breaking of the wrestlers and their coaches indicates their refusal to accept the social roles imposed upon them. This can be read specifically, as the conflict between wild, 'natural' masculinity and social control, or it can signify more generally the arbitrariness of rules and roles, and the 'naturalness' of breaking or exceeding them. Similarly, in *TV Bloopers and Practical Jokes* what appears to be the 'naturalness of the real' breaks through the roles and the rules of normal, conventional television. Both programs are playful and pleasurable in similar ways for they demonstrate that rule-governed systems are both arbitrary and fragile. Rules are one of the hegemonic forces through which the dominant try to win the consent of the subordinate to the control of their 'unruliness.' The pleasures of breaking rules or exposing their arbitrariness are resistive pleasures of the subordinate.

Many of the shows that give pleasure to children play with the limits of rule-governed systems. Shows like *Ripley's Believe It or Not,* or *Arthur C. Clarke's Mysterious World*, explore the wonders of nature that exist on or beyond the margin of rational scientific explanation. The shows demonstrate how nature itself keeps breaking through the rules that have been devised in order to understand and master it. Natural history documentaries, which are adult versions of these shows, are much less interrogative and skeptical of the rules. They tend to be either scientific and educational, in which case they exemplify science's power to explain and account for the wonders of nature, or they are unabashedly anthropomorphic, such as many of those produced by Walt Disney. In this case they either construct nature as a microcosm of the American suburbs, in which cute baby animals are protected and provided for by their hard-pressed parents until they are old enough to fend for themselves, or they make nature into something for human beings to wonder at, a wonder that celebrates an ingenious and intricate system of life on earth of which we are implicitly a part (see Turner, 1985). In either case they are rule-bound, and their pleasures are ideologically conformist and celebratory, and available mainly to those who have accommodated, or are in the process of accommodating, themselves to the social system. This type of natural history program is frequently parentally approved viewing for children: *Ripley's Believe It or Not* is more likely to be parentally frowned upon but enjoyed by the children.

Empowering Play

The play that produces this multiplicity of pleasures for the subordinate has a number of defining characteristics. First, it is structured according to rules and conventions that replicate, but often invert, those that operate in society. Unlike the rules of the social world, the rules of play are voluntarily adopted for they delimit the space within which the player can exercise control over meanings and events. Second, the player adopts a role of his or her choosing: even though the repertoire of roles may be limited, the sense of choice is far greater than in the adoption of the already written roles that society prepares for us. This voluntary adoption of player-chosen roles within player-chosen rules is liberating in that it inverts the process of social subjection. The player can implicate him- or herself into a role in play in a way that makes that role appear as 'real' as the roles played in social life: the difference lies in the player's ability to implicate him/herself in, or extricate him/herself from, the role at will in an empowering and controlled movement between the world of play and the world of the social.

In so far as play is a representation of certain aspects of the social world, the power of play involves the power to play with the boundary between the representation and the real, to insert oneself into the process of representation so that one is not subjected by it, but conversely, is empowered by it. The pleasures of play derive directly from the players' ability to exert control over rules, roles, and representations — those agencies that in the social are the agencies of subjection, but in play can be agents of liberation and empowerment. Play, for the subordinate, is an active, creative, resistive response to the conditions of their subordination: it maintains their sense of subcultural difference in the face of the incorporating forces of the dominant ideology. The pleasures of television are best understood not in terms of a homogeneous psychological model, but rather in those of a heterogeneous, sociocultural one.

In many ways play is a more productive concept than pleasure because it asserts its activity, its creativity. Play is active pleasure: it pushes rules to the limits and explores the consequences of breaking them; centralized pleasure is more conformist. Television may well produce both sorts of pleasure, but its typical one is the playful pleasure that derives from, and enacts, that source of all power for the subordinate, the power to be different.

Pleasure and Textuality

Television's playfulness is a sign of its semiotic democracy, by which I mean its delegation of production of meanings and pleasures to its viewers. The reading relations that it invites are ones of greater or lesser equality. Its unwrittenness means that it does not set itself up as the *authority* (the pun between 'author' and 'authority' is far from accidental): it has no singular authorial voice proposing a singular way of looking at the world. The author role is delegated to, or at least shared with, its viewers. Television is a producerly text that invites a producerly set of reading relations: the production of meaning is shared between text and viewer so that television does not preserve its authorial power and privilege.

By foregrounding its authorial role and therefore its textuality, it offers the viewer access to its discursive practice. In sport and news, for instance, the discursive struggle of the author function that is involved in making sense of events as they happen is made visible and therefore accessible. Showing events, or rather representations of them, alongside their narrativization into commentary or news story, opens up the process of that narrativization, and the difference between it and the 'live' events differently represented by the camera make the process of representation visible and thus part of the meanings and pleasures of the program.

In sport the authorial role is played by the commentators — but their 'story' is told as the viewer watches the game 'live'. This 'live' game is, of course, still mediated but it has a higher modality than the commentary, and any contradictions between the high modality of the (less written) game and the low modality of the commentator's story of the game invite the viewer to disagree, to produce his or her meanings (and one has only to watch a football game with a group of fans to see how eagerly this invitation is accepted). Television sport sets itself up to be disagreed with, its producerliness invites viewer-made meanings. This invitation to disagree can be part of the authorial function, as when two or more of the on-screen commentators/ experts offer different 'stories' of events in the game. More importantly, however, television's own discursive repertoire gives to the viewer authorial knowledge and the power to produce meanings that goes with it. The constant flow of background and statistical information, of replays from all angles and at all speeds, of diagrammatic explanations of tactics, all give the viewer the insider information that is normally the preserve and privilege of the author, to be released by him/her in controlled doses throughout the progress of the narrative. We don't need Foucault to tell us that knowledge and power are closely linked, though he was the first to propose that the matrix of knowledge/power/pleasure formed one of the most important forces in society. The sharing of authorial knowledge and authorial power is productive of pleasure.

In television news the author role of the studio anchor is set in a similar relationship to the events represented in the actuality film or interviews as that of the sports commentators to the game. So when the 'author' makes a 'management sense' of an industrial dispute resulting in power cuts, but the union spokesperson on film says that it was management who switched off the lights, the invitation to the viewer to disagree may be less explicit than in sport, but it is there none the less, and is an essential part of the pleasure of watching it. News, like sport, also uses electronic effects and graphics that draw attention to its own textuality, its own constructedness.

There is a similar trend, too, in the television shows that appear to be most 'realistic', by which I mean the ones that are most similar to a novel or a film with their invisible authors. Cop and crime shows are increasingly foregrounding their own textuality. In *Moonlighting*, perhaps the most sophisticated of them, the characters David and Maddy may suddenly walk off the set, or in their dialogue blame the writers for its shortcomings. In one episode, for example, Maddy is depressed and refuses to rise to David's teasing. When she asks why they have to argue, his reply is, 'You know we always do, you watch the show on Tuesday nights.' When caught in a locked hotel room with a corpse and a gun in his hand, David looks at the cops and says, 'What a situation! Thank God I'm only an actor!' This self-reflexivity (which MacCabe and Kaplan list as a requirement of a radical text) has long been a staple of comedy: shows like *Saturday Night Live* (see Marc, 1984), and *Monty Python's Flying Circus* depend upon their viewers' awareness of television's discursive practices for their humor. A more recent example of this textually deconstructive comedy is *The Young Ones*. In one episode of this, for instance, the following dialogue occurs:

Rick: (*looking out of the window*) Ah, here comes the postman.
Viv: Rick, you're so boring, why do you always tell us what's going to happen?
Rick: Because this is a studio show and they can't afford to use location shots.

Television's foregrounding of its own textuality is not always as explicit as here or in *Moonlighting*. In shows like *Miami Vice* and others that have been influenced by it, such as *Stingray*, or, to a lesser extent, *Hunter*, devices such as excessive stylishness, self-conscious camera work, unmotivated editing, and the occasional breaking of the 180° rule (see Turner, this volume), bring its textuality forward as a source of pleasure in its own right. The mode of representation is made visible and thus the relationship between the representation and the real is brought into question.

Of course, the viewers were ahead of the producers in this. Hobson (1982) and Ang (1985) have both shown that much of the pleasure of the viewers of soap opera lies in playing with the boundary between the representation and the real. Their power to do this has been increased by the fan magazines and other secondary texts which give them an insider knowledge that is broadly similar to that given by television itself to the sports fan or the news viewer. This can, in some instances, double the textual pleasure by providing a 'ghost text' like the ghost image on a poorly tuned television set. So the fan with the insider knowledge of the 'real' relationship between, say, George Peppard and Mr T, can read the ghost image of this relationship as s/he watches Hannibal and B. A. interact on *The A-Team*. The presence of this ghost text, of course, draws attention, however mutedly, to the textuality of the representation.

Television's increasingly sophisticated viewers are demanding access to television's mode of representation. Their pleasure in television is not explained by the ease with which they can accommodate themselves to its ideologically produced meanings and subject positions. A better explanation of the pleasures of television lies in understanding it as a text of contestation which contains forces of closure and of openness and which allows viewers to make meanings that are subculturally pertinent to them, but which are made in resistance to the forces of closure in the text, just as their subcultural identity is maintained in resistance to the ideological forces of homogenization. But we need a theory of pleasure that goes beyond meanings and ideology, a theory of pleasure that centers on the power to make meanings rather than on the meanings that are made. This is the thrust of what I have called television's 'semiotic democracy', its opening up of its discursive practice to the viewer. Television is a 'producerly' medium: the work of the institutional producers of its programs requires the producerly work of the viewers and has only limited control over that work. The reading relations of a producerly text are essentially democratic, not autocratic ones. The discursive power to make meanings, to produce knowledges of the world, is a power that both program producers and producerly viewers have access to.

Television's foregrounding of its discursive repertoire, its demystification of its mode of representation, are the central characteristics of its producerliness. They require, and, more importantly, are required by, the active, sophisticated, and televisually literate viewer. They offer the viewer two sorts of producerly pleasures: the one is the pleasure of making subculturally pertinent meanings, but the more important one is the pleasure in the process of making meanings, that is, over and above any pleasure in the meanings that are made. The pleasure and the power of making meanings, of participating in the mode of representation, of playing with the semiotic process — these are some of the most significant and empowering pleasures that television has to offer.

References

Ang, I. (1985) *Watching Dallas*. London: Methuen.
Barthes, R. (1975) *The Pleasure of the Text*. New York: Hill and Wang.
— (1977) From work to text. In R. Barthes *Image–Music–Text* (pp. 155–64). London: Fontana.
Brown, M. E. (1987) The politics of soaps: Pleasure and feminine empowerment. *Australian Journal of Cultural Studies* 4(2), 1–25.
Fiske, J. (1987) British cultural studies. In R. Allen (ed.) *Channels of Discourse: Television and Contemporary Criticism* (pp. 254–89). Chapel Hill: University of North Carolina Press.
Gilligan, C. (1982) *In a Different Voice: Psychological Theory and Women's Development*. Cambridge, MA: Harvard University Press.
Hobson, D. (1982) *Crossroads: The Drama of a Soap Opera*. London: Methuen.
Huizinga, J. (1949) *Homo Ludens*. London: Routledge and Kegan Paul.
Lovell, T. (1980) *Pictures of Reality: Aesthetics, Politics, Pleasure*. London: British Film Institute.
— (1983) Writing like a woman: A question of politics. In F. Barker (ed.) *The Politics of Theory 8*. Colchester: University of Essex.
Marc, D. (1984) *Demographic Vistas: Television in American Culture*. Philadelphia: University of Pennsylvania Press.
Mulvey, L. (1975) Visual pleasure and narrative cinema. *Screen* 16(3), 6–18. Also in T. Bennett, S. Boyd-Bowman, C. Mercer and J. Woollacott (eds) (1981) *Popular Television and Film* (pp. 206–15). London: British Film Institute/Open University.
Palmer, P. (1986) *The Lively Audience: A Study of Children Around the TV Set*. Sydney: Allen & Unwin.
Radway, J. (1984) *Reading the Romance: Feminism and the Representation of Women in Popular Culture*. Chapel Hill: University of North Carolina Press.
Schwichtenberg, C. (1987) Sensual surfaces and stylistic excess: The pleasure and politics of *Miami Vice*. *Journal of Communication Inquiry* 10(3), 45–65.
Singer, J. L. and Singer, D. G. (1980) Imaginative play in preschoolers. Some research and theoretical implications. Paper presented in symposium on 'The Role of Pretend in Cognitive-Emotional Development'. American Psychological Association Annual Convention, Montreal, September 1980.
Turner, G. (1985) Nostalgia for the primitive: Wildlife documentaries on TV. *Australian Journal of Cultural Studies* 3(1), 62–71.
Waites, B., Bennett, T. and Martin, G. (eds) (1982) *Popular Culture: Past and Present*. London: Croom Helm/Open University Press.
Williamson, J. (1986) The making of a material girl. *New Socialist* October, 46–7.

18 Texts, Readers and Contexts of Reading: Developments in the Study of Media Audiences

SHAUN MOORES

Mass communications research, in its varied and changing forms, has long been concerned with the relationship between media products and the audiences which consume them. Within different theoretical frameworks and modes of investigation, different understandings of this relationship have been produced. Historically, one important division was between those perspectives which asked 'what the media do to people' and others which considered 'what people do with the media' (Halloran, 1970). Although a tension of this sort has remained present in Media Studies over recent years, the terms of the debate have shifted.

A number of questions about the mass media and their audiences have been raised: How do media texts construct for their readers particular forms of knowledge and pleasure, making available particular identities and identifications? How do readers' differential social positionings and cultural competencies bear upon their interpretation or decoding of texts? How does the context of reading influence the ways in which the media are made sense of in everyday life? This article situates these questions in a series of developments which have taken place in media theory and research since the mid-1970s, attempting a broad overview of approaches to the study of audiences.

Screen: Spectator–Text Relations

My point of departure will be work in film studies which drew on psychoanalysis, linguistics and Marxism to provide a theory of spectator–text relations in the cinema. Although such work primarily considered the structure of the text, it nevertheless had important implications for our understanding of audiences — investigating the relations of looking and knowing which texts construct for their readers. In Britain, this type of analysis was most closely associated with Stephen Heath, Colin MacCabe, Laura Mulvey and Peter Wollen, who were all contributors to the film journal, *Screen*. Their approach owed much to advances in French film theory, and in particular, to the writings of Christian Metz and the political critique of mainstream cinema which followed the events of May 1968 (see Harvey, 1978).

In his essay, 'Le Signifiant Imaginaire', translated and published in *Screen*, Metz (1975: 18–19) argued for a broadened conception of the cinematic institution, stating that it 'is not just the cinema industry, it is also the mental machinery — another industry . . . i.e. the social regulation of the spectator's metapsychology . . . The institution is outside us and inside us, indistinctly collective and intimate.' Crucially, his formulation saw the cinema as an apparatus for the production of subjectivities. As MacCabe (1985: 6) has acknowledged, it was 'the attempt to link questions of significa-tion to questions of subjectivity' which characterized *Screen's* project during that period.

For *Screen*, as for Metz, psychoanalysis appeared the theoretical tradi-tion best suited to the study of film spectatorship. Jacques Lacan's reading of Freud was concerned precisely with the interrelation of signfication and subjectivity (Lacan, 1977). It offered a theory of the constitution of the human subject in and through language — a subject constructed and divided upon entry into the symbolic order of culture (for useful commentaries on Lacan, cf. Lemaire, 1977 and Coward & Ellis, 1977).

Central to *Screen's* approach was the proposal that film does not simply capture a pre-given external reality. Images are not transparent windows on the world. Instead, film was seen to be structured according to distinctive narrative conventions and codes of representation. Images are productive rather than reflective — they produce ways of seeing the world and thereby organize consumption in certain ways. They construct the 'look' or 'gaze' of the spectator, binding her or him into the fiction and into a position of imagi-nary knowledge.

The concept of 'suture' was used to theorize this 'constant welding together' (Heath, 1976: 90) of text and spectator in the flow of the film nar-rative. Originally elaborated within Lacanian psychoanalysis to refer to 'the relation of the individual as subject to the chain of its discourse' (Heath, 1976: 98), the concept was taken up within film theory by Jean-Pierre Oudart (1977–78) in France and by Stephen Heath in Britain. In order to come to terms with these arguments about cinema, it is first necessary to outline some of the basic principles of Lacan's model of language and subjectivity.

Psychoanalysis made a significant break with earlier conceptions of subjectivity found in western philosophy. The Cartesian subject — a conscious, rational human agent at the centre of thought and action — was displaced and de-centred. In Lacanian theory, there is no pre-existent consciousness which finds expression in language, rather it is language which provides the possibility of subjectivity. The biological individual is constituted as a subject 'through its positioning in a meaning-system which is ontologically prior to it and more extensive than it' (Frosh, 1987: 130). According to Lacan, this process involves a fundamental misrecognition. Although we feel as though we are the source of meaning and the site of origin for our sense of self, identity is always constructed on the site of 'the Other' — language, representation.

The constitution of subjectivity thus entails a subjectification in which the subject is divided upon entry into language. There is necessarily a split between the subject of speech and the speaking subject — between subject positions in language and the speakers who occupy them. As Heath (1977–78: 55) has noted, 'the subject of the enounced and the subject of the enunciation never fully come together'. The Lacanian, Jacques-Alain Miller, introduced the concept of 'suture' to account for the momentary and incomplete stitchings of that gap or wound (Miller, 1977–78). It names the flickering play of absence and presence in which subjectivity is constantly produced and reproduced in linguistic utterances.

To study film as discourse for Heath and others, was to identify the textual strategies whereby subject positions are generated for the spectator. This is to ask how a ceaseless stitching of viewer and screen fiction is effected — how the reader is sewn into the text in an ongoing and constantly renewed process. Film is not only concerned with constructing a scene, but also, and at the same time, with putting the viewer in a place before it — 'in place, the spectator completes the image as its subject' (Heath, 1976: 99). While cinematic language has no direct equivalent of the personal pronouns, it was argued that we can still distinguish certain procedures for the production of subjectivity.

The shot/reverse shot formation is often cited as an example of cinematic suture. This involves a complex interplay of looks between camera, spectator and characters in the fiction. It is a linking of two shots 'in which the second shot shows the field from which the first shot is assumed to have been taken' (Silverman, 1983: 201). For instance, an exchange between characters is edited so that Shot 2 reveals the protagonist whose point-of-view had been displayed in Shot 1, and the image 'of a fictional character looking in Shot 2 usually proves sufficient to maintain the illusion that Shot 1 visually "belongs" to that character' (Silverman, 1983: 292). A structure of this kind serves to construct a subject position which is occupied by the spectator in the auditorium who 'stands in' for the protagonist by identifying with a viewpoint which is simultaneously that of the camera and a character in the fiction. The shot/reverse shot sequence was understood as a suturing device in which the reader is caught up in the text's enunciation, 'spoken' by the text.

As Laura Mulvey (1975) pointed out, the business of looking and being looked at in the cinema is strongly marked by gender difference. In the shot/reverse shot formation of the classic text, it is usually men who look at women, Mulvey argued that, 'In a world ordered by sexual imbalance, pleasure in looking has been split between active/male and passive/female' (1975: 11). within the signifying practices of Hollywood, man is constituted as bearer of the look and woman as its object. This system of looks is one which matches a voyeuristic male gaze with the exhibitionism of the female displayed as spectacle. The camera, taking up the point-of-view of the male protagonist, produces a masculine subject position. That is not to say that it is only male spectators who occupy this place, but that the mode of cinematic address had 'coded the erotic into the language of the dominant patriarchal order' (Mulvey, 1975: 8).

Whereas Oudart tended to concentrate on the shot/reverse shot structure in his discussion of suture, Heath warned against too narrow a use of the concept and looked more generally at the relation between film and viewing subject. When considering the construction of looks in the cinema, the conventions of realistic representation — in which film denies its own status as image — were seen as important because they place the spectator 'in an identification with the camera as the point of a sure and centrally embracing view' (Heath, 1976: 77). This cinematic strategy has its roots in the codes of Renaissance perspective, and through the development of devices such as depth-of-field, long takes and continuity editing (Bazin, 1967), the cinema has perfected a visual illusion in which the viewer is positioned as an all-perceiving subject gazing directly onto an objective reality. Such a relation is, of course, imaginary. The 'impression of reality' (Heath, 1976: 78) is the product of a signifying practice which erases its own discursive basis. MacCabe (1976: 17) proposed that 'it is necessary to consider the logic of that contradiction which produces a position for the viewer but denies that production'.

Metz (1975: 44–45) went some way towards identifying a logic when he wrote that

> the cinematic signifier does not work on its own account but is employed entirely to remove the traces of its own steps, to open immediately onto the transparency of a signified, of a story, which is in reality manufactured by it but which it pretends merely to 'illustrate', to transmit to us after the event, as if it had existed previously (= referential illusion) . . . Hence what distinguishes fiction films is not the 'absence' of any specific work of the signifier; but its presence in the mode of

denegation, and it is well known that this type of presence is one of the strongest there are.

Elsewhere, using a term borrowed from Benveniste's linguistics, Metz has called this narration without a narrator 'histoire' (Metz, 1982). It constitutes a meta-language which 'simply allows reality to appear . . . lets the identity of things shine through' (MacCabe, 1974: 8–9). For *Screen,* the key feature of the classic realist text was the illusion of transparency — the discursive production of 'obviousness' which, argued Althusser (1971), is exactly that mechanism by which individuals are hailed as subjects in ideology.

Against the ideological operations of realist film, *Screen* posed a different tradition — the avant-garde practices of Jean-Luc Godard's cinema (Mac-Cabe, 1980; Wollen, 1982), and before it, the theatre of Bertolt Brecht (Brecht, 1964). In contrast with Hollywood, Godard and Brecht were concerned to foreground the machinery of representation. Their political art was deemed to be properly 'materialist' because it refused to efface the materiality of the signifier. This refusal, it was suggested, made for very different spectator–text relations which were characterized by alienation rather than identification — 'passionate detachment' (Mulvey, 1975: 18). MacCabe and others were attracted to such practices because they seemed to make possible 'the breaking of the imaginary relation between text and viewer' (MacCabe, 1976: 21).

While *Screen* was concerned principally with the analysis of film texts, there were also occasional discussions of television as a signifiying practice. Heath, in an essay written with Gillian Skirrow (1977), did attempt to open up questions about the specificity of television's mode of address and its differences from cinematic discourse — although their analysis of a TV documentary is typical of *Screen's* more general approach at that time. Heath and Skirrow stated that their work set out to examine 'the positionings of the viewer as subject . . . the kinds of construction and address of view and viewer' (1977: 9–10). The focus remained on the structure of the text and on the production of a place for its reading subject.

CCCS: Inscribed Readers and Social Subjects

By the end of the 1970s, a valuable critique of 'screen theory' had been developed by members of the Media Group at the Centre for Contemporary Cultural Studies in Birmingham. This critique, built on the foundations of Stuart Hall's earlier work on the encoding/decoding model, is found most clearly in the writings of Charlotte Brunsdon and David Morley (Brunsdon & Morley, 1978; Morley, 1980a; Morley, 1980b; Brunsdon, 1981; Morley,

1981). It was not, however, limited to the work of the Birmingham group, for dissenting voices could already be heard from within the pages of *Screen* itself (Willemen, 1978; Neale, 1977). At the root of these objections was the assertion that 'screen theory' failed to distinguish between the reader implied by or inscribed in the text and the actual social subjects who interpret or decode texts.

As Brunsdon (1981: 32–37) put it:

> We can usefully analyse the 'you' or 'yous' that the text as discourse constructs, but we cannot assume that any individual audience member will necessarily occupy these positions. The relation of the audience to the text will not be determined solely by that text, but also by positionalities in relation to a whole range of other discourses . . . elaborated elsewhere, already in circulation and brought to the (text) by the viewer.

While recognizing the text's construction of subject positions for the spectator, Brunsdon and Morley pointed to readers as the possessors of already-constituted cultural knowledges and competencies which are drawn on at the moment of interpretation — 'the repertoire of discourses at the disposal of different audiences' (Morley, 1980a: 171). It was argued that in the work of MacCabe, Heath and others, the text is 'not so much "read" as simply "consumed/appropriated" straight, via the only possible positions available to the reader — those . . . inscribed by the text' (Morley, 1980a: 166–67). Against such a model of spectator–text relations, Morley came to put particular emphasis on viewers as active producers of meaning and on media consumption as the site of potentially differential readings.

To counter 'the single, hypostatised text–subject relation' (Morley, 1980b: 162) found in much of *Screen's* analysis, the concept of 'interdiscourse' was introduced. Reading was not to be theorized as an abstract, isolated relationship between one text and its implied reader. There could be no reduction in which the reader is seen only as the occupant of a single textual positioning. In the encounter between text and subject, 'other discourses are always in play besides those of the particular text in focus — discourses . . . brought into play through "the subject's" placing in other practices — cultural, educational, institutional' (Morley, 1980a: 163). In the words of the former Director of the Centre for Contemporary Cultural Studies, Richard Johnson (1986: 299), 'The whole pressure of formalistic work is to isolate the text for closer scrutiny. But the real tendency of the reading moment . . . is the opposite of this . . . The reality of reading . . . is inter-discursive'.

The Birmingham Centre's *Nationwide* project was an attempt to apply some of these theoretical perspectives in a specific analysis of television texts

and audiences. In its later stages, Morley sought to chart differential interpretations of the programme made by viewing groups drawn from various
occupational and educational backgrounds — and as an empirical investigation into the relation of texts and readers, the research remains an important
landmark in modern media studies. A more detailed discussion of the project will follow, but this must be prefaced by some comments on Hall's early
paper written in 1973, 'Encoding and Decoding in the Television Discourse',
an abridged version of which was later published (Hall, 1980). (Also this
volume.)

Hall had conceptualized the production and reception of the television
message within a semiotic framework. Televisual communication was to be
understood as a complex social construction of meaning. At both ends of the
communicative chain — the encoding and decoding moments — symbolic
'work' is being done. To grasp the relationship between these moments and
thereby specify the nature of the work performed should, Hall suggested, be
the task of media research.

Drawing on the insights of structural linguistics, he rejected notions about
the 'transparency' of media representation in terms which were similar in
many respects to those used by *Screen:* 'Discursive "knowledge" is the product not of the transparent representation of the "real" in language but of
the articulation of language on real relations and conditions' (Hall, 1980:
131). Language, in the broadest sense, does not offer up a faithful reflection
of the world. Signification is dependent upon the operation of a code — for
example, conventions of selection and combination. In a television news
broadcast, an event cannot be transmitted in a 'raw' form. It has to be made
to mean and is therefore encoded in particular ways. But in Hall's model, the
codes of encoding and decoding 'may not be perfectly symmetrical' (1980:
131). There will be differing 'relations of equivalence' between the two
moments and the reasons for this potential asymmetry are twofold.

Firstly, television texts are all, to some extent, polysemic. There are
always several possible readings of the text. Especially at the connotative
level of signification — the realm of what Roland Barthes has called second-
order or associative meanings — signs possess a fluidity which enables them
to be articulated in multiple ways (Barthes, 1971; 1973). However, as Hall
(1980: 134) warns, 'Polysemy must not . . . be confused with pluralism . . .
there exists a pattern of "preferred readings".' The text is not open to be
read in any way the viewer freely chooses, since 'encoding will have the
effect of constructing some of the limits and parameters within which decodings will operate' (1980: 135).

In a similar fashion, the Soviet linguist, Valentin Volosinov (1973), has
remarked on the 'multi-accentuality' of the sign. For Volosinov, there are no
fixed meanings in language because the sign is continually the site of a class

struggle — 'a little arena for the clash and criss-crossing of differently oriented social accents' (1973: 41). So signs such as, say, 'the nation' or 'the people' are not wholly closed around a singular meaning (Hall, 1982: 78). They constitute a sphere in which meaning is contested, although as Hall would say, the competing accentuations will be 'structured in dominance' (Hall, 1980: 134). Indeed, Volsoinov (1973: 23) argued that the dominant social class will always seek to reproduce the conditions of its dominance by making certain meanings appear taken-for-granted and obvious — by trying 'to impart a supraclass, external character to the . . . sign, to . . . make the sign uni-accentual'.

The second, and related, reason for the possible non-correspondence of encoded and decoded meanings is the interrogative and expansive nature of reading practices. Umberto Eco (1972: 110) has said that the reader may 'decode the message in an aberrant way'. In an essay published in the CCCS's journal, *Working Papers in Cultural Studies,* Eco suggested that the determinations for such decodings were to be found in the reader's 'general framework of cultural references . . . his ideological, ethical, religious standpoints, his psychological attitudes, his tastes, his value systems, etc.' (1972: 115). This is not to propose a theory of selective perception, where individuals make random, private readings. There exist what Hall has called 'significant clusterings' (1980: 135). Audience decoding studies would have to map out the connections between these clustered readings and the social-discursive positionings of readers — to sketch the boundaries of various interpretive communities (cf. Morley, 1975 for an early attempt to approach audiences as cultural subgroupings).

Making use of categories first outlined in the work of the sociologist, Frank Parkin (1971), Hall tentatively identified 'three hypothetical positions from which decodings of a televisual discourse may be constructed' (1980: 136). In the first, the viewer operates within the dominant code and reads the meaning which has been encoded 'full and straight'. The second position is one in which readers adopt a negotiated code which 'acknowledges the legitimacy of the hegemonic definitions . . . while, at a more restricted, situational level . . . operates with exceptions to the rule' (1980: 137). Here, the preferred reading is not fully accepted. In addition, Hall referred to a third, oppositional, position — decoding the message 'in a globally contrary way' (1980: 137–38). Although there remained the problem of precisely how these meaning systems are related to the socioeconomic positions of readers, Hall's notes on differential decodings opened up a space for later research.

In *Everyday Television: 'Nationwide'* (1978), Brunsdon and Morley presented a textual analysis which marked the first stage of an encoding/decoding study. An examination of the programme's visual and verbal discourses, the analysis considered the distinctive ways in which *Nationwide* addressed its viewers. They argued that the programme's preferred reading of events was 'articulated, above all, through the sphere of domesticity', pointing to 'its emphasis on the ordinary, everyday aspects of issues, on the effects of general issues and problems on particular individuals and families' (1978: 74). This 'common sense' mode of presentation revolved around a certain image of the audience as a nation of individuals, united in their regional diversity and bound together through a shared experience of domestic life. The text's ideological effectivity was seen in terms of its construction of subject positions for viewers — its production of an imaginary relation, a misrecognition.

But as Morley clearly demonstrated in the second stage of the project, published in 1980 as *The 'Nationwide' Audience,* the programme's preferred reading was not necessarily accepted by actual viewers who were never reducible to the subject positions inscribed in the text. Morley carried out field research 'to establish how the messages previously analysed have in fact been received and interpreted by sections of the media audience in different structural positions' (1980b: 23). The research took the form of twenty-nine interviews conducted in institutional settings, in which groups drawn from different levels of the education system and from various occupations discussed recorded programme extracts.

Working with the pattern of the dominant, negotiated and oppositional positions set out in Hall's essay, Morley sought to classify the differential group decodings — 'to see how the different subcultural structures and formations within the audience, and the sharing of different cultural codes and competencies amongst different groups and classes, "determine" the decoding of the message' (1980b: 15). Readings did not correspond directly to economic class position. Morley noted, for instance, that apprentices, shop stewards and black F.E. students 'all share a common class position, but their decodings are inflected in different directions by the influences of the discourses and institutions in which they are situated' (1980b: 137). This was not to suggest that the ideological/discursive level of the social formation is autonomous or free-floating, but that 'it is always a question of how social position plus particular discourse position produce specific readings; readings which are structured because the structure of access to different discourses is determined by social position' (1980b: 134).

The 'Nationwide' Audience still stands as a ground breaking study of audience decodings and a challenge to the theory of text–reader relations advanced in *Screen,* although there were significant limitations to the work which Morley himself recognized. In the encoding/decoding model there seemed to be little room to account for readers' pleasures, or for the extent to which a variety of media genres are relevant to the concerns of viewers and comprehensible in the light of the reader's cultural capital. There also remained the problem of the context in which reading takes place. In the *Nationwide* decoding research, readers responded to the text as members of groups situated in the institutional environments of education or work. Would the same viewers have made sense of the programme differently if placed in the more usual reading context of the domestic household? As Morley (1980b: 27) admitted, 'The absence of this dimension in the study is to be regretted and one can only hope that further research might be able to take it up.'

Towards an Ethnography of Reading

In a critique of his own work on decoding, Morley (1981: 13) declared his interest in 'the development of what might be termed an 'ethnography of reading'. Such an approach would address precisely those limitations found in the *Nationwide* study, investigating the habits and tastes of different 'reading publics' and focusing in particular on the context of media consumption. It is with these questions that his later work on television audiences was concerned (Morley, 1986), but he was not alone in turning to the study of reading as a 'system of cultural behaviour'. Dorothy Hobson — also based at the CCCS — had already carried out audience research in an ethnographic tradition. She considered the significance of radio and television in the day-to-day lives and routines of housewives (Hobson, 1980). Her analysis was based on observations of women at home with young children, and on tape-recorded interviews with the women about their everyday use of mass media.

In accounting for the appeal of daytime radio in the lives of the housewives, she pointed to the specific context in which it is heard. Hobson argued that radio serves, in part, to combat the loneliness experienced by women as a result of their location in the domestic sphere. Despite its usual status as background sound, she saw daytime radio as an 'important means of negotiating or managing the tensions caused by the isolation in their lives' (1980: 109). Broadcasting also provides a series of punctuations in the working day of the housewife. Unlike the highly segmented temporal structures of industrial labour, housework is characterized by its 'structurelessness'. Michele Mattelart (1986: 65) has referred to this as 'feminine time . . . interiorized and lived through as the time of banal everyday life, repetition and monotony'. According to Hobson's research, 'the time boundaries provided by radio are important in the women's own division of their time' (1980: 105). The regular daily features of programming, as well as constant time-checks, enable women to sequence their domestic activities while listening to the radio.

When looking at her interviewees' accounts of their television consumption, Hobson concluded that there is 'an active choice of programmes which are understood to constitute the "woman's world", coupled with a complete rejection of programmes presenting the "man's world"' (1980: 109). Where Morley's decoding research had seen the audience as a number of cultural subgroupings defined primarily by class position, Hobson's work pointed in addition to the importance of understanding television viewing in the domestic context as gender-differentiated. The women in the study clearly distinguished 'two worlds' of television. News and current affairs, as well as much documentary and adventure fiction output — such as war films — were designated as masculine and avoided, if possible, by many of the women. The genres which they most readily related to were quiz shows — especially those with a domestic, familial theme — movies with a 'fantasy' content and, most notably, soap operas.

In a subsequent study of the audience for the British television soap opera, *Crossroads,* Hobson (1982: 105–36) returned to these issues of gender-differentiated readings and domestic contexts of consumption. Once again, the research involved an observation of audiences in the household setting — followed by a recorded discussion of the programme. A coincidental shift in the scheduling slot from 6.30 p.m. to 6.05 p.m. provided her with an excellent opportunity to see how women viewers made space in hectic tea-time routines to watch their favourite programme.

Describing one of the domestic viewing situations, Hobson wrote: 'the woman with whom I had gone to watch the programme was serving the evening meal, feeding her five- and three-year-old daughters and attempting to watch the programme on the black and white television situated on top of the freezer opposite the kitchen table' (1982: 112). As she made clear, a viewing context of this sort is a far cry from the darkened room in which an academic might usually conduct a textual analysis. For Hobson, television consumption was to be understood as 'part of the everyday life of viewers' (1982: 110). In much the same way, John Ellis has reminded us of the difference between the cinematic context, 'the relative privacy and anonymity of a darkened public space' (Ellis, 1982: 26), and the setting of the television in the home — 'a profoundly domestic phenomenon . . . another domestic object, often the place where family photos are put: the direction of the glance towards the personalities on the TV screen being supplemented by the presence of "loved ones" immediately above' (1982: 113). It was in the context of home and family that the women in Hobson's research had to arrange their viewing of *Crossroads.* Watching television was not a separate, solitary activity, rather it was woven into the routine duties and responsibilities of household management.

There was also a tendency for 'some women to feel almost guilty and apologetic that they watch the programme . . . they excuse themselves for liking something which is treated in such a derogatory way by critics and sometimes by their own husbands' (Hobson, 1982: 110). Perhaps the rejection of soap opera by husbands might be explained by the genre's focus on personal and emotional matters. One of Hobson's viewers perceptively suggested that 'men are not supposed to show their emotions and so if they watch *Crossroads* . . . then they think it's just stupid and unrealistic because they are not brought up to accept emotional situations (1982: 109). It is interesting to note that this speaker refers to men's frequent dismissal of soap opera as 'unrealistic', for as Ien Ang (1985) has argued, the popularity of the genre lies in its 'emotional realism' for many women viewers.

Similar work on the reading of popular television and literature was being done in the United States by feminist academics like Tania Modleski (1984) and Janice Radway (1987). Modleski considered the form and flow of daytime television in relation to the rhythms of women's work in the home, while Radway's research into women's consumption of romantic fiction looked not only at their interpretation of texts, but more generally at the importance of romance-reading as a social event performed in the context of family relations and domestic obligations.

Radway saw the appeal of romance-reading in its potential to transport women, albeit temporarily, from their domestic routines. Her study of a community of women romance-readers in the midwestern town of Smithton was originally intended as an inquiry into their interpretation of the literature, but during the course of the research there was a shift in focus. Radway explained that 'the Smithton women repeatedly answered my questions about the meaning of romances by talking about the meaning of romance-reading as a social event' (1987: 7). For the Smithton women, the very act of reading the romance was significant, because it enabled them to mark out a time and space of their own in a day which was otherwise devoted to the care of others.

Rosalind Coward (1984: 199) has written of fantasy as 'the "other place" of the mind . . . like a secret room or garden, to be visited in a spare moment', stating that 'women talk of looking forward to the moment of escape when they can enter the rich and creative world of their own minds, hidden from the rest of the world'. It is precisely this sort of experience which is pleasurably anticipated by the Smithton readers, for as one of the women said, 'when I am reading . . . my body is in the room but the rest of me is not' (Radway, 1987: 87). This led Radway to critically unpack the notion of 'escapism', traditionally used in a derogatory sense. She suggested that when contextualized within the day-to-day setting of home and family life, the will to be transported elsewhere through the medium of fantasy literature clearly makes sense. It makes possible an escape in two senses of the world, both of which were expressed by Radway's readers:

On the one hand, they used the term literally to describe the act of denying the present, which they believe they accomplish each time they begin to read a book and are drawn into its story. On the other hand, they used the word in a more figurative fashion to give substance to the somewhat vague but none the less intense sense of relief they experience by identifying with a heroine whose life does not resemble their own in certain crucial respects. (1987: 90)

The second sense of the term defined here by Radway is important in answering why it is that these women seek their escape via the genre of romance and not through other types of literature. They see in the romance's heroine a character who — although she often suffers humiliation and rejection from the male object of her desire — is finally united with a man who shows himself to be capable of caring. Crucially, the readers identify with a woman who is, in the end, nurtured — for in their own day-to-day lives they are destined to nurture others.

Morley's *Family Television* (1986) had many parallels with Radway's research on popular literature — a debt he acknowledged — especially in its call for questions of interpretation and questions of use to be posed together. To borrow Radway's phrasing, we might say that Morley's most recent book focused on the meaning of television viewing as a social event in a familial context. Other influences for the book came both from within media research and from some unexpected sources outside it. Hermann Bausinger's study of how the Meiers, a German family, interacted with the media and with each other over the course of a weekend convinced Morley of the importance of seeing media reception 'as an integral part of the way the everyday is conducted' (Bausinger, 1984: 349). Switching on the television set, for example, does not necessarily signify an interest in the programme being broadcast. It may well be an excuse not to talk to someone else in the room, or again, it could be an attempt to engineer a shared experience with others. In connection with this question, Morley also referred to work in the field of family psychology carried out by Irene Goodman and others (Morley, 1986: 22–30). Just as psychologists studying family life have often observed the interactive rituals which take place around the dining-table, so Goodman looked to the domestic uses of television as a way of comprehending the formulation and negotiation of rules within the family unit.

To uncover the rules and rituals of television viewing is also to investigate what Sean Cubitt (1984: 46) has called 'the politics of the living-room', for family relations are power relations. Questions of age difference — of generation — were not developed in Morley's work, but were explored in more detail in a subsequent collection of essays edited by Philip Simpson (1987), where parents discussed the place of television in relationships with their children. Morley's primary concern was with the ways in which gender relations within the household structure TV-viewing as a form of cultural behaviour.

Drawing on material from eighteen recorded interviews with families living in South London, Morley identified a number of themes and consistencies with regard to gendered viewing practices. He began by pointing out that the domestic space itself has very different meanings for men and for women. For men, it is primarily a site of leisure, defined in relation to 'work time' which is spent outside the home. For women, such a separation is often not evident. Even if she is employed in work outside the home, the woman remains responsible for household duties while situated in the domestic context. Morley argued that this makes for different styles of viewing, with most women only able to participate in distracted consumption. Indeed, while the men interviewed by Morley expressed a preference for watching quietly and attentively, the women described their viewing as 'a fundamentally social activity, involving ongoing conversation, and usually the performance of at least one other domestic activity (ironing, etc.) at the same time' (1986: 150). Only at times when the rest of the family are absent can women indulge in the 'guilty pleasures' of a solo viewing, taking a break from domestic responsibilities. Morley cited the case of one woman who 'particularly enjoys watching early morning television at the weekends — because, as these are the only occasions when her husband and sons "sleep in", these are, by the same token, the only occasions when she can watch television attentively, without keeping half an eye on the needs of others' (1986: 160).

Morley's current work confirms his commitment to ethnographic audience studies. In a joint paper with Roger Silverstone, presented at the 1988 International Television Studies Conference a further investigation of television as a domestic technology is proposed. This would involve developing a more detailed account of its contemporary and historical position in the geography and routine of the private sphere, and of its relationship with other information and communication technologies in the home. It would also require an examination of the ways in which broadcasting mediates between private and public domains, reproducing the mundane nature of everyday domestic life and familiarizing the social world beyond (Moores, 1988; Scannell, 1988). Such a project, they argued, 'reframes' mass communications research within a broader analysis of the time–space structuration of day-to-day social life.

The 'reframing' advocated by Morley and Silverstone is not intended to replace a concern with texts and readers, although they noted that 'the text–reader model does now require some reworking' (1988: 27). In the case of television, they pointed to two major qualifications which would have to be built into the model. First, they signalled the variability of television viewing as an activity. As part of domestic ritual, viewing may involve a number of

different levels of attention and engagement — and ethnographic research
has already shown that there will be changing combinations of viewers in
various household settings. Secondly, in conducting analyses of television
output it is important to recognize the multiplicity of television's modes of
address across different genres of programming. Morley and Silverstone
clearly feel that the text still requires close analysis, but suggested that 'what
is necessary is to examine the varieties of viewing and attention which are
paid to different types of programmes at different parts of the day by different types of viewers' (1988: 27). This calls for a survey of the rhetorical
relations between television texts and readers in specific temporal and
spatial contexts.

References

Althusser, L. (1971) *Lenin and Philosophy, and Other Essays*. London: Verso.
Ang. I. (1985) *Watching Dallas: Soap Opera and the Melodramatic Imagination*.
    London: Methuen.
Barthes, R. (1971) The rhetoric of the image. *Working Papers in Cultural Studies* 1.
— (1973) *Mythologies*. London: Paladin.
Bausinger, H. (1984) Media, technology and daily life. *Media, Culture and Society* 6
    (4).
Bazin, A. (1967) *What is Cinema?* Vol. 1. H. Gray (ed.). USA: University of Califor-
    nia Press.
Benveniste, E. (1971) *Problems in General Linguistics*. USA: University of Miami
    Press.
Bourdieu, P. (1984) *Distinction: A Social Critique of the Judgement of Taste*. Lon-
    don: Routledge and Kegan Paul.
Brecht, B. (1964) *Brecht on Theatre*. J. Willett (ed.). London: Methuen.
Brunsdon, C. (1981) *Crossroads*: Notes on soap opera. *Screen* 22 (4).
— (1984) Writing about soap opera. In L. Masterman (ed.) *Television Mythologies:
    Stars, Shows and Signs* (pp. 82–87). London: Comedia.
Brunsdon, C. and D. Morley (1978) *Everyday Television: 'Nationwide'*. London:
    BFI TV Mono. 10.
Coward, R. (1984) *Female Desire: Women's Sexuality Today*. London: Paladin.
Coward, R. and J. Ellis (1977) *Language and Materialism: Developments in Semiol-
    ogy and the Theory of the Subject*. London: Routledge and Kegan Paul.
Cubitt, S. (1984) Top of the pops: The politics of the living room. In L. Masterman
    (ed.) *Television Mythologies* (pp. 46–48).
Dahlgren, P. (1985) The modes of reception: For a hermeneutics of TV news. In
    P. Drummond and R. Paterson (eds) *Television in Transition* (pp. 235–49). Lon-
    don: BFI.
— (1988) What's the meaning of this?: Viewers' plural sense-making of TV news.
    Media Culture and Society 10 (3).
Eco, U. (1972) Towards a semiotic inquiry into the television message. *Working
    Papers in Cultural Studies* 3.
Ellis, J. (1982) *Visible Fictions: Cinema, Television, Video*. London: RKP.
Frosh, S. (1987) *The Politics of Psychoanalysis: An Introduction to Freudian and
    Post-Freudian Theory*. London: Macmillan.
Gray, A. (1987) Behind closed doors: Video recorders in the home. In H. Baehr and
    G. Dyer (eds) *Boxed In: Women and Television* (pp. 38–54). London: Pandora.

Hall, S. (1980) Encoding/Decoding. In S. Hall *et al.* (eds) *Culture, Media, Language: Working Papers in Cultural Studies, 1972–79* (pp. 128–38). London: Hutchinson.
— (1982) The rediscovery of 'Ideology': Return of the repressed in media studies. In M. Gurevitch *et al.* (eds) *Culture, Society and the Media* (pp. 56–90). London: Methuen.
Halloran, J. (ed.) (1970) *The Effects of Television.* London: Panther.
Harvey, S. (1978) *May '68 and Film Culture.* London: BFI.
Heath, S. (1976) Narrative space, *Screen* 17 (3).
— (1977–78) Notes on suture. *Screen* 18 (4).
Heath, S. and G. Skirrow (1977) Television: A world in action. *Screen* 18 (2).
Hirst, P. (1976) Althusser's theory of ideology. *Economy and Society* 5 (4).
Hobson, D. (1980) Housewives and the mass media. In S. Hall *et al.* (eds) *Culture, Media, Language.* London: Hutchinson.
— (1982) *Crossroads: The Drama of a Soap Opera.* London: Methuen.
Jensen, K. (1986) *Making Sense of the News: Towards a Theory and an Empirical Model of Reception for the Study of Mass Communication.* Denmark: Aarhus University Press.
Johnson, R. (1986) The story so far: And further transformations? In D. Punter (ed.) *Introduction to Contemporary Cultural Studies.* London: Longman.
Lacan, J. (1977) *Ecrits: A Selection.* London: Tavistock.
Lemaire, A. (1977) *Jacques Lacan.* London: Routledge and Kegan Paul.
MacCabe, C. (1974) Realism and the cinema: Notes on some Brechtian theses. *Screen* 15 (2).
— (1976) Theory and film: Principles of realism and pleasure. *Screen* 17 (3).
— (1980) *Godard: Images, Sounds, Politics.* London: BFI.
— (1985) *Theoretical Essays: Film, Linguistics, Literature.* Manchester: Manchester University Press.
Mattelart, M. (1986) Women and the cultural industries. In R. Collins *et al.* (eds) *Media, Culture and Society: A Critical Reader* (pp. 63–81). London: Sage.
Metz, C. (1975) The imaginary signifier. *Screen* 16 (2).
— (1982) *Psychoanalysis and Cinema.* London: Macmillan.
Miller, J-A. (1977–78) Suture (Elements of the logic of the signifier). *Screen* 18 (4).
Modleski, T. (1984) *Loving with a Vengeance: Mass-Produced Fantasies for Women.* London: Methuen.
Moores, S. (1988) The box on the dresser: Memories of early radio and everyday life. *Media, Culture and Society* 10 (1).
Morley, D. (1975) Reconceptualising the media audience. *CCCS Stencilled Paper* 9. Birmingham: University of Birmingham.
— (1980a) Texts, readers, subjects. In S. Hall *et al.* (eds) *Culture, Media, Language* (pp. 163–73). London: Hutchinson.
— (1980b) *The 'Nationwide' Audience: Structure and Decoding.* London: BFI TV Mono. 11.
— (1981) The *Nationwide* audience: A critical postscript. *Screen Education* 39.
— (1986) *Family Television: Cultural Power and Domestic Leisure.* London: Comedia.
Morley, D. and R. Silverstone (1988) Domestic communication: Technologies and meanings. International Television Studies Conference paper, University of London Institute of Education.
Mulvey, L. (1975) Visual pleasure and narrative cinema. *Screen* 16 (3).
Neale, S. (1977) Propaganda. *Screen* 18 (3).

Oudart, J-P. (1977/8) Cinema and suture. *Screen* 18 (4).

Parkin, F. (1971) *Class Inequality and Political Order*. London: MacGibbon and Kee.

Radway. J. (1987) *Reading the Romance: Women, Patriarchy and Popular Literature*. London: Verso.

Richardson, K. and J. Corner (1986) Reading reception: Mediation and transparency in viewers' accounts of a TV programme. *Media, Culture and Society* 8 (4).

Rose, J. (1986) *Sexuality in the Field of Vision*. London: Verso.

Scannell, P. (1988) Radio times: The temporal arrangement of broadcasting in the modern world. In P. Drummond and R. Paterson (eds) *Television and its Audience* (pp. 15–31). London: BFI.

Silverman, K. (1983) *The Subject of Semiotics*. USA: Oxford University Press.

Simpson, P. (ed.) (1987) *Parents Talking Television: Television in the Home*. London: Comedia.

Thompson. J. B. (1988) Mass communication and modern culture: Contribution to a critical theory of ideology. *Sociology* 22 (3).

Volosinov, V. (1973) *Marxism and the Philosophy of Language*. USA: Seminar Press.

Willemen, P. (1978) Notes on subjectivity: On reading Edward Branigan's 'Subjectivity Under Siege'. *Screen* 19 (1).

Wollen, P. (1982) *Readings and Writings: Semiotic Counter-Strategies*. London: Verso.

Wren-Lewis, J. (1985) Decoding television news. In P. Drummond and R. Paterson (eds) *Television in Transition* (pp. 205–34). London: BFI.

Index